your friendship and support

Audrey

"Both the scientific and religious communities need this book. It is a competent review of past efforts to address the challenges and opportunities presented by the genetic revolution. An extensive and thoughtful critique of the literature is accompanied by the description of concepts and methods needed for the future. This approach is then applied to the critical issues of cloning, gene patenting, and the genetic basis of human nature. The underlying theme is that the field of religious ethics has a role that cannot be replaced by either secular ethics or theology."

—*V. Elving Anderson, Professor Emeritus of Genetics, University of Minnesota*

THEOLOGY AND THE SCIENCES

Kevin J. Sharpe, Series Editor

BOARD OF ADVISORS

Ian Barbour
Emeritus Professor of Physics and Religion
Carleton College, Northfield, Minnesota

Philip Hefner
Director, Chicago Center for Religion and Science
Professor, Lutheran School of Theology at Chicago

Sallie McFague
Carpenter Professor of Theology
The Divinity School, Vanderbilt University, Nashville

Arthur Peacocke, S. O. Sc.
Saint Cross College
Oxford, England

John Polkinghorne, F. R.S.
Past President, Queens College
Cambridge, England

Robert John Russell
Director, Center for Theology and the Natural Sciences
Professor, Graduate Theological Union, Berkeley

TITLES IN THE SERIES

Unprecedented Choices

Religious Ethics at the Frontiers of Genetic Science

Audrey R. Chapman

FORTRESS PRESS   MINNEAPOLIS

To our children—Kris, Erica, Hafeez, and Cassandra—
and our hopes for their future.

UNPRECEDENTED CHOICES
Religious Ethics at the Frontiers of Genetic Science

Chapman, Audrey R.
    Unprecedented choices : religious ethics at the frontiers of
genetic science / Audrey R. Chapman.
        p.   cm.
    Includes bibliographical references.
    ISBN 0-8006-3181-1 (alk. paper)
    1. Human genetics—Moral and ethical aspects.   2. Human genetics—
Religious aspects.   3. Human genetics—Religious aspects—
Christianity.   I. Title.
QH438.7.C475   1999
241'.64957—dc21   99-22222
                                                                      CIP

The paper used in this publication meets the minimum requirements for American National Standard for Information Sciences—Permanence of Paper for Printed Library Materials, ANSI Z329.48–1984.   ∞ ™

Manufactured in the U.S.A.   AF 1-3181

03   02   01   00   99   1   2   3   4   5   6   7   8   9   10

Contents

Chapter Five: Theological Reflections on Genetics and Human Nature

Preface

Every month, sometimes every week, announcements appear of new break-throughs in understanding genetics and controlling life processes. Many, per-haps most, of these scientific advances pose fundamental ethical issues. The power to alter the biological basis of life through genetic engineering raises questions about the appropriate role and limits of human activity and alter-ations in nature. Genetic testing, the procedure to analyze particular segments of DNA, can disclose information about the genetic makeup of an individual. But what does it mean to have knowledge about a predisposition toward a spe-cific disease or disorder when there is no certainty of ever developing the condition and no effective therapy available? Evidence linking genetics to behavior potentially challenges concepts of human freedom, moral agency, and responsibility. How will we interpret and use this knowledge? Various genetic applications and proposed interventions suggest that humanity may have the ability in the not-too-distant future to reshape aspects of human nature and behavior. Should we go ahead and do so? Some of the issues emerg-ing from genetic research are completely new—whether to create transgenic forms of life and release them into ecosystems, the appropriateness of cloning human beings, whether we have the wisdom to serve as our own co-creators and alter the human genetic constitution. Others complicate already difficult moral quandaries, like the always divisive and difficult issue of therapeutic abortion.

I came to reflect on these issues through an unusual career change. After nearly ten years as a staff member at the United Church Board for World Ministries, the international agency of the United Church of Christ (UCC), in 1991 I began a new position at the American Association for the Advancement of Science (AAAS). My primary responsibility at AAAS was to serve as the director of the Science and Human Rights Program, but a few months after my arrival I had the opportunity to participate in an initial AAAS project dealing with the ethical, legal, and social issues arising out of genetic science. As AAAS's involvement with this topic grew, mine did as well and I began to engage in research on the ethical and religious implications of genet-ic science. In 1996, I became the director of a second AAAS program, initial-ly called the Dialogue between Science and Religion and recently renamed the Dialogue on Science, Ethics, and Religion. In that capacity I have codirected AAAS projects related to genetic patenting, potential human germ-line inter-ventions, and human stem cell research.

It became increasingly clear to me that our society faces unprecedented choices, and the decisions we make at this point in human history are likely to shape the human future. How do we respond ethically to biotechnical developments, and on what basis should we make any of these determinations? Like many others, I believe that the technical ability to do something does not necessarily mean we should use these powers. Moreover, I do not believe that science can provide the answers or that scientists should be given the task of making ethical determinations for society.

As I deliberated on this situation, I came to believe that the religious community can potentially make an important contribution to societal efforts to grapple with the choices and dilemmas arising from the genetics revolution. I also realized that the religious thinkers often come to genetics without deep knowledge of the science and with relatively little experience of developing ethics on frontier scientific issues.

This study was undertaken to explore approaches to interfacing religious ethics and genetic science, and to assess their contributions and limitations. The emphasis in this book, therefore, will be on the content and methodology of these works and not on the issues per se. Chapters are topically oriented and focus in turn on discussions and literature within the religious community dealing with the ethical issues related to genetic developments, cloning, and gene patenting, and efforts to engage in theological reinterpretations of human nature in light of genetic findings.

The research and reflections on which this book is based have taken place over several years' time. My efforts have been stimulated and enriched by participation in several AAAS projects and discussions with colleagues and friends. I have also been a member of several other working groups during this period, including a UCC task force on genetics and a group convened by the Hastings Center on genetic patenting.

Earlier versions of three of the chapters in this volume were the basis of papers given at conferences. In 1994, I presented a paper entitled "Christian Ethics at the Frontiers of Science" at the Society of Christian Ethics, and then in 1997 another paper on genetic patenting. I also delivered a paper entitled "Theological Reflections on Genetics and Human Nature" at the 1998 meeting of the American Theological Society. In all three cases I found the comments from and dialogue with other participants to be helpful.

It is difficult to acknowledge all of those who have contributed to this exploration and writing project. I would particularly like to thank two AAAS colleagues, Al Teich, the director of the Directorate on Science and Policy Programs, who has supported my various projects and initiatives to interface science and religion; and Mark Frankel, director of the Program on Scientific Freedom, Responsibility and Law, who served as my codirector on several

AAAS projects. The John Templeton Foundation provided a small grant that enabled me to begin the task of converting several preliminary papers into a book. Several religious ethicists, particularly Roger Shinn, Ted Peters, and Ronald Cole-Turner, provided intellectual companionship during this period. I am especially grateful to V. Elving Anderson, who undertook a detailed review of several of my chapters and offered many helpful revisions. My husband, Karim Ahmed, improved my scientific literacy and lovingly accepted my spending many, many hours writing at home on weekends and evenings.

Chapter One

The Framework

A half-century after the discovery of the double-helix structure of the chemical deoxyribonucleic acid (DNA), accelerating knowledge about and applications of genetics have given rise to a series of unprecedented ethical choices and dilemmas. The power to alter the biological basis of life through genetic engineering raises questions about the appropriate role and limits of human activity and alterations in nature. Genetic testing, the procedure to analyze particular segments of DNA, can disclose information about the genetic make-up of an individual. But what does it mean to have knowledge about a predisposition toward a specific disease or disorder when there is no certainty of ever developing the condition and no effective therapy available? Evidence linking genetics to behavior potentially challenges concepts of human freedom, moral agency, and responsibility. How will we interpret and use this knowledge? Various genetic applications and proposed interventions suggest that humanity may have the ability in the not-too-distant future to reshape aspects of human nature and behavior. Should we go ahead and do so? How do we absorb the import and respond ethically to biotechnological developments when each month, sometimes each week, seems to bring breakthroughs in understanding and controlling living processes, many of which have long-term consequences? And, on what basis should we make any of these determinations?

As some ethicists and religious thinkers have pointed out, the revolution in genetics brings awesome responsibilities, risks, and choices. At a 1992 conference on religion and genetics, the Anglican Archbishop of York, John Habgood, who was originally trained as a biologist and pharmacologist, addressed the perils of trying to know too much. "Knowledge is more than an abstract pattern in the mind or in the computer," he reminded his audience.

It is an understanding of what to do with such patterns, how to use them. It is a claim to be able to take responsible decisions about some more or less reliable bit of the natural world. And, where that knowledge relates to human beings, it is important that its connections with other aspects of human life are not broken or ignored.[1]

His concerns were several. Will an understanding of the genetic components of behavior affect our sense of personal responsibility? Will the awareness of genetic differences diminish our commitment to the equality and worth of all peoples? And, even more fundamentally, will society have the wisdom, the powers of discernment, and the appropriate commitments to apply its new knowledge and capabilities for ethical ends?

This study is an exploration of the manner in which religious thinkers and communities have responded to the challenges and opportunities of the genetics revolution. To do so, it will survey and analyze the literature on genetics written by a wide range of religiously trained ethicists and theologians, and in a few cases scientists, or commissioned by various religious bodies. Religious ethics is understood inclusively as efforts to deal with the moral implications of genetics from a religious perspective. Such a broad conception includes various types of ethical analysis and theological interpretation, as well as the development of norms and guidelines. A particular work or author is considered religious in nature if the intent is to write for a religious audience, if the author is trained in a seminary or other professional religious institution, and/or if the thinking is set within the context of a religious tradition, theology, or concepts. Most, but not all, of the sources analyzed are Christian in origin, reflecting the current availability of religious work on genetics.

My primary goal is to explore approaches to undertaking religious ethics at the frontiers of genetic science and to assess their contributions and limitations. The emphasis here, therefore, is on the content and methodology of these works of religious ethics and not on the issues per se. Nevertheless, it is difficult to discuss conceptual building blocks apart from the way they are used. Each chapter focuses on discussions of the ethical issues related to genetic developments, cloning, and gene patenting, and efforts to engage in theological reinterpretations of human nature in light of genetic findings.

This study focuses on the religious response to genetic developments for two primary reasons. First, many of the issues raised by genetic developments have significant theological as well as ethical import. The ability to alter nature, and possibly human nature as well, seemingly makes us creators, or, to use

---

1. The statement of the Archbishop of York, "The Perils of Trying to Know Too Much," is quoted in J. Robert Nelson, *On the New Frontiers of Genetics and Religion* (Grand Rapids, Mich.: Wm. B. Eerdmans Publishing Co., 1994), 48.

theologian Philip Hefner's terminology, created co-creators,[2] albeit without a transcending sense of purpose and direction. The science of genetic research has implications for understanding what it means to be human, and the nature and limits of human freedom and responsibility, topics very much within the domain of religious thought. To make decisions about genetic applications requires judgments about human moral agency and responsibility to God, to other humans, to future generations, and to the created order. Genetic findings have implications for theological interpretations of human nature, often referred to as theological anthropology. Fundamentally religious and theological questions require a religious and theological response.

Second, the religious community can make an important contribution to societal efforts to grapple with the choices and dilemmas arising from the genetics revolution. A resource commissioned by the Evangelical Lutheran Church quite appropriately comments, "The church has significant and distinctive things to say about a society wrestling with the questions and the meaning of genetic developments."[3] That observation should be extended to encompass a wide range of religious communions. Religious perspectives on genetics can offer broad frameworks of understanding and commitment so necessary to deal with these complex issues. Religious thinkers can draw on centuries, indeed millennia, of thought about human relationships and responsibilities. In contrast with the radical individualism so prevalent in our society, most religious traditions offer a concept of the common good, an understanding of the individual as a person-in-community, and a vision of human beings as basically social and interdependent beings. Religious thinkers also tend to avoid the anthropocentric bias of our culture, interpreting human life and destiny in more inclusive contexts of meaning and purpose.

Nevertheless, religious ethics is only potentially relevant to the task of shaping a moral response to the genetics revolution. Religious thinkers bring many liabilities, as well as assets, to ethical and moral analysis of genetic developments. Lack of scientific training or even basic scientific literacy is an obvious problem for many religious ethicists and theologians. Written within the context of prescientific societies, the foundational texts of most religious communities do not directly address the types of issues raised by genetic advances. Moreover, it is quite difficult to apply philosophical, ethical, and theological concepts developed for other purposes to the interpretation and analysis of scientific

2. Philip Hefner, *The Human Factor: Evolution, Culture, and Religion* (Minneapolis: Fortress Press, 1993).

3. Roger A. Willer, "Introduction," in Roger A. Willer, ed., *Genetic Testing and Screening: Critical Engagement at the Intersection of Faith and Science* (Minneapolis: Kirk House Publishers for the Evangelical Lutheran Church in America, 1998), 7.

developments. At the least, these ethical and theological building blocks need to be informed by and perhaps altered through a dialogue with science. How this may happen is the subject of this book. This study will evaluate the extent to which various religious communities and thinkers are rising to these challenges.

THE GENETIC REVOLUTION AND ITS IMPLICATIONS

The groundwork for the genetic revolution was laid in 1953 when two researchers, James Watson and Francis Crick, published a brief article in *Nature* magazine describing the structure of deoxyribonucleic acid or DNA, the genetic material found in all living organisms. Nearly a century earlier, Gregor Mendel, an Austrian monk, had conducted initial landmark experiments in genetics showing that traits can be inherited, and he also postulated the existence of a discrete unit of inheritance that we now call a gene. His findings, while initially ignored, were rediscovered at the end of the nineteenth century and led to further genetic research. By the 1940s scientists began to discover the composition of DNA. Determining the symmetrical, twisted structure of DNA, referred to as a double helix, was a decisive breakthrough, however, because it helped to explain how DNA served as the chemical basis of the gene.

DNA may be compared to a blueprint. It contains the instructions for making cells and doing the work that goes on inside of them. Genes are segments of DNA that provide the information to synthesize a specific protein molecule. Proteins are essential to the structure, function, and regulation of cells in the body because of their role in catalyzing chemical reactions. When a gene is altered or mutated it produces a change in the components, arrangement, or molecular sequence of a gene. This affects the production of specific proteins, and by doing so sometimes causes abnormalities or genetic diseases.

Sometimes described as the book of life, DNA contains the code for every inherited characteristic. For the past four billion years, all life-forms have contained some version of DNA. Today all living things, regardless of their species or level of complexity, contain the same DNA. The unique characteristics of each result from the amount of DNA in their cells and the messages that DNA carries. Thus human beings share much of our DNA with other forms of life from the simplicity of the bacteria to the far greater complexity of our nearest genetic relatives, the chimpanzee and the bonobo.

DNA also serves as the basic unit of heredity. Each gene determines one trait or characteristic. Human DNA, termed the human genome, is formed at the moment of conception when two sets of genes, one from the mother and one from the father, unite to create a new and genetically distinct person or, in the case of multiple births, persons. DNA conveys heritable characteristics, susceptibilities, and dispositions from one generation to another.

Scientists have discovered that DNA is made up of tiny chemical bits called nucleotides, each composed of four groups of chemicals—adenine, guanine, thymine, and cystosine, usually abbreviated as A, G, T, and C. These chemicals or bases, sometimes referred to as the alphabet of heredity, always occur in pairs and are repeated over and over in different sequences along the double helix. An average chromosome or string of genes has approximately 140 million alphabetic base pairs of nucleotides. The human genome has twenty-three pairs of chromosomes, containing a total of about eighty thousand genes. Altogether the human genome consists of approximately six billion letters organized in three billion base pairs. It is estimated that a printout of the information in a single human genome would be the equivalent of thirteen sets of the *Encyclopedia Britannica*.[4]

A series of discoveries in the twenty years following Watson's and Crick's work enabled scientists to begin to alter the genetic structure of life. Genetic engineering or, more technically, recombinant DNA technology, refers to the procedures utilized to manipulate, replicate, and modify DNA. First, scientists learned that, far from genetic material being fixed, the breaking and relinking of different pieces of DNA is quite common in nature. These mechanisms permit the exchange of genetic material between chromosomes. Second, in the early 1970s, scientists found that an enzyme generated in cells, of which some 150 types have now been identified, makes it possible to cut DNA at points where specific DNA sequences occur. These restriction enzymes serve as tiny biological scissors to slice DNA. Once cut, the exposed ends are able to stick to another fragment that has been cut by the same restriction enzyme, making it possible to rearrange or recombine DNA. In 1973, scientists used these techniques to add foreign genetic material, that is, fragments of DNA from another kind of organism, into a bacterium. Each time the cell divided it produced copies of the modified hybrid form. With this knowledge genetic engineering was now possible. One commentator describes the accomplishment of these scientists: "They had done in biology what medieval alchemists had unsuccessfully attempted in metallurgy. Or, according to some, they were the Drs. Frankenstein who could create new forms of life."[5]

As singular as this accomplishment is, it is important to recognize that genetic engineering rests on a long history of human efforts to alter and improve nature. From the dawn of civilization, humans have sought to adapt

4. Roger Lincoln Shinn, *The New Genetics: Challenges for Science, Faith and Politics* (Wakefield, R.I., and London: Moyer Bell, 1996), 29.
5. Quoted in Nelson, *New Frontiers*, 7.

nature to their own ends. Initial attempts to bring about deliberate genetic changes in plants and animals took place some ten thousand years ago. Selective breeding of plants and animals has been part of agriculture since its inception. Many of the domestic plants in existence today were developed through generations of planting seeds with specific characteristics. Our stock of domestic animals was similarly developed through breeding to produce offspring with particular traits.

Nevertheless, genetic engineering does represent a major threshold in new capabilities. Theologian Ronald Cole-Turner identifies four differences between genetic engineering and selective breeding: the nature of the human intervention, the speed of change, the ability to transform DNA, and the nature and volume of knowledge gained from developments in molecular biology.[6] Genetic engineering technology enables scientists to harness processes of "natural recombination" at the microbiological level to attain specific human objectives and ends. Moreover, scientists are able to transfer genes from radically different species that are unlikely to be combined in nature and impossible to mix through selective breeding. The process of selective breeding is relatively slow, usually requiring several generations, and, because it depends on the manifestation of outward traits, is something of an erratic process. In contrast, the ability to alter genetic material directly offers significantly greater specificity and speed than do traditional breeding techniques. Genetic engineering makes it possible for human beings to go beyond the selection of traits to act directly upon the genetic material itself.[7]

Advances in molecular biology have brought the unprecedented ability to manipulate, replicate, and modify DNA. This capacity to rearrange the very building blocks of life has made it possible to alter plants, animals, and potentially even human beings. Genetic engineering has enabled scientists to create transgenic animals and plants through the insertion of genes from one species into another. This technology therefore raises the issue of whether we are inappropriately playing God. Some argue, for example, that "scientists are now intruding upon an inner sanctuary of life, a sacred mystery of genetic givenness that should only be received (from God or from nature) with gratitude, never manipulated or engineered."[8] Learning how to manipulate the genetic basis of all of life also provides the potential of altering the course of evolution.

6. Ronald Cole-Turner, *The New Genesis: Theology and the Genetic Revolution* (Louisville: Westminster/John Knox Press, 1993), 42.
7. President's Commission for the Study of Ethical Problems in Medicine and Biomedical and Behavioral Research, *Splicing Life: The Social and Ethical Issues of Genetic Engineering with Human Beings* (Washington, D.C.: U.S. Gov't. Printing Office, 1982), 9.
8. Cole-Turner, *New Genesis,* 44.

What does it mean for us to be able to do so, and how should we use this power?

The explosion of knowledge about the biological basis of human life has been further accelerated by the inception of the Human Genome Project (HGP). A $3 billion initiative begun in 1990 by the United States government, with international cooperation, HGP's primary objective is to learn the sequence and map the position of the 50,000 to 100,000 genes in the human genome. Learning the sequence entails deciphering the three billion base pairs (the A,G,C,T alphabet) that constitute the DNA chains on our twenty-three pairs of chromosomes. Constructing a DNA map involves locating the position and spacing of the full complement of genes that provide the instructions for making proteins in each of our body's cells. Sequencing and mapping are steps toward the even more daunting endeavor of understanding what the genetic instructions mean. As of 1998, with the program halfway through its fifteen-year course, scientists had mapped some 4 percent of the total human genome. During the course of 1998, however, two private commercial initiatives, each utilizing a new generation of computer technology and high-speed sequencing machines, announced that they planned to decode the entire human genome by 2001. Spurred by this competition, the United States National Human Genome Research Institute, the coordinator of HGP, accelerated its own effort so as to produce a working draft of the genome by 2001 and a full version by 2003.[9]

The implications of having this knowledge are profound. For the first time, humans are analyzing the physical basis of life, our DNA sequences. Scientists, granted with considerable hyperbole, have compared the decoding of the human genome with the discovery of a biological Holy Grail and a biological Rosetta Stone.[10] James Watson, whose discovery of the helical structure of DNA laid the groundwork for the biotechnology revolution, has celebrated the project as nothing less than the attempt "to find out what being human is."[11] Recognizing the potential societal implications of HGP, Watson, who served as the first director of the project, emphasized a need to study the ethical and social issues involved. In response to his recommendation, Congress agreed to allocate 3 percent of the $200 million annual budget for research on its potential ethical, legal, and social consequences. Eventually the levels were increased to 5 percent of the budget of National Human Genome Research Institute at

9. Eliot Marshall, "NIH to Produce a 'Working Draft' of the Genome by 2001," *Science* 281 (18 September 1998): 1774–75.
10. Quoted in Ted Peters, *Playing God: Genetic Determinism and Human Freedom* (New York and London: Routledge, 1997), 6.
11. Quoted in Cole-Turner, *New Genesis,* 20.

the National Institutes of Health (NIH) and 3 percent of the Office of Health and Environmental Research in the Department of Energy, NIH's partner in the project, amounting to some $11 million by 1997.[12] Research sponsored by the Ethical, Legal, and Social Issues Program has helped clarify the issues genetic science raises but has not provided answers.

In addition to decoding the human genetic structure, HGP also seeks to identify the genes whose defects or mutations are assumed to be the cause of genetically based diseases. While all people share the same genome or genetic structure, we each have alternative forms of these genes, known as alleles. Different alleles produce variations in inherited characteristics. Genetic abnormalities, some of which are inherited and others that develop from exposure to environmental agents, affect the proteins produced by genes and thereby result in various disorders. They also are a factor in the development of cancer. Most of the public support and excitement generated by the project derives from the promise it holds for the diagnosis and eventual development of therapies to treat these diseases. It is estimated that genetic diseases afflict upwards of twenty million United States citizens and may account for 25 to 30 percent of admissions to children's hospitals.[13] Cancer is one of the leading causes of death. Human gene therapy has been described as "a symbol of hope in a vast sea of human suffering due to heredity."[14]

Thus far, scientists have made considerable progress in identifying the genes linked to genetic disorders in which an error in a single gene coding for a specific protein is the cause of the disease. They have found the genes associated with such conditions as Huntington's disease, Tay-Sachs disease, cystic fibrosis, Duchenne muscular dystrophy, Lesche-Nyhan syndrome, and sickle cell anemia. Researchers have also discovered some of the genes associated with increasing the predisposition toward certain diseases, such as breast and ovarian cancer. Nevertheless, investigators are only just beginning to characterize more common complex diseases in which several genes are involved, such as certain forms of cancer, diabetes, and heart disease.

While medical science can offer an increasing repertoire of tests to reveal some genetic risk factors, this information has not yet led to effective treatments. NIH gave permission for the first cautious experiments in somatic cell (nonheritable) gene modification in 1990. As of 1997, more than two thou-

12. Eliot Marshall, "The Genome Program's Conscience," *Science* 274 (25 October 1996): 488.
13. Ian Barbour, *Ethics in an Age of Technology: The Gifford Lectures* (New York: HarperSanFrancisco, 1993), 194.
14. John C. Fletcher and W. French Anderson, "Germ-Line Gene Therapy: A New Stage of Debate," *Law, Medicine, and Health Care* 20 (Spring/Summer 1992): 31.

sand subjects were enrolled in controlled trials for diseases ranging from rare metabolic defects to common cancers. Of the one hundred gene therapy protocols approved by the NIH Recombinant DNA Advisory Committee between 1990 and 1995, twenty-two were for genetic diseases (with cystic fibrosis accounting for the largest number).[15] Most of the other test protocols were for forms of cancer. Gene therapy to date has entailed efforts to insert a good copy of a gene into a cell that has a defective gene. By so doing, it is hoped that the corrective gene will compensate for the defective one and restore the cell to its proper function. Gene addition may be done through *in vivo* methods (directly into the patient's cells) or *ex vivo* methods (cells taken from the patient are genetically altered). These efforts have encountered three technical sets of problems: developing an effective delivery system that brings the corrected gene to the appropriate site or location in the chromosome of the cell, having the corrected gene expressed (turned on) at the right level and timing, and assuring safety in the process.[16]

The results to date have been promising but certainly far short of categorical success. In 1997 an eminent geneticist claimed that thus far "no approach has definitively improved the health of a single one of the more than two thousand patients who have enrolled in gene therapy trials worldwide."[17] Other scientists assess the field more positively, arguing that some patients have indeed been helped, if not cured. Moreover, the newness of genetic therapy makes it difficult to predict future developments, particularly if the technical problem of finding vectors able to direct the corrective gene to its appropriate site can be resolved. And, there are signs of technical progress. Targeted gene repair based on harnessing the cell's own ability to correct faulty genetic sequences, a wholly new approach, known as chimeraplasty, may provide the answer to many of the technical problems in first generation therapies.[18]

Given the imbalance between testing and treatment opportunities, the current state of genetic knowledge requires new and often agonizing decisions. Is

15. LeRoy Walters and Julie Gage Palmer, *The Ethics of Human Gene Therapy* (New York: Oxford University Press, 1997), 151.

16. This description of the current state of the technology is drawn from a presentation made by R. Michael Blaese, then Chief, Clinical Gene Therapy Branch, National Human Genome Research Institute, National Institutes of Health, to a working group of the American Association for the Advancement of Science (AAAS) in May 1998.

17. Theodore Friedmann, "Overcoming the Obstacles to Gene Therapy," *Scientific American* 276 (June 1997): 96.

18. Betsy T. Kren, Paramita Bandyopadhyay, and Clifford J. Steer, "In Vivo Site-Directed Mutagenesis of the Factor IX Gene By Chimeric RNA/DNA Oligonucleotides," *Nature Medicine* 4 (March 1998): 285–90.

it better to know or not to know genetic risk factors when there are no treatments available, particularly for disabling late-onset disorders that only appear later in life? Is such genetic information an intolerable burden imposing a sense of personal doom? Since genetic testing can be quite costly, who should be given access—only those who can afford to pay or have comprehensive health insurance that will cover the testing, or those in high-risk groups? Under what circumstances do couples planning to have a child have the responsibility to undergo carrier screening for genetic disorders, and how should this information be used for reproductive planning? Furthermore, how do we understand and interpret the existence of genetic disorders?

Prenatal testing that can find genetic abnormalities in the fetus raises another set of painful and troubling choices. Abortion, already a divisive and difficult social issue, is made even more so. Since few therapies are currently available for genetic anomalies that are discovered, genetic testing leads to the question of whether and under what circumstances an abnormal pregnancy should be interrupted or ended. Does genetic testing imply that a pregnancy is only tentative, dependent on a favorable genetic screen, and if so, what are the implications for our sense of human dignity and our perceptions of the disabled living among us? Is a therapeutic abortion ever warranted? Are some genetic disorders so disabling, so painful, and so injurious to the prospective child's quality of life that it is preferable for the birth not to occur? How do we make such determinations?

Each new genetic advance seems to bring yet another set of ethical, theological, and policy conundrums. To date, gene therapy has dealt only with the somatic or body cells of the subject being treated, but researchers appear to be on the threshold of having the technical means to attempt human germ-line interventions that will be inherited by future descendants of the patient. Do we have the right to alter the genetic composition of future generations? Scientists have managed to clone and produce genetically identical copies of several species of animals through two different techniques, each with the prospect of human application. Thus far scientists have not proceeded with human cloning, largely because of the risks involved, although several have indicated a desire to do so. But, what if animal models show human cloning to be feasible and relatively safe? Should we then permit human cloning, and what would be the implications for the family and for the cloned child?

Pushing the frontiers of biology even further, scientists have isolated and cultivated human stem cells, the primordial cells from which the entire individual develops. Because stem cells are the basis of more specialized cells, human stem cells may have the potential to grow into replacement tissue of virtually any kind for transplantation into a patient's body. Stem cells may also offer more effective routes to human cloning than the techniques used to date for the cloning of sheep, cattle, and mice. Therapies developed from stem cells may also be able to treat a wide range of chronic diseases. Stem cell research and applications, however, raise yet another series of issues related to the moral status of human primordial stem cells and the sources from which they are derived, either blastocysts left over from fertility clinics, *in vitro* fertilization efforts, or aborted fetuses. How is it possible to weigh and balance moral obligations to the future health and welfare of people with respect for the human embryo? This issue may escalate the already wrenching debate over abortion.

Biomedical science is advancing at an unprecedented rate. Seemingly, every month, every week brings announcements of new breakthroughs in understanding and controlling life processes. Does the technical ability to do something mean that we should use those powers? If not, who should and how do we make ethical decisions that will affect both contemporary society and future generations? Should scientists be given unfettered opportunities for genetic research and applications, or will doing so doom our society to being shaped by a technological determinism? And if we wish to draw a line so that we can control this evolving technology rather than have it control us, how do we do so?

Some of the issues emerging from the genetic developments are completely new—whether to create transgenetic forms of life and release them into ecosystems, the appropriateness of cloning human beings, whether we have the wisdom to alter the human genome. In other cases, genetic discoveries and developments complicate already difficult moral quandaries, like the issue of therapeutic abortion. Some of these issues are most appropriately addressed at a societal level through public policy. Others, particularly genetic testing and screening, increasingly confront individuals and families with a personal need to respond to the tide of genetic developments. With each wave of new discovery, these fundamental questions become more pressing, not to mention ever more complex to address.

MAKING UNPRECEDENTED CHOICES

Clearly, the choices we make today will shape the human future. In 1966, the World Council of Churches (WCC) Fourth Assembly, anticipating further discoveries in genetic science and the development of biotechnology, issued a caution: "We are faced with the second technological revolution. Basic human values are at stake. They may be enhanced, stabilized, degraded, or destroyed depending on the way we use technology."[19] Whether we will determine or be

19. Quoted in David M. Gill, *Technology, Faith and the Future of Man: Report on an Exploratory Conference* (Geneva: WCC, 1970), 11.

determined by genetic science and technology will depend on our capacity to discern the challenges and respond wisely.

Yet, in a period of human history in which science and technology are conferring powers of life and death far beyond those of previous generations, society seems singularly incapable of reflecting upon and engaging in shared moral reasoning about these discoveries. Although we face unprecedented choices, we seemingly have lost the ability to engage in meaningful corporate moral discourse. As ethicist Larry Rasmussen notes, "Our society [the United States] currently lives from moral fragments and community fragments only, and both are being destroyed faster than they are being replenished."[20] He anticipates that this bodes trouble for basic moral formation because this process requires community as the matrix of the moral life.[21] So it does, but it is also problematic for addressing frontier scientific issues. Cultural pluralism and moral fragmentation make it difficult to reach consensus about societal priorities and goals, let alone to summon the spiritual and ethical resources necessary to respond to the challenges posed by science and technology. These are identified by theologian Ronald Cole-Turner as "the power to guide, to envision the ideal, the good, the true, and the beautiful, and thus to define our presence on the planet."[22]

Contemporary society seems morally numbed and fatigued by the burden of responding to the many developments emerging from the accelerated genetic revolution. Many, perhaps the majority of persons, seem to lack the basic scientific literacy required to understand the nature of these discoveries, and there are currently few effective channels of public education. Because the mass media frames societal consideration, these issues are often sensationalized and trivialized into sound bites. Typically an initial flurry of concern is not sustained long enough to have meaningful debate of any kind. Public opinion frequently vacillates between fearfulness of the new and a heady, almost reckless excitement and affirmation. The glamour and mystique of science often make it difficult to raise questions about the appropriateness and ethical implications of particular applications and technologies. During much of the period of rapid advances in genetics and biotechnology, there has not been a mechanism in this country for public bioethics, like a national bioethics advisory body, as a means of providing expert analysis and recommendations.[23] Much of the time,

20. Larry Rasmussen, *Moral Fragments and Moral Community: A Proposal for Church and Society* (Minneapolis: Fortress Press, 1993), 11.
21. Ibid., 11–12.
22. Cole-Turner, *New Genesis*, 9.
23. A National Bioethics Advisory Commission (NBAC) of eighteen independent experts was finally constituted in 1996, with a mandate covering the rights and wel-

Congress seems either unable or at least reluctant to deal with these developments. This leaves issues related to genetic science and technology to be determined by the courts on narrow legal grounds or directed by the market. And, given the nature and significance of these unprecedented choices, we require more ethically sensitive, balanced, and appropriate instruments of reflection than either the courts or market can provide.

Science cannot provide the answers. Nor should scientists be given the task of making ethical determinations for society. As society has become more sensitive to concerns about the potential dangers of biological science to human subjects and its significant potential consequences, the regulation of science has become part of our public policy landscape. The National Bioethics Advisory Commission (NBAC) notes, "Because science is both a public and social enterprise and its application can have profound impact, society recognizes that the freedom of scientific inquiry is not an absolute right and scientists are expected to conduct their research according to widely held ethical principles."[24] In other words, appropriate ethical constraints are a matter for both scientists and the broader public to formulate and implement. Similarly, molecular biologist Robert Pollack warns that the dream of pure and unfettered research is ultimately dangerous because the path of science is not self-correcting. According to Pollack, science can meet its responsibilities only by openly sharing concerns with others and requesting the broadest possible societal participation in setting its agenda. He counsels fellow scientists as follows:

> Molecular biologists have two choices. They can continue working out the meanings of individual genes, going into business for themselves with the discoveries they have made in tax-supported laboratories, shortcutting peer review using news conferences and patent secrecy, taking tax money from their forty million Americans who cannot afford any health insurance at all, and ignoring any potential eugenic uses of their work. Or they can begin to rethink what it is they do and why they do it.[25]

Further complicating matters, narrow specialization, an analytic approach, and an instrumental frame of reference have rendered secular philosophy and ethics often unable even to ask appropriate questions, let alone shape a meaningful discussion, or provide a substantive, moral judgment. Gerald McKenny comments in his book *To Relieve the Human Condition* that modern moral discourse provides

---

fare of human subjects, the management and use of genetic information, and genetic patenting.

24. NBAC, *Cloning Human Beings: Report and Recommendations* (Rockville, Md.: NBAC, 1997), 6.

25. Robert Pollack, *Signs of Life: The Language and Meanings of DNA* (Boston: Houghton Mifflin, 1994), 180.

no vocabulary to deliberate about the moral purposes the body serves, the goods health should promote, or the limits technology should observe in controlling our bodies. Hence, according to McKenny, it becomes difficult to discuss and discern what kinds of suffering should be eliminated, what choices we should make, or what role technology should play.[26] Given these limitations, it becomes tempting to try to resolve genetic dilemmas by resorting to narrow perspectives and orientations offered by specific disciplines—particularly law and economics—or ideologies. But this carries grave risks. As the theologian Richard McCormick cautions,

> The dangers that confront us in facing the bioethical problems cast up by advancing technology are quite well known, but easily overlooked in practice. The dangers are that such problems will be "solved" by one-eyed approaches such as power, fiat, prestige, economics or even tradition in its narrow and, I think, untenable sense (the application of old and presumably invariable injunctions to new data). That is why it is important to ask: "Where do we start?" Our beginnings are like the first chapter of a novel: They foreshadow and sometimes even determine what is to come.[27]

Bioethics, also known as biomedical ethics or medical ethics, is the subfield or specialty closest to genetics. Critiques of secular bioethics, many by long-time practitioners, point to the degree to which its orientation reflects the unchallenged individualism in United States cultural tradition and how this has shaped and distorted its issues, social construction of realities, and priorities. Perhaps the single most influential book in the field, *Principles of Biomedical Ethics,* written by Tom Beauchamp and James Childress, puts forward an approach based on four principles, sometimes referred to as principlism.[28] Of the four principles—autonomy, nonmaleficence, beneficence, and justice—the first is by far the most dominant. Toward the end of his career, Daniel Callahan, a pioneer in bioethics and founder of the prestigious Hastings Center, wrote about the degree to which liberal individualism had led bioethics to neglect substantive questions about the goals of medicine and its service to the human good, arguing that it was insufficient to guide medicine through the biomedical revolution and the technological innovations it has spawned.[29]

---

26. Gerald P. McKenny, *To Relieve the Human Condition: Bioethics, Technology and the Body* (Albany: State University of New York Press, 1997), 21.
27. Richard A. McCormick, "Bioethics and Method? Where Do We Start?" *Theology Digest* 29 (Winter 1981): 303.
28. Tom L. Beauchamp and James F. Childress, *Principles of Biomedical Ethics,* 4th ed. (New York and Oxford: Oxford University Press, 1994).
29. Daniel Callahan, "The Goals of Medicine: Setting New Priorities," A Special Supplement to *The Hastings Center Report* 26 (November/December 1996): S1–25.

Others have commented on the inadequacies of the individualistic focus on doctor-patient relationships, namely, that it has led to the failure to address wider questions of social justice. Some critics are disturbed about the way health is cast as a commodity rather than a social good, also that health and illness are understood as conditions that happen to individuals one at a time, obscuring the sense in which the health of all depends upon the health of each.[30] Still other bioethicists castigate the field for diverting its gaze from considering social issues, especially those that affect persons who are poor.[31]

When medical ethics first developed in the late 1960s and early 1970s, religious thinkers and questions played an important role, but as the field developed and the work became more focused and specialized, it became increasingly secularized. In an autobiographical essay written in 1990, Callahan commented that the loss of a distinctively religious voice in medical ethics encourages a form of moral philosophy for use in the marketplace. He believed the net result of the narrowing of philosophy and the disappearance or denaturing of religion in public discourse left us too heavily dependent on the law as the working source of morality. It deprived society of the accumulated wisdom and knowledge of long-established religious traditions, according to Callahan, and it enshrined the discourse of wary strangers speaking in a form of moral Esperanto that suppresses the pluralism of particular moral communities.[32]

THE POTENTIAL ROLE OF RELIGIOUS COMMUNITIES

Religious ethics is potentially relevant to the task of shaping a moral response to the impact and implications of science and technology, for a variety of reasons. First and foremost, many of the issues that the genetics revolution raises have significant theological components and therefore require a religious and theological response. Not only are these questions religious in nature, but for persons of faith the choices genetic developments pose cannot be addressed apart from fundamental theological precepts about human nature and standing before God and our role in creation. Writing in a resource commissioned by the Evangelical Lutheran Church in America, Roger Willer calls church members to a critical engagement that "recognizes that genetic developments

30. Bruce Jennings, "Beyond Distributive Justice in Health Reform," *The Hastings Center Report* 26 (November/December 1996): 14–15.

31. Renée C. Fox, "More than Bioethics," *The Hastings Center Report* 26 (November/December 1996): 5–7.

32. Daniel Callahan, "Religion and the Secularization of Bioethics," *Theology, Religious Traditions, and Bioethics*, Supplement to *The Hastings Center Report* 20 (July/August 1990): S4.

are occasions in which God is at work. Genetic testing and screening are part of God's creative enterprise and evoke religious concern at every level."[33] Cole-Turner proposes that "the purpose of genetic engineering is to expand our ability to participate in God's work of redemption and creation and thereby to glorify God."[34]

The genetic revolution offers both a challenge and an opportunity to the religious community: a challenge to apply religious values and frameworks to new and unprecedented issues and an opportunity to help interpret and illuminate significant ethical choices before their members and the broader society. Taking Patrick Nowell-Smith's definition, genetic developments have potential import for all three dimensions of a system of morality: understandings about the nature of human beings and their world, beliefs about what is good or appropriate, and rules laying down what ought or ought not to be done.[35] Genetic science also has significant implications for some traditional faith-based concepts and understandings, particularly those relating to theological anthropology. The task of religious thinkers in every period is to attempt to formulate conceptions of God, humanity, and the world relevant to contemporary human life and draw their ethical implications. To meet these requirements in our age, these constructions must take science into account. This type of critical engagement with genetic developments is obviously difficult and complex. Nevertheless, by refraining from doing so and not wrestling with the questions and meaning of genetic developments, religious communities risk becoming irrelevant to important ethical and policy decisions.

One of the contributions religious perspectives can provide is to offer the broad frameworks of understanding and commitment so necessary to deal with these complex issues. In contrast with the radical individualism prevalent in secular ethics, religious ethicists can draw on traditions with a concept of the common good, an understanding of the individual as a self-in-community, and a vision of human beings as a basically social and interdependent species. The ethicist Sondra Wheeler comments, "The picture of the self-possessed individual deciding his or her own fate in splendid isolation is one wholly alien to the Christian understanding of moral existence."[36] Elizabeth Bettenhausen,

33. Willer, "Introduction," in Willer, ed., *Genetic Testing,* 8.

34. Cole-Turner, *New Genesis,* 51.

35. Patrick H. Nowell-Smith, "Religion and Morality," in *Encyclopedia of Philosophy,* vol. 7 (New York: Macmillan and the Free Press, 1967), 150, cited in Philip Hefner, "Theological Perspectives on Morality and Human Evolution," in W. Mark Richardson and Wesley J. Wildman, eds., *Religion and Science: History, Method, Dialogue* (New York and London: Routledge, 1996), 403.

36. Sondra Ely Wheeler, *Stewards of Life: Bioethics and Pastoral Care* (Nashville: Abingdon Press, 1996), 46.

another ethicist, conceptualizes personhood as a "matter of living reciprocally in the presence of God, of oneself, of other persons, and of all creation."[37] Judaism, Christianity, and Islam conceptualize persons as moral and social beings created to live in communities linked by relationships of mutual caring and responsibility. The religious concept of covenant captures this sense of interconnectedness between humanity and God and the interrelationships among persons in a moral community in which both the common good and the good of each member are sought as a dimension of faithfulness to God's mandates.

A religious centering by its very nature offers a vision in which persons are responsible beyond their own self-interest to the ultimate source of grounding of their lives and being. James Gustafson argues in his monumental two-volume *Ethics from a Theocentric Perspective* that the central moral question for a theocentric perspective is, "What is God enabling and requiring us to be and to do?"[38] While I agree with Gustafson's characterization, I would like to add a caveat, namely, that no faith community, no religious thinker has ready-made answers regarding divine mandates for genetic research and applications. The interface between religious belief and genetics calls for a complex and sometimes ambiguous process of discernment. Religious ethics at the frontiers of science has no place for religious fanaticism or fundamentalism.

In postindustrial societies, religious communities constitute one of the most important intact sources of moral formation and discourse. Religious communities are not necessarily free of the particularisms, inadequacies, and prejudices of other communities, but at a minimum the historical religious traditions are centers of moral judgment and criticism. Ethicist Larry Rasmussen explains, "*Religio* means 'a uniting bond.' It is a special bond, a tether to the sacred and divine, that strong link to God which holds fast the precious cargo of abiding meaning."[39] At their best, religious communities provide dedication to significant issues of meaning and interpretation within the framework of responsibility to the Divine and a commitment to human well-being. They seek to inculcate a catholic moral vision, offer moral leadership, and constitute centers of moral formation and reformation. And even when they fall short of this ideal, which is not infrequently, they at least retain a commitment in principle to an ethical orientation that transcends self-interest, short-term benefit, and economic aggrandizement.

---

37. Elizabeth Bettenhausen, "Genes in Society: Whose Body?" in Willer, ed., *Genetic Testing and Screening,* 113–14.
38. James M. Gustafson, *Ethics from a Theocentric Perspective,* vol. 2, *Ethics and Theology* (Chicago: University of Chicago Press, 1984), 1.
39. Rasmussen, *Moral Fragments,* 16.

Many religious communities and thinkers early realized the importance of genetic developments. A few theologians began to address issues related to genetics and genetic engineering as early as the 1960s. In 1980, the general secretaries of three major faith-based organizations, the National Council of Churches in the U.S.A., the Synagogue Council of America, and the U.S. Catholic Conference wrote a letter to President Jimmy Carter warning of the perils that genetic engineering posed to humanity.[40] A 1984 publication of the National Council of Churches of Christ in the U.S.A. anticipates that the discoveries in human genetics may revolutionize our fundamental understandings of the world and the role of humanity:

> It may well be that this new turning point in molecular science is as radical as Copernicus's discovery in the sixteenth century that the earth revolved around the sun and not vice versa. It may be as far-reaching as Darwin's theory of evolution. It may be as crucial to our understanding of reality as Einstein's theory of matter. With each discovery we had to rethink our scheme of the universe and the role of humanity in it.[41]

The National Council of Churches Panel on Bioethical Concerns goes on to compare the current "bioethical pilgrimage" brought about by the discoveries of genetic science to the journeys of Abraham, Moses, and other persons of faith.[42] During the past twenty years, religious thinkers have contributed a relatively extensive literature on issues related to genetics, cloning, and genetic patenting.

Religious thinkers and communities also have taken a leadership role in making the claim that science and technology should be held to an ethical standard of evaluation. A 1986 policy statement of the National Council of Churches of Christ in the U.S.A. on the topic of genetics, for example, states: "We cannot agree with those who assert that scientific inquiry and research should acknowledge no limits. All that can be known need not be known if in advance it clearly appears that the process for gaining such knowledge violates the sanctity of human life. . . . Remembering its own history, the church should not oppose scientific advances, but it must speak out in judgment when

---

40. Letter from Dr. Claire Randall, General Secretary, National Council of Churches; Rabbi Bernard Mandelbaum, General Secretary, Synagogue Council of America; and Bishop Thomas Kelly, General Secretary, U.S. Catholic Conference to President Carter, 20 June 1980. The letter is reproduced in the President's Commission, *Splicing Life,* App. B, 95.
41. Panel of Bioethical Concerns, *Genetic Engineering: Social and Ethical Consequences,* Frank M. Harron, ed. (New York: Pilgrim Press, 1984).
42. Ibid., 20.

the quest for new knowledge supersedes all ethical concern."[43] That many religious thinkers are sensitive to the negative effects of science and technology does not make them Luddites opposed to scientific advancement or warriors in an unending battle between science and religion. As theologian Ronald Cole-Turner commented in a perspective published in *Science* magazine regarding the opposition of a wide coalition of religious leaders to genetic patenting,

> Recent scholarship is showing that the "warfare between science and religion" is turning out to be mostly myth, kept alive by those who want to push these two great human endeavors—the need to focus in communities on our deepest moral and spiritual yearnings, and the longing to understand the natural world of which we are a part—into opposing camps. The fact is that many religious leaders have seen science as a means to achieve the goals of religion, namely, to help and to heal. Religion gives science its purpose, and science gives religion its eyes and its hands.[44]

The issue is not so much an either/or, that is, a categorical acceptance of the legitimacy of all scientific applications that are technically feasible or a Luddite rejection of science and technology. Instead, the goal of many religious thinkers has been an effort to determine how to direct science and technology toward realizing human and environmental values.

To argue that religious thinkers and communities can make a significant contribution to ethical analysis and guidelines on frontier scientific issues is not to make a claim for theological privilege, however. The relevance of theological ethics for undertaking analysis of the implications of scientific and technological breakthroughs rests on its ability to ground, orient, and inform the task.[45] Theology and theological ethics should be an important voice in societal discussions because they offer a comprehensive and foundational orientation commensurate with the nature of the critical issues that scientific advances raise. Put in another way, developments that raise theological questions deserve a theological analysis. Given the importance of placing scientific developments within a context of basic moral commitments and values, the choice appears to be having theologians and religious ethicists contribute a theological perspective or having scientists attempt to be moral philosophers. Clearly society is better served by the former alternative.

43. National Council of Churches of Christ in the U.S.A., "Genetic Science for Human Benefit" (New York: Office of Research and Evaluation, adopted by the Governing Board 22 May 1986), 15.
44. Cole-Turner, "Religion and Gene Patenting," *Science* 270 (6 October 1995): 52.
45. James M. Gustafson, *Intersections: Science, Theology, and Ethics* (Cleveland: Pilgrim Press, 1996), 3.

It is important to emphasize what I am not claiming. I am not stepping out of a naturalistic frame of reference to assert that theology has a special status by virtue of its grounding in revelation or its foundations in sacred scriptures, doctrine, or religious tradition. Nor is Scripture or any specific sacred text the source for ready-made answers. Theological ethics is not the only appropriate discipline or approach. And, the appropriate relationship between religion and science is not unidirectional from religion to science.

I would also like to acknowledge that religious thinkers bring many liabilities, as well as assets, to ethical and moral analysis of genetic developments. Lack of scientific training is an obvious problem. It is simply not possible to deal with the ethical implications of particular genetic discoveries without understanding the science involved. At the very least, it requires some knowledge of basic biology and genetic science. Moreover, a fairly sophisticated level of scientific expertise may enhance an ethical evaluation of whether to go forward with particular applications.

Written within the context of prescientific societies, Scripture, or for that matter the foundational texts of most religious communities, does not directly address the types of issues raised by genetic advances. An interchange at the AAAS Dialogue Group on Genetic Patenting highlights this situation. A scientist generally sympathetic to the concerns of the religious community questioned why a theologian's paper had not cited any specific biblical references. The theologian responded that he had in fact included every relevant passage on gene patenting. Obviously, religious texts offer norms and values that provide a significant starting point; but the challenge, and it is a significant one, is how to discern and apply them to the complex and sometimes ambiguous choices before us today.

Traditional theological concepts and doctrinal formulations are only *potentially* applicable to thinking about the ethical conundrums cast up by advancing technologies. While theologians and ethicists have considered the nature and purpose of life for millennia, it is quite difficult to apply philosophical, ethical, or theological concepts developed for other purposes to the interpretation and analysis of scientific developments. As one theologian commented about cloning, "You can't just take a [religious] tradition that has been worked out in centuries of cultural shift and apply it like a cookbook to a new discovery."[46] Faith traditions set important parameters and perspectives, but unless their concepts are modernized through a dialogue with science and their content

---

46. Robert Russell, Executive Director of the Center for Theology and the Natural Sciences, quoted in "To Clone or Not to Clone," *Christian Century* 16 (19 March 1997): 286.

made more concrete and specific, they may be more suited to ask appropriate questions than to provide clear-cut answers.

Complicating the interface with science is that theology and ethics are based on sweeping, first-order principles, such as love of neighbor, and abstract concepts, for example, human dignity. Moreover, two thousand years of Western philosophical influence have kept Christian theology and ethics abstract and global. Thus, religious thinkers can more easily expound in the abstract on such topics as human dignity than evaluate the long-term implications of particular technologies within specific societal contexts for human dignity. Claims that humans are created in the image of God underscore that persons have moral responsibility and dignity; but unless the concept is made more specific, these claims will offer little concrete guidance as to whether to proceed with particular genetic applications.

TOWARD A DIALOGUE BETWEEN GENETIC SCIENCE, THEOLOGY, AND ETHICS

Much like what James Gustafson suggested, the most fruitful relationship between religion and science is a two-way dialogue, an interactional, dialectical process. Gustafson raises the possibility that "theological and ethical theory will be informed and even altered by concepts, information, and theories that they meet at particular intersections."[47] In contrast with the belief that theology and ethics cannot be substantially altered by other disciplines, theology can intersect science in a meaningful way, but it must be ready and open to being informed by and even altered by that relationship. Perhaps one mark of a real encounter is that both disciplines will be changed in some way by the process.

Religious metaphors, concepts, and narratives developed in response to very different contexts than we face today at the very least need further conceptualization, specification, and "operationalization" to be relevant for ethical analysis of genetic science. This requires developing methodologies that enable an interaction between science and norms, concepts, and metaphors drawn from theological ethics. That the interaction between science, ethics, and theology tends to be dynamic adds to the complexity of this task. While inherited theological and ethical concepts might serve as basic building blocks, such a dialogue is more likely to redefine them and evoke new meanings. Beliefs about the nature of human beings in their world, so central to the construct of an ethical system, may themselves be altered by the findings of genetic science. Thus the necessary dialogue can in some ways be compared with simultaneous translation of two languages on a changing conceptual field.

47. Gustafson, *Intersections,* 4.

To proceed with a meaningful dialogue, six questions related to the inter-face between religious thought and genetic science must be addressed. First, what are the methodological options for undertaking religious ethics at the frontiers of genetic science? Second, what types of conceptual building blocks do various religious thinkers use to address these topics? Third, what implica-tions does the interface between religion and genetic ethics have for theolo-gy, particularly theological anthropology? Fourth, in what ways do religious thinkers tend to differ from their secular counterparts? Fifth, is religious ethics on science and technology necessarily bound by historical religious traditions, or is it possible to engage meaningfully in broader theological and ethical analysis on science and technology across boundaries within the religious community? And sixth, how can religious thinkers best contribute to deliber-ations on genetics in a pluralistic secular society, and what are the costs and trade-offs of attempting to develop a public theology on genetics that address-es the wider society?

Methodological Options

What types of methods are most relevant for undertaking religious ethics at the frontiers of genetic science and seeking some kind of meaningful interface between science and faith? As noted, the ability of religious communities to address cutting-edge scientific and technological issues requires the develop-ment of new ways to apply abstract theological concepts and ethical norms to complex scientific innovations. This is largely unchartered terrain. Particularly formidable to traverse, all cross-disciplinary research, analysis, and efforts at dialogue must cope with differences in methodological approaches, priorities, and vocabularies in the distinct fields. Science and religion have disparate ori-entations, approaches to framing and testing truth statements, terminologies, and worldviews.[48] Each individual ethicist and every committee or task force convened for this purpose therefore has had two tasks. The first of these is defined by the goals and objectives of the proposed inquiry, and the second by the development of a methodology by which to proceed.

Gustafson delineates a variety of ways in which other disciplines, including the sciences, have been and are related to theological ethics, ranging from per-spectives which maintain that theology and ethics cannot be substantially altered by other disciplines to those which seek consonance or some form of integration. Of the eight patterns of relationship he presents, four have partic-ular relevance to the encounter of religious ethics with genetic science. In the

---

48. See, for example, Ian Barbour, *Religion in an Age of Science: The Gifford Lectures* (San Francisco: HarperSanFrancisco, 1990), 66–92, on the similarities and differences in sci-entific and theological/religious methodologies.

first, it is acknowledged that information, explanations, interpretations, and valuations from other disciplines have implications for the substance or content of theological ethics, thus requiring a revision of traditional theological and ethical theses. In the second, theological ethics redescribes, reexplains, or confers meaning to events or findings from other disciplines by placing them in a larger religious and ethical context. In the third, other disciplines offer the descriptions and analyses to which religious ethical principles are applied. And in the fourth, some general coherence is sought between theological and ethical premises, the information and explanations used from other disciplines, and how these data are interpreted and applied.[49] It is important to ask which of these approaches or discourse modes are being applied by religious thinkers at the intersection between ethics and genetic science and to what end.

Conceptual Building Blocks

The manner in which thinkers select, weigh, develop, and apply fundamental conceptual building blocks plays an important role in structuring their evaluation of the ethical implications of particular scientific and technological innovations. To do justice to the complexity of the task, this process of "operationalizing" abstract theological concepts requires a multifaceted, multidisciplinary dialogue between the science and the theology. This is made all the more complex because many religious concepts function more like metaphors or symbols. Various religious claims, for example, the assertion that humans are created in the image of God, tend to evoke a range of meanings. As such, these metaphors are sometimes described as multivalent, indicating that a variety or surplus of meanings can be assigned to or inferred from the concept. Jan Heller points out that this characteristic has fostered the growth and endurance of religious traditions because it enables adaptability without loss of their original meaning. Yet, it makes the concepts difficult to serve as standards or criteria by which to develop guides for action.[50] It is therefore important to identify the key conceptual building blocks that ethicists use and whether these concepts and metaphors are defined and developed sufficiently to illuminate ethical discernment on frontier scientific issues.

Implications for Theology

The implications of the dialogue with genetic science for faith-based concepts and understandings presents another set of issues. In what ways, if any, do the

49. Gustafson, *Intersections,* 137–40, 143.
50. Jan Christian Heller, "Religiously Based Objections to Cloning," in James M. Humber and Robert F. Almeder, eds., *Human Cloning* (Totowa, N.J.: Humana Press, 1998), 161.

findings of genetic science challenge traditional religious doctrines, and which communities are most affected? What is required to develop an updated theological anthropology consonant with the findings of genetic science? How does this enterprise affect religious teachings about the human essence or soul? Are we our genes, and if so, what does this mean for our sense of moral freedom and responsibility? In what ways can an interface with genetic science play a constructive role in redefining and developing religious ethics?

Distinctiveness of Religious Ethics

This study is predicated on the assumption that religious etheicists can make a distinctive contribution because they differ in some fundamental ways from their secular counterparts. What then are some of the salient differences between secular and religious ethicists working on genetics? Do these two communities generally address the same topics and have similar concerns? Are there themes and orientations that set religious ethicists apart from their secular counterparts? Do religious thinkers offer distinctive methodologies, approaches, emphases, and/or perspectives informed by their traditions? What kinds of religious insights are most relevant and helpful in helping to discern the potential benefits, as well as harms, related to genetic science?

Relevance of Traditional Confessional Orientations

Postmodernists tend to emphasize the distinctiveness and relevance of particular traditions. As a corollary, they argue that it is futile to attempt to establish a common framework for morality or ethical analysis. Editors of *Christian Bioethics,* a journal begun in 1995, explain this perspective.

> Rather than revealing itself as a single, unified, ecumenical faith, Christianity is sundered with Christians united neither in one communion nor in one baptism. *Christian Bioethics* seeks to examine the traditional content-full moral commitments which the Christian faiths bring to life, sexuality, suffering, illness and death within the context of medicine and health care. Seeking to understand the differences which separate the bioethics of Roman Catholics, Protestants, and the Orthodox, *Christian Bioethics* explores the manners in which the faiths diverge.[51]

The thesis of the journal is this: "Christian bioethics, like the Christian Scriptures, Christian love, Christian belief, and Christian action, can only be understood within a particular community with a particular tradition." But is this necessarily the case, particularly on a topic like genetics, in which elements

---

51. H. Tristam Engelhardt, Jr., "Toward a Christian Bioethics," *Christian Bioethics* 1 (1995): 1.

of a tradition, whether Christian or others, cannot be applied to the issues at hand without a significant development and interpretation? While there are likely to be diverse interpretations and views within the religious community on any topic related to genetics, are these differences necessarily shaped by the thinker's religious background? Will all members of a particular community view the relevance of their own traditions in the same way? Arguing for the need to recover a Christian rather than a denominational approach to bioethics, Nicholas Capaldi cautions, "We cannot escape post-modernism by retreating into 'our' community because we have lost a sense of what it means even to understand 'our' community."[52] Given the wide range of theological approaches, methodologies, and emphases among theologians and religious ethicists, how do these intersect with tradition so as to shape ethics on genetics?

Role of Religious Discourse in a Pluralistic Secular Society
It is entirely appropriate for religious thinkers and communities to engage in public theology, but to do so is likely to entail costs and trade-offs. Tensions between religious discourse and the challenges of public accessibility and meaning tend to be difficult to resolve. In fact, problems of translating religious discourse into a common moral language appropriate to an interdisciplinary and public audience propelled many religiously trained thinkers into writing as secular bioethicists.[53] Leon Kass suggests, "Perhaps for the sake of getting a broader hearing, perhaps not to profane sacred teachings or to preserve a separation between the things of God and the things of Caesar, most religious ethicists entering the public practice of ethics leave their special insights at the door and talk about 'deontological vs. consequentialist,' 'autonomy vs. paternalism,' 'justice vs. utility,' just like everybody else."[54] This is a bit of an overstatement, but it does pose the challenge before religious thinkers of retaining and conveying the full meaning of religious concepts to a secular audience.

Genetic engineering, cloning, and genetic patenting are all topics on which members of the religious community have sought to address the wider society. What does their experience tell us about the public limits of religious discourse? Can substantive religious perspective be communicated in a pluralistic society without attenuating or transforming their meaning? Is it feasible or even appropriate to use religious language and concepts in a public forum on genetics? If not, what are the alternatives?

52. Nicholas Capaldi, "From the Profane to the Sacred," *Christian Bioethics* 1 (1995): 77.
53. Courtney S. Campbell, "Religion and Moral Meaning in Bioethics," *Theology, Religious Traditions, and Bioethics: A Special Supplement to The Hastings Center Report* 20 (July/August 1990): 4–7.
54. Quoted in Campbell, "Religion and Moral Meaning in Bioethics," 5.

Chapter Two

Genetics in Religious Perspective

In June 1980, leaders of three major religious communities—Protestant, Catholic, and Jewish—took the unusual step of writing to the president of the United States to express their concerns about a scientific development. The letter from the general secretaries of the National Council of Churches, the Synagogue Council of America, and the U.S. Catholic Conference to President Jimmy Carter warned of the perils genetic engineering posed to humanity:

> We are rapidly moving into a new era of fundamental danger triggered by the rapid growth of genetic engineering. Albeit, there may be opportunity for doing good; the very term suggests the danger. Who shall determine how human good is best served when new life forms are being engineered? Who shall control genetic experimentation and its results which could have untold implications for human survival? Who will benefit and who will bear any adverse consequences, directly or indirectly?[1]

The letter went on to state that these were not ordinary issues. "These are moral, ethical, and religious questions. They deal with the fundamental nature of human life and the dignity and worth of the individual human being."[2]

Advances in molecular biology have brought the unprecedented power to manipulate the genetic basis of life. This ability to rearrange the very building blocks of life makes it potentially possible to modify plants, animals, and even

---

1. Letter from Dr. Claire Randall, General Secretary, National Council of Churches; Rabbi Bernard Mandelbaum, General Secretary, Synagogue Council of America; and Bishop Thomas Kelly, General Secretary, U.S. Catholic Conference to President Carter, 20 June 1980. The letter is reproduced in the President's Commission for the Study of Ethical Problems in Medicine and Behavioral Research, *Splicing Life: The Social and Ethical Issues of Genetic Engineering with Human Beings* (Washington, D.C.: U.S. Gov't. Printing Office, 1982), App. B, 95.
2. Ibid., 96.

human beings, as well as to create new life-forms. The general secretaries acknowledged the ethical and religious significance of these developments by raising a series of fundamental questions: Would the knowledge be used for human betterment, for example, to correct genetic deficiencies, or would it be applied for other purposes contrary to human and societal well-being? Was it likely, as they contended, that "those who would play God will be tempted as never before"?[3] Would scientists and corporations make decisions about the development of this new technology primarily on economic grounds or would society impose wider criteria to determine priorities? Further, who and how would decision makers determine whether to go forward with specific applications of genetic engineering?

The significance of these issues points to the need to establish adequate mechanisms for public review and oversight of genetic engineering. The general secretaries underscored the importance of representing the broader public interest in making decisions related to the development, experimentation, and ownership of new life-forms. To that end, they requested that the president convene a group to consider these matters and advise the government. In turn, they pledged their own efforts: "The religious community must and will address these fundamental questions in a more urgent and organized way."[4]

In the past two decades members of the religious community, on both a corporate and an individual level, have sought to raise and address these questions in a variety of ways. Noted ethicist James Gustafson identifies two points of intersection between the work of theologians and geneticists.[5] He terms the first of these the "ethical intersection," referring to determinations about the morality of certain forms of genetic research and therapy and the criteria used to make those assessments. The second, "scientific-theological intersection," alludes to the implications of genetic science for central questions of the meaning and purpose of life. This chapter and the next two on genetic patenting and cloning focus on the first of these intersections. Chapter 5, on the implications of genetic research for developing an updated theological anthropology, explores the second. Most, but not all, of the moral theology discussed in this chapter is Christian in character, reflecting the body of work in this field.

INITIAL RESPONSE

Genetic engineering, or more technically recombinant DNA technologies, initially evoked deep anxieties and fundamental ethical and religious questions,

---

3. Ibid.
4. Ibid.
5. James M. Gustafson, "Where Theologians and Geneticists Meet," *Dialog* 33 (Winter 1994): 7–16.

even among some members of the scientific community. For example, in a 1967 editorial entitled "Will Society Be Prepared?" published in *Science,* Marshall Nirenberg, a staff member at the National Heart Institute, cautioned that "man may be able to program his own cells with synthetic information long before he will be able to assess adequately the long-term consequences of such alterations, long before he will be able to formulate goals, and long before he can resolve the ethical and moral problems which will be raised."[6] He proposed that humanity defer from utilizing this capability until we had developed sufficient wisdom to use this knowledge for the benefit of humankind.[7] Similar concerns are reflected in some of the early theological and ethical literature on human genetics. In this context, it is important to note that questions raised by moral theologians about some types of human genetics applications do not amount to a Luddite rejection of the science. Indeed, some of the religious literature reviewed in this chapter may even be faulted for an overly optimistic assessment of genetic engineering's potential benefits.

Early work by theologians often reflects a diffuse sense of uneasiness or anxiety about the implications of altering the genetic basis of life. Karl Rahner, an eminent Catholic theologian, published two essays in 1966 in which he considered the theological significance of a range of new technologies, including "genetic manipulation." Writing in advance of the actual development of genetic engineering, Rahner uses the term to refer more to what would currently be described as forms of assisted reproduction, particularly artificial insemination by donor. On a theoretical level, Rahner appears to affirm human freedom to shape or manipulate its own essence and future. "According to Christian anthropology man really is the being who manipulates himself. . . . Man, as the being who is free in relation to God, is in a most radical way empowered to do what he wills with himself, freely able to align himself toward his own ultimate goals."[8] Rahner defines Christianity as the religion of the absolute future and affirms that God, as intimate presence, both judges and confirms human efforts at self-definition.[9] Counterbalancing this openness, Rahner underscores that human beings proceed from existential limits that constrain our ability to make choices. Self-manipulation sets humanity on a one-way irreversible historical course, forcing those who come later to live

6. Quoted in LeRoy Walters and Julie Gage Palmer, *The Ethics of Human Gene Therapy* (New York: Oxford University Press, 1997), 141.
7. Cited in ibid., 143.
8. Karl Rahner, "The Experiment with Man: Theological Observations on Man's Self-Manipulation," in *Theological Investigations* IX, G. Harrison, trans. (New York: Seabury, 1996): 225–52, cited in Ronald Cole-Turner, *The New Genesis: Theology and the Genetic Revolution* (Louisville: Westminster/John Knox Press, 1993), 64.
9. Rahner, "The Experiment with Man," cited in Cole-Turner, *New Genesis,* 65.

with our mistakes. Changes in our genetic code that reflect the current historical context may reduce the freedom or well-being of future generations. Because Rahner believes that the genetic uniqueness and individuality of each person originated in the intimacy of sexual union, he opposes artificial insemination as a technological intrusion upon the sexual intimacy of marriage through which foreign genetic material is introduced.[10]

Paul Ramsey, a leading Methodist moral theologian, also took an active role in evaluating the implications of genetic engineering. Like Rahner, Ramsey subsumed a panoply of reproductive technologies, particularly artificial insemination, in his critique of genetic control, and like Rahner, he was opposed to the separation of the unitive and procreative ends of human sexuality. In contrast with Rahner, Ramsey had a less hopeful, almost apocalyptic anticipation of the human future. His 1970 book *Fabricated Man* conveys a sense of pessimism about the survival of the human species: "Religious people have never denied, indeed they affirm, that God means to kill us all in the end, and in the end he is going to succeed."[11] While the book does not categorically rule out genetic technologies, if they are proven to be consistent with human dignity and freedom, it contains a much cited maxim that has served as a rallying cry for opponents: "Men ought not to play God before they learn to be men, and after they have learned to be men they will not play God."[12] Arguing against the "revolutionary biologists" who were advocates of genetic manipulation for eugenic purposes, Ramsey warns that "playing God" with emerging genetic technologies would more likely result in human self-destruction than improvements in the species.[13]

In 1980, a few days after the United States Supreme Court issued a precedent-making decision accepting the patenting of genetically engineered microorganisms, the general secretaries of the National Council of Churches, the Synagogue Council of America, and the U.S. Catholic Conference wrote the letter cited at the beginning of this chapter. Their concern that "no government body was exercising adequate oversight or control, nor addressing the fundamental ethical questions," prompted the President's Commission for the Study of Ethical Problems in Medicine and Biomedical and Behavioral Research, an already existing body, to expand its agenda to explore these issues.[14] To assist in the process, the commission assembled a panel that includ-

10. Karl Rahner, "The Problem of Genetic Manipulation," *Theological Investigations* IX, 205–22, cited in Cole-Turner, *New Genesis,* 64–65.
11. Paul Ramsey, *Fabricated Man: The Ethics of Genetic Control* (New Haven: Yale University Press, 1970), 136.
12. Ibid., 136.
13. Ibid., 140–51.
14. President's Commission, *Splicing Life,* 1.

ed representatives from medicine and biology, philosophy and ethics, law, social policy, and the industrial private sector. The commission also invited the general secretaries to identify scholars who could address uniquely theological concerns related to genetic engineering from the perspective of their traditions.[15] The commission eventually received testimony from a total of nineteen theologians and ethicists as well as from representatives of the federal agencies most actively involved in human genetics.

The 1982 report issued by the commission, *Splicing Life: The Social and Ethical Issues of Genetic Engineering with Human Beings,* reflected this input. It considered religious as well as social and ethical issues, particularly whether genetic engineering amounts to assuming God-like powers. *Splicing Life* generally gave genetic engineering a favorable assessment. Acknowledging that genetic engineering techniques challenged some deeply held feelings about the meaning of being human and of family lineage, the report ultimately concluded that public concerns about manipulating nature were exaggerated.

> The Commission could find no ground for concluding that any current or planned forms of genetic engineering, whether using human or nonhuman material, are intrinsically wrong or irreligious per se. The Commission does not see in the rapid development of gene splicing the "fundamental danger" to world safety or to human values that concerned the leaders of the three religious organizations. Rather, the issue that deserves careful thought is: by what standards, and toward what objectives, should the great new powers of genetic engineering be guided?[16]

Although the commission did not find the issues related to genetic therapy appreciably different from those related to any new diagnostic and therapeutic techniques, it called for "especially stringent" precautions on the development of new diagnostic and therapeutic techniques that would influence future generations. It also recommended "periodic reassessment" of issues.

ECUMENICAL AND DENOMINATIONAL INITIATIVES

In a considerable body of literature on genetic engineering, churches have sought to define and address basic theological and moral issues related to this new technology. Ecumenical and denominational bodies have commissioned committees or individual experts to study aspects of genetic research, testing, and engineering; develop resources; and draft position statements. Some of these documents have become the basis of official policy approved by the

15. Ibid., 110.
16. Ibid., 3.

church's or the relevant ecumenical governing body. In addition, statements from the pope and the Congregation for the Doctrine of the Faith have framed the position of the Roman Catholic Church on some aspects of genetic science application.

Ecumenical efforts to explore the implications of genetic science and genetic engineering frequently preceded denominational initiatives. The World Council of Churches, long concerned with the ethical significance of science and technology, organized its first consultation on genetics as early as 1973.[17] This consultation, which was coorganized by the Christian Medical Commission, dealt with issues of genetic counseling that emerged from new techniques for diagnosis of genetic defects. It commissioned nineteen papers, later published in *Genetics and the Quality of Life,* and issued a concluding "finding and recommendations."[18] Like many other study groups, the findings represented the views of the panel and did not have official standing. The 1979 WCC-sponsored World Conference on Faith, Science and the Future had one plenary session on the biological revolution, and one of its ten sections was devoted to the topic, "Ethical Issues in the Biological Manipulation of Life." Following that conference, the WCC convened a working group that prepared the 1982 report *Manipulating Life: Ethical Issues in Genetic Engineering.*[19] Proposals and recommendations contained in the August 1989 report by the WCC's Subunit on Church and Society, entitled *Biotechnology: Its Challenges to the Churches and the World,*[20] were formally adopted by the WCC's Central Committee and sent to its member churches for study and implementation.

In 1980, the National Council of Churches of Christ in the U.S.A. organized its first task force, whose membership included both scientists and theological ethicists. The task force, which worked for some three years, was commissioned to speak on its own authority, and not formulate positions or policies for the National Council of Churches. Its fifty-seven-page report, *Human Life and the New Genetics,*[21] is notable for its pastoral tone, aiming to help laypeople

17. This chronology of ecumenical discussions on genetics follows Roger Lincoln Shinn, "Genetics, Ethics, and Theology: Ecumenical Discussions" (prepared for the Genome Consultation of the Center for Theology and the Natural Sciences, August 1992).

18. Charles Birch and Paul Abrecht, *Genetics and the Quality of Life* (Elmsford, N.Y., and Potts Point, New South Wales, Australia: Pergamon Press, 1975).

19. WCC Church and Society, *Manipulating Life: Ethical Issues in Genetic Engineering* (Geneva: WCC, 1982).

20. WCC Church and Society, *Biotechnology: Its Challenges to the Churches and the World* (Geneva: WCC, 1989).

21. *Human Life and the New Genetics: A Report of a Task Force Commissioned by the National Council of Churches of Christ in the U.S.A.* (New York: NCC, 1980).

understand the issues and make decisions. Subsequently, the National Council of Churches appointed another panel that in 1984 produced an eighty-one-page book entitled *Genetic Engineering: Social and Ethical Consequences.*[22] Despite the involvement of ten members of the Governing Board and several staff, the book carries a disclaimer that it is a study document and not an official policy statement. Then in 1986 the Governing Board formally adopted a statement entitled "Genetic Science for Human Benefit," which was published as a sixteen-page pamphlet.[23]

Of the documents within the Roman Catholic tradition with implications for genetic engineering, "Instruction on Respect for Human Life in Its Origin and on the Dignity of Life (Donum Vitae)," issued by the Congregation for the Doctrine of the Faith in 1987, is perhaps the most significant.[24] Unlike most of the ecumenical Protestant documents described above, it has the status of a magisterial statement seeking to clarify and restate official teaching. Other resources setting forth a Catholic perspective include an address Pope John Paul II made on medical ethics and genetic manipulation to participants in the 1983 World Medical Association convention[25] and *Human Genetics: Ethical Issues in Genetic Testing, Counseling, and Therapy,*[26] a forty-four-page pamphlet issued in 1990 by the Catholic Health Association of the United States and developed by an interdisciplinary research group. Like many of the Protestant statements, *Human Genetics* serves as a resource for ethical consultation and decision making. A working party of the British Catholic Bishops Joint Committee on Bioethical Issues undertook a four-year study of human genetics and produced a resource that considers both somatic (nonheritable) and germ-line (heritable) interventions.[27]

22. Panel of Bioethical Concerns, *Genetic Engineering: Social and Ethical Consequences,* Frank M. Harron, ed. (New York: Pilgrim Press, 1984).

23. National Council of Churches of Christ in the U.S.A., "Genetic Science for Human Benefit" (New York: Office of Research and Evaluation, adopted by the Governing Board 22 May 1986).

24. Congregation for the Doctrine of the Faith, "Instruction on Respect for Human Life in Its Origin and on the Dignity of Life (Donum Vitae)," 1987, reproduced in Kevin D. O'Rourke, O.P., J.C.D., S.T.M., and Philip Boyle, *Medical Ethics: Sources of Catholic Teaching,* 2d ed. (Washington, D.C.: Georgetown University Press, 1993).

25. Pope John Paul II, "The Ethics of Genetic Manipulation," *Origins* 13 (17 November 1983): 386–89.

26. *Human Genetics: Ethical Issues in Genetic Testing, Counseling, and Therapy* (St. Louis: Catholic Health Association of the United States, 1990).

27. Working Party of the Catholic Bishops Joint Committee on Bioethical Issues, *Genetic Intervention on Human Subjects* (London: Catholic Bishops Joint Committee on Bioethical Issues, 1996).

Eight major North American Protestant denominations have addressed genetics issues in some form, and at least one European communion, the Church of Scotland, has also done so. As might be anticipated, these denominational documents are very different in focus, purpose, and emphasis, as is the process by which they were drafted. Of the group, seven—the United Methodist Church, the United Church of Christ (UCC), the Episcopal Church, the Presbyterian Church (U.S.A.), the Reformed Church in America, the Evangelical Lutheran Church in America, and the Southern Baptist Convention—have drafted reports, policy statements, or study resources on genetic science, genetic engineering, or procreational ethics. An eighth, the United Church of Canada, has prepared a brief.

Responding to the revolution in biomedical technology, in 1983 the newly reunited Presbyterian Church (U.S.A.) General Assembly devoted a section of its report on biomedical issues to the topic "Genetic Choices and the Ethics of Domination,"[28] and in 1990 adopted a second resolution.[29] After a process that involved development of a provisional study by its Commission on Christian Action, congregational study, and a series of consultations, the General Synod of the Reformed Church in America approved a statement on genetic engineering in 1988.[30] In 1989, the General Synod of the UCC voted a pronouncement, "Church and Genetic Engineering,"[31] and a related resolution, "The Church and Reproductive Technologies."[32] Two years later, the General Conference of the Episcopal Church passed a resolution providing guidelines in the area of genetic engineering. A report of the United Methodist Church Genetic Science Task Force was adopted by the 1992 General Conference under the title "New Developments in Genetic Science."[33]

---

28. Presbyterian Church (U.S.A.), 195th General Assembly (1983), "The Covenant of Life and the Caring Community" and "Covenant and Creation: Theological Reflections on Contraception and Abortion," *Social Policy Compilation* (Louisville: Advisory Committee on Social Witness Policy, 1992).

29. Presbyterian Church (U.S.A.), 195th General Assembly (1983), "The Covenant of Life and the Caring Community," *Social Policy Compilation* (Louisville: Advisory Committee on Social Witness Policy, 1992), 97, 846. The resolution of the 202d General Assembly (1990), untitled in the compilation, is on p. 776.

30. "Genetic Engineering," *Reports on Christian Action, Minutes of the General Synod 1988* (New York: Reformed Church in America, 1988).

31. UCC, "Pronouncement: Church and Genetic Engineering," *Minutes, Seventeenth General Synod* (St. Louis: United Church Resources, 1991), 45–47.

32. UCC, "Resolution: The Church and Reproductive Technologies," in ibid., 45–47.

33. United Methodist Church, "New Developments in Genetic Science," in *The Book of Resolutions of the United Methodist Church* (Nashville: United Methodist Publishing House, 1992), 325–38.

Somewhat ironically, the text, which arguably is reasoned most clearly from a theological foundation, is not a denominational resolution but a brief to the Royal Commission on New Reproductive Technologies prepared on behalf of the United Church of Canada by its Division of Mission.[34]

On a more pastoral level, the American Lutheran Church, the Association of Evangelical Lutheran Churches, and the Lutheran Church in America, predecessor denominations of the Evangelical Lutheran Church in America, collaborated to commission a series of essays that were published in 1985, three of which deal with genetic manipulation, *in vitro* fertilization, and genetic screening and counseling.[35] The Christian Life Commission of the Southern Baptist Convention also commissioned and published two pamphlets for members, one on the ethics of human embryo research and the other on genetic engineering.[36] In 1996, the United Church Board for Homeland Ministries of the UCC published a resource paper on genetics and pastoral theology.[37]

Several second-generation studies of human genetics and genetic engineering are under way or in some cases completed. The Committee on Medical Ethics of the Episcopal Diocese of Washington published a work in 1998 entitled *Wrestling with the Future: Our Genes and Our Choices,* which offers an overview of issues related to prenatal and adult genetic testing.[38] In the same year, the Office of Theology and Worship of the Congregational Ministries Division of the Presbyterian Church (U.S.A.) published a collection of essays entitled *In Whose Image? Faith, Science, and the New Genetics,* intended for personal as well as group study. The volume focuses on the "challenge that contemporary developments in the biological sciences pose to the church's theology, and especially to the church's understanding of what it means to be

34. "A Brief to the Royal Commission on New Reproductive Technologies on Behalf of the United Church of Canada, prepared by the Division of Mission in Canada" (approved by the executive of the Division of Mission, 17 January 1991).

35. Edmund N. Santurri, "The Ethics of Prenatal Diagnosis," Paul T. Jersild, "In Vitro Fertilization," and James H. Burtnes, "Genetic Manipulation," pamphlet series (New York: Lutheran Church in America, 1986).

36. C. Ben Mitchell, "Genetic Engineering: Bane or Blessing," and C. Ben Mitchell, "Was Jesus an Embryo? The Ethics of Human Embryo Research and the Brave New World" (Nashville: Christian Life Commission, n.d.).

37. Brent Waters, *Ministry in an Age of Science and Technology: Genetics and Pastoral Theology* (Cleveland: The Division of Education and Publication, United Church Board for Homeland Ministries, 1996).

38. Cynthia B. Cohen, Chair, Committee on Medical Ethics, Episcopal Diocese of Washington, *Wrestling with the Future: Our Genes and Our Choices* (Harrisburg, Pa.: Morehouse Publishing, 1998).

human before God."[39] Likewise, *Genetic Testing and Screening: Critical Engagement at the Intersection of Faith and Science,* sponsored by the Division for Church in Society of the Evangelical Lutheran Church in America, is an edited volume, with study questions following each chapter.[40] In contrast with the Episcopal resource on genetic testing, which emphasizes the explication of options and their implications, this volume places these issues within a more substantive theological and ethical framework. A resource on the ethics of genetic engineering in nonhuman species developed by a working group of the Society, Religion and Technology Project of the Church of Scotland was also published in 1998.[41] At the time of writing, the UCC is completing work on a collection of essays based on a series of cases, each dealing with a different dimension of the moral dilemmas raised by genetics.

These second-generation works often have more in common with the writings of scholars described in the next section than with the initial round of denomination-commissioned resources. Perhaps that should not be surprising, given the composition of the working groups, many of which have the same scholars as members. In contrast with the earlier denominational efforts that sought primarily to establish baseline policies, these are efforts to develop serious, in-depth treatments of the way genetics intersects with and challenges traditional theological understandings. The focus on the ethical and theological issues genetic testing raises reflects the realization that "It is largely through genetic testing and screening that the nonspecialist will personally confront the personal, social, theological, and pastoral dilemmas that attend genetic developments."[42] Although these resources were prepared under the sponsorship of particular denominations, they are only loosely linked with historical confessions and earlier documents outlining policy positions.

Despite their limitations, the resources analyzed in this section represent an important contribution to efforts to come to terms with genetic engineering. These and future institutional church initiatives have the potential of filling needs that individual ethicists or theologians, no matter how profound or insightful, cannot. With the exception of scientists in the early years of genetic engineering, religiously based communities have been virtually the only

---

39. John P. Burgess, ed., *In Whose Image? Faith, Science, and the New Genetics* (Louisville: Geneva Press for the Office of Theology and Worship, Congregational Ministries Division, Presbyterian Church [U.S.A.], 1998), xi.

40. Roger A. Willer, ed., *Genetic Testing and Screening: Critical Engagement at the Intersection of Faith and Science* (Minneapolis: Kirk House Publishers for the Evangelical Lutheran Church in America, 1998).

41. Donald Bruce and Ann Bruce, eds., *Engineering Genesis: The Ethics of Genetic Engineering in Non-Human Species* (London: Earthscan Publications, 1998).

42. Roger A. Willer, "Introduction," in Willer, ed., *Genetic Testing and Screening,* 5.

groups that have even attempted to engage in corporate-level ethical reflection and discourse on genetics engineering and HGP. Whereas individual ethicists and theologians usually work alone and can only speak for themselves, the development of denominationally or ecumenically based social policy statements provides an opportunity for interaction among a wider community of thinkers and experts, with the possibility of formulating a broader-based perspective. The process itself affords potential for educating and involving members. In addition, these denominational and ecumenical statements can have a standing both among members of these bodies and the wider society that the works of individual persons are unlikely to achieve. Clergy called upon to render advice and counsel parishioners about genetics-related issues are more likely to turn to and be guided by a denominational statement or resource than a work by an individual ethicist.

Yet, as a veteran of these processes, serving at different times as staff and as a participant, I am well aware of the problems implicit in these corporate efforts. To list but a few, they are typically drafted by diverse committees whose membership is intentionally chosen to incorporate a range of and sometimes fundamentally conflicting theological and ethical perspectives and professional backgrounds. Theology or ethics by committee, particularly a committee with shifting membership depending on attendance at specific meetings, rarely produces as coherent, well-reasoned a document as the work of a single author. It inclines drafts to either be compromise statements or to gloss over major issues on which the members cannot agree. And because of the difficulties in melding subject competence and ethical and theological discourse, the task is frequently segmented or compartmentalized with different subcommittees drafting the various sections of the statements.

Attitudes toward Genetic Science

Many of these sources have a respectful attitude toward genetic science, taking care that the concerns expressed will not appear unqualifiedly critical. The 1986 National Council of Churches policy statement acknowledges, "Churches are well equipped to speak of the Bible, the Gospel, Christian doctrines and ethics; but they have no privileged wisdom about science as such."[43] It goes on to note that nothing will be gained by alienating scientists from the religious community by an unqualified and unwarranted criticism of their work. Given these acknowledged limitations of the competence of religious thinkers, drafting committees frequently included prominent scientists in their membership, with scientists sometimes even constituting a majority of members or serving as cochairs.

43. National Council of Churches, "Genetic Science for Human Benefit," 2.

Despite cautions against alienating scientists, the National Council of Churches statement also rejects a position of unconditional acceptance of scientific achievement untempered by humane and ethical considerations.[44] Similarly, a 1992 Methodist statement cautions that the prevalent principle in scientific research, that what can be done should be done, does not provide an adequate grounding for genetic science. Instead it emphasizes the importance of ethical and legal oversight in research design. Even more, it underscores that applications of research to technologies need moral and ethical guidance. To that end, it urges adequate public funding of genetic research as a means to promote greater accountability to the public by those involved in setting the direction and priorities.[45] A recent Lutheran resource takes a position described as "critical engagement" that in principle affirms genetic knowledge and its applications, but also critically examines particular applications. The resource both recognizes that genetic developments are occasions in which God is at work and in which sin is just as assuredly present.[46]

Given the importance of understanding genetic science, several of the documents appear to consider basic science education to be one of their central tasks. Almost all of the reports and several of the policy statements have sections with such titles as "The Very Least We Need to Know about Genetic Engineering." Others have glossaries of common terms used in discussing genetic engineering. Sometimes the science sections are longer than those on theological perspectives. The 1988 statement of the Reformed Church in America, for example, devotes nearly four pages to describing the science, another two pages to raising questions about basic research and its regulation, and an additional three to delineating potential applications of human genetic engineering, but allocates only three to its theological affirmations and analysis.[47] Both the Presbyterian and Lutheran second-generation resources have chapters that serve as basic primers on genetic science. One of the major purposes of both the Lutheran and the Episcopal resources is to explain the science of genetic testing and screening in considerable detail.

In contrast with the hopeful tone in many of these documents, resources developed by the WCC tend to be characterized by a hermeneutic of suspicion. The premise from which they proceed is that "the church must engage technology at its source and not merely at its consequences."[48] The 1989 report

44. Ibid., 2–3.
45. United Methodist Church (U.S.). Program Council, *The Book of Resolutions of the United Methodist Church* (Nashville: United Methodist Publishing House, 1992), 12.
46. Willer, "Introduction," in Willer, ed., *Genetic Testing and Screening*, 8.
47. "Genetic Engineering" in the Reports on Christian Action, *Minutes of the General Synod* 1988 (New York: Reform Church of America).
48. Quoted in WCC, *Biotechnology: Its Challenges to the Churches and the World*, 7, from

"Biotechnology: Its Challenges to the Churches and the World" emphasizes, "Technology is not neutral or value free: it is as much an ideology as it is a tool of science. It has in fact become an instrument of power and is itself trapped in vast networks of power which are complex, systemic, often multinational, and exists primarily to maximize profit."[49] It goes on to characterize the struggle with the misuse of science and technology as comparable to the New Testament opposition to the "principalities and powers" that have gripped the world.

One of the most systematic efforts to assess both the potential benefits and drawbacks to genetic engineering occurs in the report entitled *Engineering Genesis: The Ethics of Genetic Engineering in Non-Human Species.* Undertaken by a working group sponsored by the Society, Religion and Technology Project of the Church of Scotland, the study describes a wide range of potential positive contributions. These include feeding an increasing world population, making marginal agriculture more viable in poor regions, reducing environmental degradation from agriculture by reducing chemical inputs, offering various medical benefits through novel uses of genetics in animals, plants, and microorganisms, and understanding and treating animal diseases. The report then identifies likely negative consequences of genetic engineering, such as the tendency to treat animals more as commodities than as creatures in their own right. Like other documents, the working group mentions the uncertainties involved in releasing into the environment new life-forms that cross species barriers. It is also concerned about the possibility that genetic engineering will reduce genetic diversity by relying on a smaller pool of genetically optimized products. Other negatives mentioned include skewing research and applications toward Western consumer markets and neglecting wider world needs, and distracting attention from issues related to developing more sustainable forms of agriculture. It concludes that genetic engineering is neither wrong in itself nor universally acceptable. Without resolving these tensions, the document comes down on the side of public accountability and the need to protect the interest of less powerful groups in society.[50]

Theological Framework and Premises
Despite their status as documents prepared by and for religious bodies, the theological grounding, particularly in first-generation documents, tends to be perfunctory. While denominational task forces and study groups typically

an earlier WCC report, *Integrity of Creation,* the report of a 1988 WCC Norway consultation, WCC: 11.
49. Ibid.
50. Bruce and Bruce, eds., *Engineering Genesis.*

include professional ethicists and theologians, early statements do not generally have a theological character. Those in the form of relatively brief resolutions formulated for and voted by church judicatory bodies, like an action of
the Episcopal General Convention, often do not even attempt to engage in
theological reflection as a basis for drawing ethical and policy guidelines. The
lack of a consistent theological character in some cases derives in part from
their rather narrow and specific focus. Some of the statements were apparently written in response to specific policy issues raised by their members and
requests for guidance in decision making. Several of the task forces and committees that drafted these documents apparently did not intend to engage in
theological reflection. Ethicist Roger Shinn, who served as the chair of one
National Council of Churches initiative, describes the status of the theological discussion as follows: "It draws from theology not a set of prescriptions but
'a context of awareness.'"[51] The same could be said of other denominational
and ecumenical literature.

While many of these reports and statements do include a section on theological perspective, theological reflection does not provide the foundation for
an evaluation of the implications of the science, ethical analysis, or formulation
of public policy. One of the major reasons is that the theology tends to be compartmentalized; that is, theological affirmations once made do not become the
grounding for subsequent ethical and policy discourse. In many cases the theological framework amounts to little more than a recitation of traditional
beliefs and dogma without any effort to examine the implications of these
affirmations for understanding the genetics revolution or to explore whether
genetics requires an extension or reinterpretation of traditional teachings. It
reads almost as if these report sections or statements were drafted by separate
subcommittees with little contact or interaction.

There are exceptions. The 1986 policy statement of the National Council
of Churches and the brief of the United Church of Canada work from a more
explicit theological perspective. And several of the second-generation resources,
particularly the Presbyterian collection of essays, consider theological issues. In
contrast with the policy orientation of many of the earlier documents and
resources, *In Whose Image?*, commissioned by the Presbyterian Church (U.S.A.)
explores questions that recent developments in the biological science pose to
the church's theology and understanding of what it means to be human, that
is, made in the image of God. While perspectives of the various authors vary,
they all identify with the Reformed tradition.[52] Given the focus of many of the

---

51. Roger Lincoln Shinn, "Genetics, Ethics, and Theology," in Ted Peters, ed., *Genetics:
Issues of Social Justice* (Cleveland: Pilgrim Press, 1998), 132.
52. Burgess, ed., *In Whose Image?*, xi–xvii.

essays in this volume on reinterpreting theological anthropology in light of the findings of genetic science, the contributions of its various authors are considered in chapter 5.

Many of the documents, particularly the initial statements described in this section, reiterate traditional theological formulations without clearly drawing out their implications for genetic research and applications. Typically they affirm God as Creator, sovereign over all of creation, God's creation as good, and redemption and salvation as the purpose of the creation. They characterize human beings as finite, contingent, interdependent, and socially oriented creatures owing their existence to God. Created in the image of God, human beings are described as having both power and responsibility. Additionally, the documents state something to the effect that the pursuit of knowledge is a divine gift to be used in accordance with God's purposes. Although some of the documents refer to the reality of sin, they tend to view positively the potential of using knowledge and technology to serve humanity and God.

In a number of cases, drafters of these documents realize that historic Christian teaching about human nature and the meaning and purpose of human life are challenged by new technologies. To provide a few examples, a 1989 WCC report reflects that "the revolution in biotechnology calls churches to reexamine the fundamental understandings of the relationship between God, humanity and the created order.[53] Similarly, the 1992 United Methodist Church policy statement "New Developments in Genetic Science" notes that "developments in genetic science compel our reevaluation of accepted theological/ethical issues, including determinism versus free will, the nature of sin, just distribution of resources, the status of human beings in relation to other forms of life, and the meaning of personhood."[54] A 1982 WCC report acknowledges that coming to terms with new technologies such as genetic screening, selective abortion, *in vitro* fertilization, surrogate motherhood, and gene transplantation will depend on churches developing "a better understanding of the meaning of faith in the full light of the new knowledge and power that the biological sciences have brought." It notes, however, that some churches have reacted apprehensively and defensively, even claiming that the treatment of creation in the first chapter of Genesis is a scientific account. A more creative response will "require study and reflection on the new knowledge that biology brings, and the working out of the relation between faith and this knowledge to an extent we have as yet hardly begun."[55]

53. WCC, *Biotechnology*, 8.
54. United Methodist Church, "New Developments in Genetic Science," 329.
55. WCC, *Manipulating Life*, 1.

While many of these sources acknowledge that genetic science raises fundamental theological issues, few go beyond doing so. Instead they seem to be flagging a future agenda item. Only the second-generation resources even begin the task. Of the resources reviewed here, the Presbyterian study of faith, science, and the new genetics most explicitly attempts to update Christian tradition in light of the new genetics. It has essays on the origins and evolution of humanity, genetic determinism, human nature, the human condition, and the soul, all in light of the findings of genetic science. These, too, are discussed in chapter 5.

Many of these documents utilize the concept of stewardship as the basis for a genetic ethic. The stewardship tradition, which is rooted in Scripture, characterizes the vocation of humanity as a servant who has been given the responsibility for the management and service of something belonging to another, in this case the Creator. However, the classical notion of stewardship predates the discovery of evolution and assumes that we live in a static, finished, and hierarchical universe in which stewardship implies respecting the natural order and not seeking to change it. For the stewardship model to be relevant, then, requires considerable updating and reinterpretation.

The book *On Behalf of God: A Christian Ethic for Biology,* written by religious philosopher Bruce Reichenbach and geneticist V. Elving Anderson, makes an effort to do so. Their approach is to draw a Christian ethic of stewardship from biblical passages, particularly the opening chapters of Genesis. They interpret this ethic as having three components: the human responsibility to fill the land, to rule the land, and to work with and care for the property of the owner. In contrast with traditional stewardship models, they draw on one of Jesus' parables (Matt. 25:14-30) to contend that stewards are charged with seemingly contradictory obligations both to preserve and change, conserve and risk, the property entrusted to them. To argue for the permissibility of change, Reichenbach and Anderson reject tenets of classical theology, which portray God as knowing all possibilities, controlling all actualities, and instead portray God as a risk taker, especially in the divine relationship with free human beings. Given this understanding of the human mandate, they then wrestle with the central questions of what we are obligated to change, what other kinds of changes are permissible, for what purposes are we to change creation, and what are the limits of the change.[56]

The dilemma is that Scripture does not provide ready answers, even for the prescientific society for which it was written, let alone clear guidelines for

---

56. Bruce R. Reichenbach and V. Elving Anderson, *On Behalf of God: A Christian Ethic for Biology* (Grand Rapids, Mich.: Wm. B. Eerdmans Publishing Co., 1995), 65–66, 40–72.

complex contemporary conundrums related to science and technology. Reichenbach and Anderson posit that science and technology should be held to the same accounting as all other stewards: "They must address concerns about what is worth knowing in light of human needs, about what is worth doing in light of potential human good, and about what scientists should be doing in light of the development of their own moral character."[57] But what does that mean in terms of setting priorities or drawing limits? Is there any scientist who would acknowledge that his or her research was not valuable in some way, if only to expand the boundaries of human knowledge? Once their stewardship model is developed, Reichenbach and Anderson do not draw middle axioms for its applications. While the chapters dealing with specific issues, two of which address aspects of genetic science, are factually illuminating and their analysis and recommendations insightful, this is largely despite, not because of, their efforts to apply their ethic of stewardship to the issues at hand.

For the most part, the denominational statements that employ a stewardship paradigm do not make an effort to update, reinterpret, or deal with the dilemmas of applying this model to a dynamic and ever-changing creation. The Methodist text, for example, describes human beings as stewards accountable to the Creator. Because human beings are created in the image of God, they have both the power and the responsibility to use power as God does, with love. Their discussion of stewardship emphasizes that humans are to participate in, manage, nurture, justly distribute, employ, develop and enhance creation's resources in accordance with their finite discernment of God's purposes. The document identifies human accountability in the pursuit and applications of knowledge in three directions: to God, to the human community, and to the sustainability of all creation.[58] Nevertheless, the affirmation that "knowledge of genetics is a resource over which we are to exercise stewardship responsibility in accordance with God's reign over nature"[59] remains little more than rhetoric. It is given little specific content, and the ethical analysis and policy recommendations in the statement do not derive from the stewardship framework.

Resources based on the alternative concepts of humans as God's partner or co-creator do a better job of interpreting and applying their theological grounding to the issues at hand. This may reflect the greater consistency and relevance of their theological model to scientific discoveries in biology and genetics. Of the documents, the United Church of Canada's brief most clearly adopts this position. It affirms: "We are called to be co-creators with God,

57. Ibid., 62.
58. United Methodist Church, "New Developments in Genetic Science," 327–28.
59. Ibid., 332.

working for wholeness in our communities and in each person. This is in the proper sense 'playing God' because it is set within the context of the search for full humanity and seeks to meet the conditions set out in God's intentions."[60] The National Council of Churches policy statement and "The Covenant of Life and the Caring Community," a report by the Presbyterian Church, also affirm the dynamic character of the creation. Without using the terminology of co-creation, the National Council of Churches notes, "Creation by divine power is not static but dynamic and ongoing. As creatures uniquely made in God's image and purpose, humans participate in the creative process through the continuing quest for knowledge, which now includes unraveling and learning to control the intricate powers compressed in genes of DNA molecules."[61] The Presbyterian report similarly acknowledges that "scientific research has revealed to us that creation is not fixed, but ongoing" and that "God calls us to be involved in the process," using the formulation that persons have the opportunity to be "co-laborers with God."[62]

That said, the theological concept of co-creation in these statements does not generate a clearer delineation of appropriate applications or limitations for genetic engineering than does the stewardship model used in other resources. Like the stewardship-oriented documents, the theological affirmations of co-creation are used primarily as metaphors to designate the human role in creation. Neither stewardship nor co-creation is translated into specific precepts or middle axioms that can then provide the basis for ethical analyses and/or policy recommendations.

Rather than stewardship or co-creation, the UCC pronouncement opts for compassion and the potential of genetic engineering for healing and wholeness as its central theme. Noting that Jesus fed the hungry and healed the sick, the statement dwells on the potential of genetic engineering to relieve suffering and increase food production. Anticipating that genetic engineering will open new ways for people of compassion to help those in need, the UCC calls on members of the church to follow the example of Jesus and to use genetic engineering capabilities to bring healing and sustenance to people everywhere.[63]

Although the pronouncement is the only statement to explicitly place developments within genetic science in the framework of healing and compassion, it is implicit in many, if not all. The theological commitment to ame-

60. The Division of Mission in Canada, "A Brief to the Royal Commission on New Reproductive Technologies," 14.
61. National Council of Churches, "Genetic Science for Human Benefit," 14–15.
62. Presbyterian Church (U.S.A.), "The Covenant of Life and the Caring Community," 10.
63. UCC, "Pronouncement," 42–43.

liorating suffering, along with the belief that genetics will provide significant new modalities for the treatments of congenital defects and human disease, plays a major role in shaping attitudes toward genetic research and therapies within the religious community. Perhaps the most categorical and enthusiastic affirmation of genetic advances to promote health and increase fertility has come from the Jewish community. This, in part, reflects contemporary interpretations of *tikkun olam,* the mandate to be an active partner in the world's repair and perfection. Despite a sensitivity to the potential use of genetics for eugenic purposes, the mandate to be a partner in creation has inclined Jewish religious leaders and thinkers to support medical advances and by extension genetic research and applications.[64]

Does the potential of genetic science to bring healing offer a relevant framework for ethical and theological analysis? The Gospels do record some thirty-five instances of Jesus healing various infirmities—blindness, deafness, leprosy, dumbness, lameness, mental illness, paralysis, and leprosy. However, several scholars claim that the healings were viewed by early Christians as evidence that the messianic age had come, and not as a commitment to health and healing per se.[65] Moreover, many of Jesus' miraculous healings involved exorcism to cure patients by expelling the demons causing their illness, which is hardly a model for genetic science. Although Paul indicated that healing was practiced in the early church as one of several "gifts of the Spirit" (1 Cor. 12:9) and the Epistle of James describes a rite of healing (James 5:14-15), suffering and affliction were understood by several New Testament writers, Paul among them, as part of the discipline through which Christians would grow toward spiritual maturity. Two biblical scholars reviewing this literature comment, "the New Testament epistles, which were intended to provide normative apostolic instruction to the churches, have little to say about physical healing."[66] Instead, they argue that healing and wholeness are imaged more in spiritual than in physical terms.

Moreover, the compassion and healing framework, at least as it is conceptualized in these texts, tends to gloss over difficult ethical issues that genetic science raises. It may be that genetic science will revolutionize medicine, but first society will have to determine the medical uses to which genetic technology should be applied, the types of diseases and abnormalities that should be given

64. Laurie Zoloth-Dorfman, "Mapping the Normal Human Self," in Ted Peters, ed., *Genetics: Issues of Social Injustice* (Cleveland: The Pilgrim Press, 1998), 190–92.
65. Darrel W. Amundsen and Gary B. Ferngren, "The Early Christian Tradition," in Ronald L. Numbers and Darrel W. Amundsen, eds., *Caring and Curing: Health and Medicine in the Western Religious Traditions* (New York and London: Macmillan Publishing Co., 1986), 42–47.
66. Ibid., 45.

priority, and the basis on which persons should be given access to genetic therapy. Unfortunately, the religious community has given far too little attention to what might be termed the hard issues related to genetic medicine. The HGP, "perhaps more than any other biomedical undertaking, raises profound issues of whether all new information is good, whether some medical information is not empowering but disempowering, whether society has the inclination or ability to afford equal access to a powerful new technology, and whether the legal system can deal effectively with the potential for discrimination, limits on autonomy, and political divisiveness of genetic information."[67]

Although human gene therapy offers a potentially effective new treatment approach to medicine, it is and will continue to be very expensive. Thus societal investments in genetic research and therapy will come at the cost of forgoing other types of medical research and care. This trade-off is not a trivial issue in a society in which more than forty-three million persons lack even basic medical insurance and the medical services it provides. Moreover, access to gene therapy will depend on the ability to pay for that treatment, or more precisely, to have medical insurance that is willing to reimburse the costs.[68] Thus there may be ever-growing disparities between rich and poor in gaining access to genetic services to alleviate disease and, perhaps at some point in the future, for purposes of genetic enhancements.[69]

Ethical and Justice Concerns

In its resolution "On Implications of Genetic Research and the Church's Response," the Presbyterian Church (U.S.A.) commits itself to engage in prophetic inquiry concerning theological and ethical issues raised by the HGP. It defines prophetic inquiry as "the means by which we use the wisdom of modern technology and science integrated with the teachings of biblical tradition in order to move more fully toward God's kingdom of wholeness and justice."[70] Yet the analysis of potential challenges posed by genetic research, testing, and applications in these documents tends not to be very prophetic. Nor is it noticeably different from most secular evaluations. That is not to say that

67. Mark A. Rothstein, "The Genetic Factor in Health Care Reform: Framing the Policy Debate," in Thomas H. Murray, Mark A. Rothstein, and Robert F. Murray, Jr., eds., *The Human Genome Project and the Future of Health Care* (Bloomington and Indianapolis: Indiana University Press, 1996), 224.

68. William J. Polvino and W. French Anderson, "Medicine, Gene Therapy, and Society," in Murray, Rothstein, and Murray, Jr., eds., *Human Genome Project*, 39–40.

69. Maxwell J. Mehlman, "Federal Entitlement Programs," in Murray, Rothstein, and Murray, Jr., eds., *Human Genome Project*, 113–32.

70. Presbyterian Church (U.S.A.), "On Implications of Genetic Research and the Church's Response," General Assembly, *Social Policy Compilation* (Louisville: Advisory Committee on Social Witness Policy, 1992), 776–77.

the religious statements and resources fail to raise significant ethical concerns, only that these documents are often quite superficial. They frequently read like laundry lists of issues with little theological or ethical analysis or development.

Ethical issues cited in a pamphlet prepared for the Christian Life Commission of the Southern Baptist Convention mirror the concerns of many of the churches and ecumenical agencies. C. Ben Mitchell, the author, recognizes that human genetic science does not so much create new ethical issues but amplifies and aggravates several preexisting concerns. One of these is the potential misuse of genetic data to discriminate against persons with genetic pre-dispositions. To respond to that possibility, the pamphlet strongly recommends protecting the confidentiality of genetic information and preventing insurance carriers and employers from having access to or utilizing these data. Like many of the other resources, this pamphlet warns against eugenic applications to improve the human stock by eliminating undesirables. Consistent with the prolife position of the Christian Life Commission, Mitchell is also concerned that prenatal screening for diseases where there is no known treatment will increase the incidence of abortion.[71]

The United Methodist resolution adopted by the 1992 General Conference deals with four sets of issues: the patenting of life-forms and access to genetic technology; genetic medicine and therapy, including issues related to both screening and diagnosis and genetic therapy; agricultural applications; and the environment. It shares the concern of other groups that genetic screening and diagnosis and the concomitant reproductive decisions people will make may have eugenic consequences. It cautions against pregnancy termination for gender selection and minor genetic abnormalities, and in situations where there is a dispute about the quality of life of a fetus with a genetic disorder. The resolution notes the complexity of dealing with the need to protect an individual's privacy and the need to provide other family members with genetic information that could affect their medical treatment and reproductive plans.

Like the Southern Baptist Convention pamphlet, this resolution anticipates the suffering and hardship that may result for persons with late-onset diseases or with a genetic predisposition to diseases because of employment or health care insurance discrimination. Given the high cost of genetic technologies, the United Methodist resolution raises concerns about resource allocation. It supports equal access to medical resources, including the right to health care and health care resources, regardless of genetic or medical conditions, and opportunities for genetic testing and counseling by appropriately trained professionals.[72] While a helpful starting point, this list parallels concerns articulated

71. Mitchell, "Genetic Engineering," 13-16.

in secular resources. And, it is just a list. There is no ethical analysis, and no indication as to why the Christian community or any denomination therein should hold these positions. Nor does the report suggest that the religious community has any particular ethical sensitivities, competence, or potential role in addressing these issues.

The relative lack of development of a justice trajectory, both in these documents and in the works of individual thinkers cited in the next section, is a surprise and a disappointment. When justice concerns are brought to the fore, they are rarely addressed within a specifically religious or theological context. For example, very few of these documents deal explicitly with the important role of commercial interests in shaping the priorities for genetic research and development and its implications. The Church of Scotland study on nonhuman applications of genetic engineering does recognize that applications of genetic engineering will be determined by commercial considerations and that those with a sound ethical justification may be disadvantaged when competing with others likely to bring economic benefits.[73] Of the religious ethicists regularly writing on genetics, Karen Lebacqz most consistently raises issues of justice. Two of her recent articles, "Fair Shares: Is the Genome Project Just?" and "Genetic Privacy: No Deal for the Poor," both in the recently published volume *Genetics: Issues of Social Justice,* are examples.[74] Some of the most penetrating critiques of genetics in edited collections, on such topics as the implications for social stratification and eugenics, are written by secular analysts, for instance, Troy Duster, who is a social scientist.[75]

ETHICAL AND THEOLOGICAL LITERATURE BY INDIVIDUAL RELIGIOUS THINKERS

There is a growing ethical and theological literature on genetics by moral theologians in the form of individually authored book-length studies, articles and edited collections of articles, and chapters of broader works. Some of these thinkers, Roger Shinn, for example, have played prominent roles on denominational and ecumenical task forces, and have explored issues with greater freedom and depth in their own works. Yet, despite the interest in genetic science within the religious community, fewer than a dozen book-length stud-

---

72. United Methodist Church, "New Developments in Genetic Science."

73. Bruce and Bruce, eds., *Engineering Genesis.*

74. Karen Lebacqz, "Fair Shares: Is the Genome Project Just?" in Peters, ed., *Genetics,* 82–110, 239–54.

75. Troy Duster, "Persistence and Continuity in Human Genetics and Social Stratification," in Peters, *Genetics,* 218–38.

ies by religious thinkers on human genetics were published between 1980 and 1998. These works, particularly the individually authored or co-authored volumes, make a significant contribution toward developing a constructive moral theology on genetics. Most, in fact virtually all, of the authors have considerable knowledge of the scientific foundations. Nevertheless, this literature is far from comprehensive on the ethical issues genetic advances raise. And many of the authors focus more on defining the meaning of genetic discoveries than on providing guidance about how to proceed.

To briefly overview the major book-length works, in 1993 the UCC theologian Ronald Cole-Turner published *The New Genesis: Theology and the Genetic Revolution.* A relatively brief work (109 pages) that provides a useful introduction to genetics and some of the theological issues the genetic revolution raises, *The New Genesis* considers the difference between traditional agricultural breeding methods and genetic engineering, the purpose of genetic engineering, and the initial response of the churches and individual theologians to developments in genetic research. Cole-Turner concludes with a series of theological affirmations that conceptualize genetic engineering as an extension of God's creating and redeeming activity. According to Cole-Turner, God works through both natural processes and human initiatives to achieve genetic changes. Nevertheless, he rejects the notion of humanity being imaged as God's co-creator in this process.[76]

Cole-Turner coauthored a second book with Brent Waters, *Pastoral Genetics: Theology and Care at the Beginning of Life,* published in 1996.[77] Its intended audience is clergy called on to counsel parishioners confronting the very difficult task of making moral decisions about procreation and abortion in an era of genetic testing. Far more than a how-to guide, the book integrates an engaging case-study approach with an explanation of the scientific basis of genetic testing and a meaningful theological commentary. Three chapters—on connecting God with genetic processes, exploring the presence of God in pain, and considering human genetics in the light of the resurrection—are particularly notable for their ability to illuminate difficult, complex, ambiguous issues without necessarily resolving them. Using a nondirective approach reminiscent of contemporary norms of pastoral counseling, their text informs pastoral genetics with sophisticated theological reflection without being prescriptive. The book concludes with an invitation to clergy to participate in an ongoing conversation in the life of the church about genetic science and technologies.

76. Cole-Turner, *New Genesis,* 109.
77. Ronald Cole-Turner and Brent Waters, *Pastoral Genetics: Theology and Care at the Beginning of Life* (Cleveland: Pilgrim Press, 1996).

In 1994, J. Robert Nelson published a work entitled *On the New Frontiers of Genetics and Religion,* which recounts presentations at the 1990 and 1992 Institute of Religion conferences and excerpts a few of the resources prepared for the conference, including the delegates' "Summary Reflection Statement" at the second conference. As might be expected, the book is a smorgasbord that bears many of the limitations of multiauthored volumes without the benefit of allowing the various voices to speak for themselves. Because this work is one of the few seeking to incorporate a diversity of religious communions beyond the Christian community, it is particularly unfortunate that virtually all such perspectives were given so little space. The one exception is an essay on Judaism and genetics by Barry Freundel, an Orthodox Jewish rabbi.[78]

Roger Shinn, who might be described as the doyen of religious ethicists working on genetics issues, published a book entitled *The New Genetics: Challenges for Science, Faith, and Politics* in 1996. Like the seventh chapter in his 1982 work, *Forced Options: Social Decisions for the 21st Century,*[79] Shinn utilizes genetics as a case study for ethical decisions required by new scientific knowledge and power. Also, in much the same manner as his approach in *Forced Options,* he argues in *The New Genetics* that responsible decisions require an understanding of both science and ethics. More specifically, he posits that public policies result from an interaction of three dynamic forces—human values and faiths, scientific information and concepts, and political activity.[80] One strength of his treatment is to show the dialectic between the potential of genetic knowledge to heal and distort the human. One weakness is Shinn's decision here, as in some of his other works, to write for a secular rather than a religious audience.[81] The problem is that religion, to the extent it is dealt with at all, is considered a kind of ideological input into decision making rather than a normative and conceptual context. Shinn does, however, use a religious frame of reference to deal with the issues related to the modification of germline cells.

Ted Peters' 1997 book *Playing God? Genetic Determinism and Human Freedom* represents the first truly comprehensive and in-depth theological analysis of human genetics. Although religious thinkers had previously recognized that

78. Barry Freundel, "Personal Religious Positions Individually Expressed: Judaism," in J. Robert Nelson, *On the New Frontiers of Genetics and Religion* (Grand Rapids, Mich.: Wm. B. Eerdmans Publishing Co., 1994), 120–35.

79. Roger Lincoln Shinn, *Forced Options: Social Decisions for the 21st Century* (San Francisco: Harper and Row, 1982), 127–46.

80. Roger Lincoln Shinn, *The New Genetics: Challenges for Science, Faith, and Politics* (Wakefield, R.I., and London: Moyer Bell, 1996), 89.

81. To be fair, I would like to note that Roger Shinn and I have had several discussions about this issue and agreed to disagree.

genetic knowledge raises issues for theological concepts and traditions, Peters is the first to systematically take on the challenge of exploring this knotty and complicated subject. The foreword, written by Francis Collins, director of the National Center for Human Genome Research, describes the work as a "remarkable book," which seems an apt characterization.[82] As the subtitle indicates, the work examines the cultural and theological struggle between genetic determinism, the notion that our genes govern us like a puppeteer, and the hope that new genetic knowledge will increase the human freedom to control its own future and destiny. Peters, professor of Systematic Theology at Pacific Lutheran Theological Seminary and the Center for Theology and the Natural Science at the Graduate Theological Union in Berkeley, California, offers an eloquent criticism of the "gene myth" of genetic determinism and a defense of human moral freedom. He argues, "responsibility includes building a better future through genetic science, a form of human creativity expressive of the image of God imparted by the divine to the human race."[83]

Jan Heller's *Human Genome Research and the Challenge of Contingent Future Persons*[84] investigates how genetic science is likely to affect future generations and explores the implications for evaluating the scientific advances associated with HGP. Recognizing that future persons will bear the burdens and/or benefits of contemporary decisions about genetic science applications, particularly germ-line interventions that will be heritable, Heller seeks to find a philosophical and theological framework for moral deliberations.

There are two edited collections on genetics based on contributions by religious ethicists. The first, *Genetic Ethics: Do the Ends Justify the Genes?*,[85] the product of a Center for Bioethics and Human Dignity project, has a wide range of articles written primarily, but not entirely, by evangelical Protestants. Its glossary of genetic terms is particularly helpful. A second volume, *Genetics: Issues of Social Justice*,[86] presents contributions from a group of researchers and guest scholars who participated in a project at the Graduate Theological Union in Berkeley, California. It incorporates a wider range of theological perspectives than *Genetic Ethics*. *Genetics* includes essays by a Jewish bioethicist and secular scholars as well as Protestant and Catholic moral theologians.

---

82. Ted Peters, *Playing God? Genetic Determinism and Human Freedom* (New York: Routledge, 1997), x.

83. Ibid., xvii.

84. Jan Christian Heller, *Human Genome Research and the Challenge of Contingent Future Persons* (Omaha: Creighton University Press, 1996).

85. John F. Kilner, Rebecca D. Pentz, and Frank E. Young, eds., *Genetic Ethics: Do the Ends Justify the Genes?* (Grand Rapids, Mich.: Wm. B. Eerdmans Publishing Co., 1997).

86. Peters, *Genetics*.

ETHICAL AND THEOLOGICAL ANALYSES

Playing God: Determination of Limits

Since the inception of the genetic revolution, religious and secular thinkers have raised questions about the appropriateness of utilizing scientific knowledge for reengineering and enhancing human beings and creating new forms of life. The phrase "playing God" has come to be used as shorthand for concerns that it is inappropriate for humans to change the way other living organisms or human beings are constituted because it amounts to usurping the creative prerogative of God. A book written by Leroy Augenstein, a biochemist, in 1969, *Come, Let Us Play God,*[87] was the first work to ascribe the role of playing God to modern medical activity. It then was linked to genetics in two separate publications in 1977: *Playing God: Genetic Engineering and the Manipulation of Life*[88] and *Who Should Play God?*[89] Although Augenstein wrote sympathetically about prospective biomedical developments, seeking to acquaint people with the unprecedented range of possibilities on the horizon, "playing God" has come to serve as a symbolic expression of concern over the extensive power of contemporary genetic technologies.[90] Claims that genetic engineering amounts to playing God have served as a rallying cry for a variety of critics, many of them secular thinkers. Theologian Ted Peters argues that the primary role of the phrase "playing God" is to serve as a warning and that it has very little cognitive value when looked at from the perspective of a theologian.[91] This section reviews the debates about playing God to ascertain whether Peters is correct and whether religious thinkers have provided sufficient content or criteria to illuminate fundamental choices about the appropriate limits of human intervention in creation.

One of the most extensive discussions of what it means to use the phrase "playing God" in relationship to genetic engineering occurs in *Splicing Life,* a 1982 report of the President's Commission for the Study of Ethical Problems in Medicine and Biomedical and Behavioral Research. Although it may seem strange for a government commission to devote some 10 percent of a report on genetic engineering to such a theological concern, the commission undertook

87. Leroy Augenstein, *Come, Let Us Play God* (Evanston, Ill.: Harper and Row, 1969).

88. Jane Goodfield, *Playing God: Genetic Engineering and the Manipulation of Life* (New York: Harper Books, 1977).

89. Ted Howard and Jeremy Rifkin, *Who Should Play God? The Artificial Creation of Life and What It Means for the Future of the Human Race* (New York: Delacourt Publishing, 1977).

90. Frank D. Seydel, "Human Gene Therapy—Playing God?" in *The Biology of Hematopoiesis* (New York: Wiley-Liss, 1990), 340.

91. Peters, *Playing God?* 2.

this particular study in response to a request from three general secretaries of religious organizations. As part of its procedure, the commission asked each general secretary to identify scholars able to elaborate on the theological considerations underlying their concern about gene splicing in humans.[92] "At its heart," the report concludes, "the term [playing God] represents a reaction to the realization that human beings are on the threshold of understanding how the fundamental machinery of life works." So understood, the phrase is not so much an objection to the research but "an expression of awe—and concern" (54).

A second meaning the commission identified was the assumption that gene splicing technology amounted to arrogant interference with nature. In response, the commission observed that in some senses all human activity that produces changes which would not otherwise have occurred can be so labeled (55). For example, human beings have been creating new life-forms ever since they learned to cultivate new characteristics in plants and breed new traits in animals. As for the notion that gene splicing technology violates God's prescriptive natural law or goes against God's purposes as they are manifested in the natural order, the commission pointed out that none of the scholars designated to represent the three major religious traditions made such a claim. Quite the contrary: "Although each scholar expressed concern over particular applications of gene splicing technology, they all also emphasized that human beings have not merely the right but the duty to employ their God-given powers to harness nature for human benefit" (56).

The commission considered a third issue: whether "breaching species barriers" violated specific religious prohibitions. Although the production of hybrids had preceded genetic engineering, the commission acknowledged that there might be two new sources of concern. First, unlike mules, which are sterile, the novel forms of life produced through genetic engineering can reproduce themselves and therefore self-perpetuate potential "mistakes." Second, given religious prohibitions against sexual relations between human beings and lower animals and people's fear that partially human hybrids would be something akin to Dr. Frankenstein's monster, the mixing of human and non-human genes was likely to be problematic (56–60).

Of the various arguments that genetic engineering represented playing God, the most cogent admonition against the use of gene splicing technology, according to the commission, was the lack of sufficient knowledge or wisdom of the uses or consequences. Nevertheless, the commission tended to downplay the significance of this caution, relegating it to little more than a variant on the Socratic injunction Know thyself, or, as they rephrased it, "acknowledge the limits of understanding and prediction" (59). Although

92. President's Commission, *Splicing Life,* 53.

undoubtedly correct that this concern places emphasis on the potential consequences rather than the problematic nature of the technology as such, it still raises significant issues. The commission "could find no ground for concluding that any current or planned forms of genetic engineering, whether using human or nonhuman material, are intrinsically wrong or irreligious per se." Nevertheless, this assessment, even if correct, does not justify dismissing, as it did, religiously grounded fears that the rapid development of genetic engineering might constitute a fundamental danger to safety or human values. This is particularly so since the report does not recommend either comprehensive criteria or adequate mechanisms to set standards and objectives to guide the powers of genetic engineering. Additionally, the range of religious views consulted, while broad by the standards of its day, certainly does not represent an adequate basis on which to draw the conclusion that there was nothing specifically irreligious about creating new life-forms or attempting to "improve" human nature.

These issues have been raised many times since by a variety of groups and individual thinkers, perhaps most carefully by the working group convened by the Church of Scotland's Society, Religion and Technology Project to study the ethics of genetic engineering in nonhuman species. Much like the president's commission, this project explored whether genetic manipulation entails usurping the creative prerogative of God and taking on an activity that is inappropriate for finite human beings. Unlike the commission, the project also considers whether genetic engineering represents a denial of the created or evolved good of animals or plants and its substitution with human goods and designs. It generally has positive view toward genetic engineering as an exercise of the potential given to human beings by God, in which we appropriately play God.

Their discussion is placed within a biblical and ethical framework. The working group's interpretation of Scripture emphasizes broad human responsibility for ordering the natural world and not just passively serving as curators of a living museum.[93] It argues that the biblical mandate to humanity to understand and to make something of the creation also justifies the technological manipulation of life to serve human welfare, a view that undoubtedly reflects its composition: the overwhelming majority of its members have backgrounds in science and technology. Additionally, the working group rejects the misgiving that genetic engineering, and to some extent biotechnology in general, is unnatural and violates the given order of the natural world. Countering this view, it points out that after centuries of human activity that have transformed the biosphere, the concepts of natural and unnatural are difficult to define in any meaningful way (88–89). The working group does acknowledge that perspec-

---

93. Bruce and Bruce, *Engineering Genesis*, 86.

tives of ecological holism articulated in some feminist and Christian approaches, which argue that genetic engineering may upset the balance, relationality, order, and diversity of nature, have some merit (98). Its book-length report also recognizes that transferring genes between species particularly disturbs some Christians—and it might be noted Orthodox Jews as well. Those who believe that genetic engineering violates the given order of nature often interpret the Genesis creation account's description of God making "everything after its kind" as setting natural barriers among the species. In arguing against this perspective, the working group claims that the Old Testament distinction of "kinds" cannot be equated with the biological notion of species. It also points out that genetic exchange occurs routinely in nature. Nevertheless, the working group affirms the idea of the natural (or divine) wisdom of the natural order and the need for humans to respect the distinction of species and orders (93–95).

Engineering Genesis concludes that genetic engineering is but the latest phase of a technological enhancement of the environment for human benefit. Its acceptance of the moral appropriateness of genetic engineering rests primarily on a consequentialist analysis weighing the potential benefits and potential drawbacks of this technology. Nonetheless the working group underscores that there can be a significant disparity between the optimistic potential which is claimed for specific applications of genetic engineering and the real results which accrue in production (101). Urging caution and care, the working group recommends against assaults on nature, such as introducing transgenic species into the wild or mixing large numbers of genes between species (95–96). It further emphasizes the importance of undertaking a case-by-case analysis of potential applications. The study's final reflections also consider the need to protect the interests of less powerful groups in society (284–85).

Allen Verhey, an evangelical Protestant bioethicist, has written an essay in which he claims that *Splicing Life* "reduced the meaning of the phrase to secular terms and made 'God' superfluous."[94] Verhey places the commission's interpretation within the framework of the post-Baconian search for scientific knowledge as a source of power over nature and warns that this effort inevitably places humanity at the center, displacing God to the periphery or boundaries of human knowledge and power. In the context of this kind of limited and defensive understanding of God's role in the creation, according to Verhey, playing God means to usurp God's authority and dominion at the boundaries of human knowledge and power, to encroach inappropriately on those areas of human life where human beings have hitherto been ignorant or powerless (64). While he objects to such a limited conception of the God of creation and Scripture, he does not claim that the affirmation that the God of

94. Allen D. Verhey, "Playing God," in Kilner, Pentz, and Young, eds., *Genetic Ethics,* 61.

creation made and sustains the order we observe and rely upon precludes scientific research or prohibits natural scientific explanations. He also points out
that indiscriminate warnings against playing God are little more than slogans
and therefore do not provide clear standards of behavior.

Verhey's construction of a more appropriate interpretation of playing God
builds on Paul Ramsey's warnings made in 1970 at the dawn of the genetics
revolution. Verhey draws from Ramsey the fundamental perspective that a religious ethic for a Christian or a Jew must be premised on a worldview in
which God is a given, and not just any old God, "but the God who creates and
keeps a world and a covenant" (67). Like Ramsey, Verhey understands such a
conception of God to impose a prohibition against separating the unitive and
procreative goods of human sexuality and therefore specifically enjoining
against artificial insemination using the sperm of a donor. In addition, he
assumes that warnings against playing God extend to deliberately killing
patients, even ones in the very early stages of life in a petri dish. While endorsing Ramsey's concerns against playing God, Verhey also invites society to "play
God in the correct way" (67). To Verhey that means looking at the creation and
its genetics with wonder and awe, to delight in the elegant structure of DNA,
and to appreciate the work of the Creator. Alternatively, it means promoting
life and its flourishing through genetic therapies that aim at health and, by
implication, apparently refraining from therapeutic abortions following from
prenatal genetic diagnoses (70). Because God takes the side of the poor, playing God for Verhey also entails assuring that the benefits of the HGP and
other genetic research are shared equitably and help the poor (69–71).

It is ironic that for all his criticisms of the secular character of *Splicing Life* and
his effort to place the discussion within a theological interpretation, Verhey
does not end up at a substantially different place than the President's
Commission. He appears to conclude that genetic engineering and research do
not in themselves raise fundamental questions, but that some of their potential
applications are questionable. The standard he puts forward to render such uses
appropriate, or to play God the way God plays God, is imprecise at the least. The
particular examples he offers seem more a selective expression of a particular
theological perspective than a clear-cut set of criteria. Why, for example, should
the principle of the unity of the unitive and procreative goods of human sexuality take center court? Since virtually all genetic therapeutic interventions
ostensibly attempt to improve health, does that mean that Verhey accepts everything, including germ-line interventions, that can be justified on those grounds?
As principles go, the justice standards he offers go beyond issues of appropriate
intervention to wider questions about the distribution of burdens and benefits.
As such, Verhey's discussion adds little beyond much of the religious literature
on genetics.

Despite the title of his book, *Playing God?,* Ted Peters, an ecumenical Lutheran in background, tends to be disparaging of the usefulness of that enigmatic phrase. He suggests that it can have three overlapping meanings. The first has to do with a sense of awe about learning fundamental secrets of nature, a kind of belief that we are on the threshold of acquiring God-like knowledge and powers. The second relates to wielding power over life and death, something the medical profession routinely exercises. The third, which Peters considers the most relevant to genetics, is the use of science to alter life and influence evolution.[95] But Peters disputes what many critics claim, that genetic engineering and other reproductive technologies go beyond the limits of a reasonable dominion over nature or at least provide temptations in that direction. Like Philip Hefner, Peters conceptualizes the human being as God's "created co-creator," a creature created by God and vested with creativity to share in the transforming work of God's ongoing creation (15). As such, Peters is more comfortable with engaging in genetic engineering than theologians who have a more static vision of the creation and a greater hesitation to transcend fixed boundaries. Nevertheless, Peters recognizes that human creativity is ambiguous, particularly when it involves technology. He describes human beings as condemned to be creative, having no choice but to express ourselves through tools and technology, but living in a context of risk because technology can be used for good or for evil (15). To the extent that the warning not to play God provides a caution against foolish Prometheanism, Peters finds it helpful, but for him the real issue is how we should play human and understand our human relationship to nature, God, and future generations. "I recommend that we take advantage of the ability to deliberate, decide, and take responsible action. . . . I recommend that we orient our free wills around the good, the long-range good for the human race and for life on our planet as a whole" (177–78). This is a noble vision, one in tune with Christian hope, but offering little in the way of specifics to help guide choices in the applications of genetic technology.

Criteria for Determining Limits and Appropriate Applications

Most religious thinkers writing on genetics tend to have generally positive views about potential applications of genetic technologies, but they are also aware of some of the risks involved. *Genetic Testing and Screening* characterizes the Lutheran position as "critical engagement" and this characterization could be applied more broadly within the religious community. According to Roger Willer, its editor, critical engagement "signifies that, in principle, the emerging genetic knowledge and its application are to be affirmed; but it simultaneously indicates that people of faith must consider any particular instance critically.

95. Peters, *Playing God?* 10–11.

This means that Christians must decide about any specific instance according to criteria informed by faith and Christian sources."[96] Thus, even if genetic engineering does not amount to playing God, there is a need for moral theologians to frame guidelines for determining whether specific applications are ethically appropriate.

Openness to genetic engineering, particularly among the moral theologians well versed in science, often derives from the realization that nature itself is constantly engaging in a process akin to human genetic engineering, albeit presumably without the element of intentionality. Theological formulations also incline some in this direction. As noted, both Philip Hefner and Ted Peters characterize the human person as God's created co-creator and think of the *imago Dei* embedded in humanity in terms of creativity.[97] In Peters's proleptic ethics, he rejects humanity playing God in the Promethean sense, but concludes that "we should play human in the *imago Dei* sense—that is, we should understand ourselves as created co-creators and press our scientific and technological creativity into the service of neighbor love, of beneficence."[98]

But what does this really mean? How do we determine whether technological creativity is truly in the service of beneficence, particularly when many of the issues at hand are complex and human motives are acknowledged to be ambiguous? Hefner, for example, raises the question if we are genetically determined to be free, and if freedom is the condition that makes serious human sinning possible, whether we are now at risk of derailing our evolutionary future. He identifies a variety of ways in which human sin is likely to affect applications of genetics: First, genetic interventions will be manipulated by social class interests to benefit the affluent and harm the poor and marginalized persons. Second, certain groups, such as insurance companies and employers, will attempt to use the information provided by genome mapping for their own interests. Third, alterations will be made both in individuals and in the germ-line that will prove to be unwise. Fourth, facets of the genome project will redefine human life in ways that violate human dignity.[99] That genetic development is being driven by profit-driven commercial interests rather than ethics suggests that these prospects are more likely than not.

Peters's writings also exhibit this tension between a theological commitment to human freedom and creativity in probing and reengineering nature and caution in concrete applications, albeit more sequentially than concurrently. Peters

96. Willer, "Introduction," in Willer, ed., *Genetic Testing and Screening*, 8.
97. Peters, *Playing God?* 15.
98. Ibid., 161.
99. Philip Hefner, "Determinism, Freedom, and Moral Failure," in Ted Peters, ed., *Genetics* (Cleveland: Pilgrim Press, 1998), 111, 120.

concludes his book with an invitation to answer God's call to be creative and transformative so as to make life qualitatively better for God's creatures.[100] Nevertheless, a second book of his, *For the Love of Children: Genetic Technology and the Future of the Family,* published only one year earlier, focuses on the risks of new reproductive technologies based on genetic science. In it Peters expresses his concerns that choices conferred by assisted reproductive technologies, such as genetic selection, will result in an effort to produce designer children as well as an increased propensity toward selective abortion when the fetus does not meet with the parents' criteria. He foresees that multiple choices in baby making, rather than making life qualitatively better, will tend to commodify children, that is, incline prospective parents to regard children as a form of merchandise in the expanding marketplace of genetic services. The dilemmas this raises are several. Bringing new life into being is one of the most important expressions of the human role as created co-creators, and it is understandable that parents would want to bring healthy babies into the world who have the potential of a full life. Yet widespread use of genetic screening of embryos and fetuses to prevent the birth of children with genetic defects would likely result in the scenario that Peters fears. It would also risk diminishing the dignity and worth of all persons born with genetic disabilities and seemingly affirm a genetic definition of personhood. Peters does not so much resolve these knotty questions as sensitively and perceptively discuss them within the context of Christian thinking on sex and baby making. He concludes that most Christians are not ethically ready for an era of selective abortion for purposes of sorting out desirable from undesirable genes.[101]

How should determinations about appropriate genetic research and applications be made? Richard McCormick, a Roman Catholic moral theologian, states that the central question or moral criterion should be this: "Will this or that intervention (or omission, exception, policy, law) promote or undermine human persons 'integrally and adequately considered'?"[102] To consider whether specific genetic interventions are likely to be positive or harmful, he offers a set of values. According to McCormick, the sacredness of life requires avoiding undue risks. The interconnection of life systems means that harm to any one will likely have a deleterious impact on others. Genetic technology must respect the uniqueness and basic equality of the individual. Decisions relating to priorities of genetic research and the enjoyment of its benefits should also

100. Peters, *Playing God?* 178.

101. Ted Peters, *For the Love of Children: Genetic Technology and the Future of the Family* (Louisville: Westminster/John Knox Press, 1996), 117.

102. Richard A. McCormick, S.J., *The Critical Calling: Reflections on Moral Dilemmas Since Vatican II* (Washington, D.C.: Georgetown University Press, 1989), 267.

be sensitive to the need for distributive justice. Given the importance of these decisions for the common human future, McCormick emphasizes the need to go beyond the exclusive expertise of the scientific community to develop public mechanisms of ongoing deliberation, oversight, and public informa- tion.[103]

The theological and ethical framework in the United Church of Canada's brief perhaps best expresses the thrust of the ethical principles cited in the var- ious ecumenical and denominational statements. In its executive summary, the brief affirms the following:

- Life is a gift of ultimate value and to be respected as such. It is an end in itself. The life and health of another person must never be treated as means to some other person's ends.

- Human beings are essentially relational rather than individual. This applies to professional as well as to personal situations and extends to national and world levels.

- Justice and compassion are at the heart of being human. The measure of our humanity is our ability to create a society in which the rights of the weak- er and the needy are protected.

- Responsible use of the resources of the earth and its people requires the establishment of priorities that reflect these values.

- While medical technologies offer hope to some, they must be carefully scrutinized for their costs to human beings and their utilization of scarce resources. Clear guidelines must be established for their use.[104]

Roger Shinn's self-described "limited attempt to identify some clues to human norms as they pertain to genetic exploration and practice"[105] is also intended to offer a beginning point for guidelines for genetic activity. While they are not framed in explicit theological terms, they do reflect religious val- ues. And they certainly overlap with the perspective outlined in some of the ecumenical and denominational documents described earlier in this chapter. Shinn's six guidelines are as follows:

- Physical health: Genetic investigation and practice, directed toward healing, are beneficent—provided they guard against excessive risk, rash denials of human frailty, and partisan definitions of normality (108).

103. Ibid., 268–69, 270–71.
104. The Division of Mission in Canada, "A Brief to the Royal Commission on New Reproductive Technologies," 3.
105. Shinn, *New Genetics,* 107.

- Humankind and nature: Nature and its awesome, intricate ecosystems deserve our profound but guarded respect. Nature does not dictate norms. We can ask of every genetic intervention in nature whether a modification of culture would be preferable. But we can intervene, with due caution, to protect significant values (110).

- Freedom in community: Freedom in community is one of the normative marks of humanity. An ethically responsible program of genetic research and practice, while recognizing that the human body includes causal mechanisms, some of them genetic, will remember that persons are more than mechanisms or collections of mechanisms. It will recognize the mystery of selfhood and will seek to protect freedom in community (112).

- Diversity: Diversity is an asset to be treasured. . . . Any general norms should include diversity. Attempts to normalize deviant types should give strong weight to the unconcerned choice of those to be normalized (114–15).

- Imagination and reason: Imagination and reason are gifts to humanity, to be valued. They do not determine human worth. But when they are threatened by genetic ailments, healing is welcome (117).

- Character: Genetic knowledge is intimately linked to human character, but character (social and personal) will direct the uses of the knowledge. . . . We cannot entrust genetic power to any elite—military, financial, or scientific— without violating the gift of human dignity (120).

While similar in many regards to the ethical framework in secular evaluations of genetic research and technology, the religiously grounded criteria or principles tend to have some distinctive themes. One is the emphasis on the relational or social character of human beings and the concomitant need to consider the implications of the genetic revolution within a social and community, as well as an individual, context. Another is that religious writings are more inclined to view issues in a wider framework, the impact of genetic engineering on animals, plants, and the environment, as well as human beings. Yet another distinctive principle appearing in several of the statements is a genetic equivalent of the preferential option for the poor, the need to evaluate the impact of the genetic revolution on the poorest and most vulnerable persons and societies. Finally, works of religious ethicists are more likely to affirm the fundamental human right of people to be involved in decisions affecting their well-being.

What is unfortunate is that these principles are rarely applied to analyze specific issues. If religious ethics had proceeded in this direction, it would have made a real contribution to dealing with some of the dilemmas genetic applications

raise. None of the principles and norms enumerated in this literature offer specific directions for the application of genetic power. Nor are they intended to do
so. Shinn characterizes his set as referring "less to precise decisions than to the personal and cultural climate in which decisions are made" (120-21). He attempts to
apply them with regard to only one issue, the modification of human germ-line
cells, and his perspective on this critical issue is not conclusive in one direction or
another. To use the distinction that Tom Beauchamp and James Childress make
in their well-known *Principles of Biomedical Ethics*,[106] religious ethicists offer broad
principles rather than specific rules for determining whether a certain kind of
application is ethical or not. Nevertheless, the most difficult aspect of moral reasoning about genetics is applying general principles or norms to specific issues and
cases.

Genetic Testing and Therapeutic Abortions

Developments in genetic science have significant implications for reproductive
decision making. Once scientists identify where the source of the genetic predispositions for many serious diseases is located, they have frequently been
able to develop diagnostic tests. Genetic testing is a laboratory procedure that
examines a sample of genetic material, usually drawn from blood, to determine
whether a particular gene known to cause a genetic condition or disease is present. Increasingly, persons with a history of genetic problems in their families
choose to have genetic tests done to determine whether they are a carrier, and
if so, what the statistical prospects are that a child conceived with their partner will be afflicted with the condition. Various types of postconception testing are also available. Prenatal diagnosis is now possible for some two hundred
genetic diseases and metabolic disorders, and others are likely to be made
available in the years ahead. Techniques have been developed to examine *in
vitro*–fertilized eggs for some types of gene abnormalities as early as the fourth
cell division. Two pregnancy tests are in widespread use, both with some risks
to the mother as well as to the fetus: amniocentesis, usually performed between
the twelfth and sixteenth week of pregnancy, and chorionic villus sampling,
which can be done as early the seventh week of pregnancy. Research is also
under way to identify fetal cells in the blood of pregnant women so as to be
able to undertake less invasive forms of genetic testing.[107] Just as testing of
newborns for elevated blood phenylalanine levels associated with phenylke-
tonuria (PKU) has been routine since the 1960s, it may become more com-

---

106. Tom L. Beauchamp and James F. Childress, *Principles of Biomedical Ethics,* 4th ed.
(New York: Oxford University Press, 1994).
107. Cole-Turner and Waters, *Pastoral Genetics,* 17.

mon to screen segments of the population for a wide range of genetic diseases. There are indications that insurance carriers and some employers are already demanding some genetic tests to reduce the risks associated with providing medical and life insurance coverage to clients or employees.

These advances pose increasing dilemmas as to how to respond to the opportunity for prenatal genetic testing and then use the information gained from these diagnoses. These painful choices, usually made by the parents with the assistance of a genetic counselor and sometimes with additional pastoral counseling by clergy, are all the more wrenching because genetic testing is still a relatively imprecise science that cannot determine the potential seriousness of a mutation or correct it *in utero*. Because the ability to diagnose genetic disorders is far more advanced than the capacity to treat them, most parents only have a choice of bearing or aborting a fetus with a genetic abnormality. Abortion is already one of the most divisive moral issues in this country, and genetic science is increasing its rancor and moral complexity.

The current state of the development of genetics raises many difficult issues that intersect with the morality of abortion and respect for life. Are parents responsible for the genetic health of their children, and if so, what are the moral implications of giving birth to a child with a serious genetic disorder? In previous generations, parents who gave birth to a child with a genetically related illness or disorder attracted sympathy, not blame, but couples having a child who does not meet "normal" or "minimal" genetic expectations are now more likely to be criticized. They may also run the risk of being penalized by their medical insurers for failing to use medical technologies that could prevent the birth of genetically "defective" infants, especially if they already have one afflicted child.[108] If parents utilize some form of prenatal testing, how should they make moral determinations when they discover a fetus has some form of genetic anomaly? Does the suffering associated with specific genetic abnormalities ever warrant a therapeutic abortion? If so, what kinds of standards should be used to make this determination? What are the implications for human dignity and for attitudes toward persons afflicted with genetic disorders and other medical handicaps? Positions on these issues often, but not always, reflect views on the moral status of the embryo and on the permissibility of abortion.

One issue on which ethicists disagree is whether an openness to genetic testing necessarily means that parents are making acceptance of the pregnancy conditional on the fetus meeting certain standards. Evangelical and conservative Protestants often have the strongest reservations about using prenatal genetic screening. C. Ben Mitchell, an ethicist who serves as a consultant for

108. Waters, *Ministry in an Age of Science and Technology,* 14.

the Southern Baptist Convention, points out that "the expansive use of pre-natal genetic screening casts a shadow of suspicion over every unborn baby. Every pregnancy becomes a 'tentative pregnancy,' pending the results of pre-natal screening." He argues that it is morally offensive to treat human babies as chattel to be disposed of when they do not meet our criteria of normalcy, warning that the effort to prevent children from being born with fatal and debilitating diseases is likely to increase discriminatory prejudice and reduce life prospects for persons with disabilities. Mitchell concludes that the church must provide support and encouragement for couples who either choose not to undergo prenatal screening or decide to maintain their pregnancy despite the diagnosis of genetic anomaly.[109]

Despite its insistence that the human being must be respected as a person from the very first instance of existence and strong opposition to abortion,[110] the Roman Catholic Church does not categorically oppose genetic testing. It does, however, impose restrictions. Pope John Paul II insists that at no moment in its development should the embryo be the subject of tests that are not ben-eficial or experimentation that would inevitably mutilate or damage it.[111] Genetic testing and intervention are deemed acceptable only when strictly therapeutic and intended to promote the well-being of the fetus without intruding on the biological nature of the human being or potentially leading to abortion.[112] The Catholic Health Association of the United States encour-ages Catholic health care institutions to consider the establishment of programs in medical genetics and recommends that the freedom of persons to partici-pate in genetic testing and counseling should be protected. To be consistent with the principle of justice, the Catholic Health Association also advocates that genetic services be available equally to persons on the basis of need.[113]

Testing for genetic anomalies has also posed challenges for Jewish ethicists. Orthodox Judaism recognizes only one warrant for abortion, direct threats to the mother's life. Yet, the incidence of Tay-Sachs disease within the Ashkenazic Jewish community, a genetic affliction that usually causes death within three years of birth, is one hundred times that in the population at large. Rabbi David Bleich, described as the most rigid of Orthodox bioethicists on this issue, states categorically that the immutability of Jewish law (*halakhah*) does not

109. C. Ben Mitchell, "The Church and the New Genetics," in Kilner, Pentz, and Young, eds., *Genetic Ethics*, 238, 240.
110. Congregation for the Doctrine of the Faith, "Dignity of Procreation," 701.
111. Pope John Paul II, "Address to a Working Party on the Legal and Ethical Aspects of the Human Genome Project," 20 November 1993, reprinted in *Genetic Intervention on Human Subjects*, 54.
112. Pope John Paul II, "Ethics of Genetic Manipulation," 385, 388.
113. *Human Genetics*, 39–40.

permit selective abortion of affected fetuses. Bleich further claims that the commandment to procreate is not suspended for carrier couples, whom he thereby condemns to the possibilities of producing children doomed to an early and painful death. His only concession is to support the screening of unmarried adults so that they can refrain from entering into unions with high risks of procreating children with genetic problems.[114]

In contrast with Bleich's position, Conservative and Reformed scholars believe that the interpretation and application of Jewish law undergoes constant change. They therefore have greater latitude in recognizing changes in the historical context of past medical decisions and their crucial differences with the contemporary situation. Elliot Dorff, a Conservative rabbi and bioethicist, argues that traditional sources refrained from identifying fetal conditions as a grounding of morally defensible abortion only because in earlier times it was not possible to know anything about the health of a fetus before its birth. Advances in genetics and neonatalogy, according to Dorff, should establish the fetus's health as an independent consideration. Like many Protestant bioethicists, his view is that some fetal anomalies are so devastating that abortion is appropriate to spare the child from suffering. He identifies two such cases, Tay-Sachs and Lesch-Nyham, but the basis of his reasoning is not clear.[115] Other Jewish ethicists are far more cautious about the development of widespread prenuptial and prenatal genetic screening among Ashkenazic Jews. Laurie Zoloth-Dorfman warns that "if the concept of prenuptial and prenatal screening is *halakhically* acceptable for Tay-Sachs, and the technology exists to uncover more and more diseases, then the process shifts perilously close to the eugenic imperative."[116]

Most mainline Protestant ethicists dealing with genetics implicitly support the genetic screening of high-risk pregnancies, but they are reluctant to be directive on the central moral issue of whether or when to terminate a pregnancy if a defect is identified. Both the Lutheran collection of essays in *Genetic Testing and Screening* and the Episcopal resource *Wrestling with the Future: Our Genes, Our Choices* take a nondirective approach. They often seem more concerned to define the ethical and theological issues than to offer concrete guidance, particularly on sensitive questions related to conception and abortion. For example, the Episcopal resource addresses the morality of abortion in a variety

114. Dena S. Davis, "Method in Jewish Bioethics," in Paul F. Camenisch, ed., *Religious Methods and Resources in Bioethics* (Dordrecht and Boston: Kluwer Academic Publishers, 1994), 115.
115. Ibid., 115–227.
116. Laurie Zoloth-Dorfman, "Mapping the Normal Human Self," in Peters, ed., *Genetics*, 192.

of situations, depending on the severity of the genetic defect revealed through prenatal testing. In each of these cases, even when prenatal testing indicates the child would have a fatal condition or would never develop consciousness, the document offers theological perspectives both supporting and opposing abortion.[117] It points out that the most recent Episcopal General Convention resolution considers abortion morally permissible only in extreme situations, without explaining how to determine whether a specific genetic anomaly would fit this characterization. *Pastoral Genetics,* by Cole-Turner and Waters, provides a very helpful discussion of the religious and moral issues that confront those coping with difficult pregnancies. But their approach is pastoral and theological rather than prescriptive. According to the authors, "The pastor's task is to engage in conversation that enables a clearer understanding and response, one that is open to the possibility of God's presence, healing, and blessing."[118] Their book affirms the uniqueness of each pregnancy as a distinct or special possibility for human life, but it does not rule out therapeutic abortion as an option. Nevertheless, they say more about theodicy than genetic counseling, more about connecting God with genetic processes than providing specific advice as to how to respond to a genetically disabled fetus.

Ted Peters's book *For the Love of Children* offers five "minimalist middle axioms" for moral analysis consistent with protection for the developing child, that illuminate the context for decision making without resolving where to draw the line. His recommendations are as follows: first, the moral status of the fertilized zygote, whether or not the conceptus has the full personhood and dignity of a living adult, means that it is better to weed out defective or undesirable genes prior to conception through screening or manipulating the sperm or ovum. Second, selective abortion should always be a last resort and decisions should always reflect the future well-being of the child. Third, compassion taken up as nonmaleficence should be the deciding principle. Fourth, compassion expressed in the concrete situation of a family making a decision about a specific child is more acceptable than eugenics, that is, efforts to reduce the incidence of a particular trait in the population at large. And fifth, in making choices it is important to distinguish between preventing suffering and enhancing genetic potential.[119] To counter the attraction of the "perfect child syndrome" and confer dignity on future children, he proposes a new biblical mandate based on a paraphrase of 1 John 4:19, "God loves each human being regardlless of genetic make-up and we should do likewise."[120]

---

117. Cohen, ed., *Wrestling with the Future,* 87–99.
118. Cole-Turner and Waters, *Pastoral Genetics,* xiii.
119. Peters, *For the Love of Children,* 117–18.
120. This maxim appears in several of his writings, most recently in Ted Peters, "Love

Human Genetic Interventions

Richard McCormick distinguishes between four types of genetic applications: somatic cell therapy, germ-line interventions, enhancement genetic engineering, and eugenic genetic engineering.[121] Somatic cell therapy refers to efforts to correct the functioning of a defective gene in an individual's body cell or to replace it and thus cure the disease at its root. In contrast with somatic interventions, germ-line therapy, if and when it becomes feasible and morally acceptable, would alter germ (reproductive) cells and thereby make changes that would affect the patient's progeny. Enhancement genetic engineering would entail utilizing these same techniques to produce in healthy individuals improvements such as greater height, increased strength, or sharper memory. Like other forms of eugenics, genetic engineering employed for these purposes would involve systematic efforts to breed superior individuals, in this case through genetic selection or alteration. In terms of our current situation, experimental forms of somatic gene therapy began in 1990. The feasibility of at least some forms of germ-line intervention seems very close, and some would argue that pressures for undertaking some form of eugenics are already upon us.

It has generally been assumed that germ-line intervention is more technically difficult and higher risk than somatic cell therapy. These reservations have applied whether the alteration is conducted on gametocytes (a cell that produces germ cells), mature germ cells (eggs and sperm prior to union), or zygotes or pre-embryos (undifferentiated very early stage embryos). Assessments of the feasibility of germ-line intervention depend in part on definitional issues, particularly whether the screening and selection of early stage embryos to ensure that pregnancies begin with genetically healthy embryos constitutes a form of germ-line therapy. Pre-embryo selection is already being used on human embryos in some research centers and private fertility clinics and is likely to become even more common in future years. Yet assumptions about rigid distinctions between somatic and germ-line therapy and the greater difficulties and higher risks of the latter may become outdated by scientific advances. Scientists anticipate, for example, that some of the most promising new techniques under development to correct somatic cell defects may have the secondary unintended effect of simultaneously modifying germ cells in the subject, presumably with no increased level of risk. Efforts to treat genetic diseases of fetuses while *in utero,* which are likely in the near future, may have the same effect. If these developments proceed, they will raise

and Dignity: Against Children Becoming Commodities," in Willer, ed., *Genetic Testing and Screening,* 129.
121. McCormick, *Critical Calling,* 265.

novel ethical issues about unintended effects as well as place decisions about embarking on germ-line interventions in a new context.

Virtually no ethicist, working within either a religious or a secular context, contests the principle that new genetic knowledge should be used to improve human health and relieve suffering, but this consensus currently applies only to somatic gene therapy for therapeutic purposes, provided that its safety is demonstrated. This is the position in the few Jewish[122] and Islamic sources[123] available, as well as of the greater number of Christian religious thinkers and bodies considering genetic therapies. As an example, a 1996 report written by a working group of the British Catholic Bishops evaluates somatic therapy as not being different in principle from other forms of medical treatment. Like other experimental medical therapies, the moral calculus for them depends on the potential benefits to the patient, the risks to the patient and to others, and the cost and other burdens of the treatment. The bishops also caution that because somatic therapy is still experimental it should be used to treat causes of serious disease only where there is no satisfactory alternative treatment.[124] Similarly, an Episcopal resolution does not identify any theological or ethical objection to somatic gene therapy, provided that the procedure proves to be effective without undue risk to the patient and attempts to prevent or alleviate serious suffering.[125] In view of the various risks, the WCC recommends that subjects of this research should be fully informed of the nature and consequences of the procedure, to the extent that the latter can be determined.[126]

As might be anticipated, germ-line alterations that will affect the genetic inheritance of future generations elicit a more cautious response. Shinn categorizes the spectrum of opinions on germ-line interventions as ranging from emphatic rejection to enthusiastic anticipation.[127] Scientists, ethicists, and religious thinkers who support human germ-line intervention, if not now then

122. Freundel, "Personal Religious Positions," 133–35; Fred D. Ledley, "Judaism," in Nelson, *On the New Frontiers,* 136–38; Laurie Zoloth-Dorfman, "Mapping the Normal Human Self: The Jew and the Mark of Otherness," in Peters, *Genetics,* 191–93.

123. Gamal I. Serour, "Islamic Developments in Bioethics," in B. Andrew Lustig, *Theological Developments in Bioethics: 1992–1994* (Dordrecht, Boston, and London: Kluwer Academic Publishers, 1997), 176, and G. I. Serour and A. Omran, eds., *Proceedings of the First International Conference on Bioethics in Human Reproduction Research in the Muslim World* (Cairo: International Islamic Center for Population Studies and Research, 1991).

124. Working Party of the Catholic Bishops Joint Committee, *Genetic Intervention on Human Subjects,* 28–29.

125. 70th General Conference of the Episcopal Church, 1991, reprinted in Cynthia Cohen, ed., *Wrestling with the Future: Our Genes and Our Choices* (Harrisburg, Pa.: Morehouse Publishing, 1998) 119.

126. WCC, *Biotechnology,* 13.

127. Shinn, *New Genetics,* 124–29.

in the future, generally offer one or more of the following rationals: Germ-line intervention is potentially the only means of treating genetic diseases that do their damage early in embryonic development;[128] germ-line engineering provides a significant vehicle for blocking the transmittal of heritable forms of debilitating illness from one generation to another;[129] and, germ-line therapy is more efficient than the repeated resort to somatic cell therapy to correct the same defect in successive generations.[130]

Positions of religious bodies on the appropriateness of germ-line therapy range from the studied and intentional silence on the matter in the National Council of Churches statement to various statements that have significant reservations about undertaking germ-line intervention. Perhaps the strongest such example of this latter category is a 1992 Methodist statement: "Because its long-term effects are uncertain, we oppose therapy that results in changes that can be passed to offspring."[131] Here it is also relevant to note that Jeremy Rifkin, a social activist and critic of genetic engineering, managed to obtain endorsements from the chief officers of most major Protestant denominations, several Roman Catholic bishops, and a few theologians and scientists for a 1983 resolution opposing all "efforts to engineer specific genetic traits into the germline of the human species." The document was released with "a call upon Congress to prohibit genetic engineering of the human germline cells."[132] This resolution did not, however, mirror the policies adopted by these communions.

It would be more appropriate to characterize the official positions of most of these bodies, at least those that have relevant policies, as expressing caution rather than categorical rejection. Various Catholic texts provide relevant examples. In a 1983 address, Pope John Paul II distinguished between strictly therapeutic genetic interventions and manipulations that would harm the origin of human life, modify the genetic store, or lead to further marginalization of groups of people. He deemed therapeutic genetic manipulation as acceptable but categorized nontherapeutic forms as arbitrary and unjust.[133] This phrasing creates considerable ambiguity because most germ-line interventions, at least those currently contemplated, would be for therapeutic purposes. The 1994 Catholic catechism builds on the papal teaching: "Certain attempts to influence

128. *Human Genetics,* 21.

129. Marc Lappé, "Ethical Issues in Manipulating the Human Germ Line," *Journal of Medicine and Philosophy* 16 (1991): 631.

130. Burke K. Zimmerman, "Human Germ Line Therapy: The Case for Its Development and Use," *Journal of Medicine and Philosophy* 16 (1991): 593–612.

131. United Methodist Church, *Book of Discipline of the United Methodist Church* (Nashville, Tenn.: United Methodist Publishing House, 1992), 97–98.

132. Quoted in Shinn, *New Genetics,* 125.

133. Pope John Paul II, "The Ethics of Genetic Manipulation."

chromosome or genetic inheritance are not therapeutic but are aimed at producing human beings selected according to sex or other predetermined qualities. Such manipulations are contrary to the personal dignity of the human being and his integrity and identity. . . ."[134] Again, this wording does not appear to rule out germ-line interventions that are clearly therapeutic. The 1996 report of the British Catholic Bishops also expresses reservations about germ-line intervention, but in doing so it assumes that germ-line therapy will necessarily involve one or more elements morally unacceptable to the Catholic church: use of *in vitro* fertilization or similar laboratory techniques, experimentation on embryos in the course of developing the therapy, discard of embryos and abortion of fetuses on whom the therapy is unsuccessful, and exposure to excessive risk. If the technology were to be made safer and it became possible for modifications to be made on ova or sperm so that conception could proceed through normal marital intercourse, the bishops indicate that they would not consider germ-line intervention theologically problematic.[135] This is also the position in a pamphlet prepared for the Catholic Health Association of the United States.[136] And, the technology is moving in that direction.

Many of the documents advocate a temporary moratorium, rather than a permanent ban, so as to assure safety and provide time for ethical reflection to guide scientists and society. According to the formulation in a WCC report, "The World Council of Churches proposes a ban on experiments involving genetic engineering of the human germline at the present time, and encourages the ethical reflection necessary for developing future guidelines in this area."[137] Similarly, the Reformed Church in America concludes that "research and experimentation with genetic intervention with individuals for the relief of disease (somatic cell therapy) be affirmed; but the intervention into the human gene pool (germ cell therapy) be proscribed until such time as the questions raised in the study be resolved satisfactorily."[138]

In many of these documents, the distinction made between the acceptability of somatic cell therapy and the problematic nature of germ-line therapies appears to be primarily on the grounds of safety rather than a more explicit theological or ethical level. Other than acknowledging that such genetic therapy would have potential long-term effects on the human species, especially

---

134. *The Catechism of the Catholic Church* (Mahwah, N.J.: Paulist Press, 1994), par. 2377.
135. Catholic Bishops Joint Committee, *Genetic Intervention on Human Subjects,* 31.
136. *Human Genetics,* 20–22.
137. WCC, *Biotechnology,* 14.
138. "Genetic Engineering," 73.

loss of genetic diversity, none of the documents specifically address the theological issues involved in permanently altering the genetic makeup of human beings. In the case of the United Methodist statement, for instance, caution appears to be motivated by practical concerns related to assuring safety, demonstrating the certainty of its effects, and documenting that risks to human life will be minimal. Similarly, reservations of the UCC derive from concerns with unforeseen effects, and the pronouncement acknowledges that future developments may resolve these anxieties. Implicitly accepting that such germ-line therapy will become a reality, the UCC advocates extensive public discussion and, as appropriate, the development of federal guidelines.[139]

The writings of several religious thinkers go beyond the absence of strong theological prohibitions in the public theology to an even greater openness to germ-line interventions. In the case of Shinn, qualified acceptance seems to reflect his acknowledgment of the dynamic nature of genetic science. While Shinn is more interested in defining the issues than in delineating his own position, he discloses that he wants to "keep the window open a crack."[140] Other moral theologians are drawn toward germ-line intervention by virtue of their theological orientation. As Peters explains, his future-oriented theology of freedom offers a vision of human creativity, self-transcendence, and the possibility for something new as central to human nature.[141] Like the Roman Catholic theologian Karl Rahner, Peters believes that human existence is open to an infinite horizon and yet to be determined.[142] Rahner's formulation is that as subject we become our own object, becoming our own creator.[143] The conception of the human being as God's created co-creator, put forward by Philip Hefner[144] and adopted by Peters, understands the role of human beings as the "modifying and enabling of existing systems of nature so that they can participate in God's purposes in the mode of freedom."[145] Hefner does not draw its implications for intentional human genetic modification, but Peters does, advocating that we "play human" and emulate God's creativity through anticipating our own self-transcendence. He argues that our ethical vision cannot

139. UCC, "Pronouncement," 43.
140. Shinn, *New Genetics,* 144–45.
141. Peters, *Playing God?* 156.
142. Karl Rahner, "Christology within an Evolutionary View," *Theological Investigations* V 22 volumes (London: Darton, Longman and Todd, 1961–1988, and New York: Crossroad, 1961), 168, cited in Peters, *Playing God?* 143.
143. Karl Rahner, *Foundations of Christian Faith* (New York: Seabury, 1978), 35.
144. Philip Hefner, "The Evolution of the Created Co-Creator," in Ted Peters, ed., *Cosmos as Creation: Theology and Science in Consonance* (Nashville: Abingdon Press, 1989), 211–34.
145. Ibid., 212.

acquiesce to a reality filled with human misery, some of which is genetically caused. Thus he contemplates a better future in which genetic technologies, including human germ-line therapy, lead us toward the promise of the New Jerusalem.[146]

Given the strong concerns some secular ethicists have about germ-line intervention and its legal prohibition in several European countries, the relative openness of the American religious community is fairly remarkable. With the exception of Paul Ramsey's apocalyptic anticipation of the consequences of germ-line engineering in the early phase of the science, the religious community in this country has not reacted to the prospect of human self-engineering with great alarm or with fundamental theological reservations. A traditional stewardship model, such as many religious communities and thinkers espouse, could have been interpreted conservatively to preclude changes in the human genome. The positions of the Parliamentary Assembly of the Council of Europe and other critics that categorically oppose germ-line modification, however, have not struck a responsive chord in the religious community. Even the recognition that human germ-line manipulation could accelerate tendencies to commodify children and evaluate them according to standards of quality control does not necessarily trump a theological openness to human self-transcendence. Peters, for example, has it both ways. Despite his theological openness to germ-line intervention, he also cautions that this development will result in new possibilities for designer children that violate the obligation to love each child and to seek his or her fulfillment regardless of the child's genetic makeup.[147]

Although our obligation to future generations has been a major theme in religious ecological ethics, it has not been prominent in religious writings on genetics, and secular ethicists have given this topic greater attention in their discussions of the implications of germ-line interventions. It is a relevant consideration because germ-line modifications would shape not the patient being treated, but the progeny of the patient. As in the case of all experimental procedures, the subjects, in this case members of future generations, might be exposed to a substantial level of risk, with the possibility of damage. What is different in this case is that neither the subjects undergoing the therapy or enhancement nor the doctors and scientists conducting the intervention would have the means of obtaining the consent of those future persons who would be affected. This situation has been a prominent factor in some secular groups, for example, the Council for Responsible Genetics, opposing all forms of

---

146. Peters, *Playing God?* 148, 184.
147. Ted Peters, "In Search of the Perfect Child," *Christian Century* (30 October 1996): 1037.

germ-line modification.[148] It should be noted, however, that the topic of intergenerational ethics is itself controversial, with philosophers and ethicists disagreeing as to the nature and basis of determining obligations to future generations. Moreover, some proponents counter these reservations by arguing that it may be wrong for us not to tamper with our genetic structure and thereby forgo the opportunity to improve the health of future generations.[149]

Religious ethicists have entered into the fray not so much to take a specific position as to analyze and evaluate the debate and to determine which philosophic position on intergenerational ethics is most promising from a theological perspective. Peters's book *Playing God?* offers a careful and insightful review of the literature, almost entirely secular, opposing germ-line interventions. He generally does not find much credibility in these critiques, including the arguments of those who oppose germ-line modification because it infringes on our responsibilities to future generations. Without clearly explaining why, he also contends that those who focus on this criticism of germ-line intervention accord moral priority to those who have not yet been born over already existing persons.[150]

In *Human Genome Research,* which seeks primarily to explore the manner in which the HGP is likely to affect future generations, or "future contingent persons," Jan Christian Heller also explores the theological implications of future persons bearing an inordinate share of certain social costs stemming from genetic applications. He comes to the conclusion that traditional personal theocentric reasoning "fails to provide concrete guidance to individual agents for choices involving contingent future persons and that it provides only very limited guidance to collective agents."[151] The limitation of the personal theocentric approach, according to Heller, is that it gives agents no reason to believe that God favors one future person over another and therefore no basis for particular choices.[152] He advocates adopting an impersonal theocentric approach modeled on James Gustafson's work as better able to resolve issues of intergenerational equity. Like Gustafson, Heller's framework conceives of value in theocentric terms, meaning that the existence of value is dependent on the existence of God, and, like Gustafson, he views the Deity impersonally, with an agent-neutral perspective. Heller's proposal by its very nature does

---

148. Council for Responsible Genetics, Human Genetics Committee, "Position Paper on Human Germ Line Manipulation," 1992.

149. John Gillot, "Germ Line Gene Therapy—Why Not?" *GenEthics News* (November/December 1995): 6.

150. Peters, *Playing God?* 153–54.

151. Heller, *Human Genome Research,* 150–51.

152. Ibid., 151.

not provide a way to consider and weigh what would be good or bad for those specific people whom our acts are likely to affect. Instead it provides warrants for evaluating better or worse states of affairs.

The implications of germ-line interventions for eugenics constitute yet another issue. First used by Francis Galton, a cousin of Charles Darwin, in the late nineteenth century, eugenics, meaning "good birth," became a movement in the early part of the twentieth century with the goal of weeding out what proponents believed were the "bad" traits of society and promoting "good" ones. Tendencies within eugenics to regard some races and nationalities as superior and the atrocities committed by the Nazis, ostensibly on eugenic grounds, have given eugenics very negative connotations.[153] It is therefore understandable that ethicists would oppose germ-line intervention for eugenic purposes, and several of the statements of public theology do so. The Methodist document is an example.[154] While it is unlikely, at least in democratic countries, that genetic science will lead to "hard eugenics," that is, centralized and compulsory policies, it may lead to a creeping "soft eugenics." This term is used by Shinn to refer to a kinder, gentler program to perfect human individuals by correcting their genomes.[155] At least one ethicist already interprets genetic counseling as amounting to a form of eugenics. Arthur Dyck claims that genetic counselors, contrary to their official ethic to be nondirective, are not "value neutral" but "zealously seek converts to their own version of the genetic gospel realized through eugenic measures."[156] Others express similar concerns. Moreover, there are likely to be increasing economic and societal pressures on parents to correct genetic abnormalities, if not through abortion, then through genetic therapy. Thus, although there may not be any organized movement to improve the hereditary lines of the human community, germ-line interventions, in conjunction with the increased use of reproductive technologies, may still be a "back door" to eugenics.[157]

Many in the religious community distinguish between the acceptability of somatic cell therapy, and possibly germ-line interventions as well, for therapeutic purposes and their inappropriateness for enhancement purposes, but the line between therapy and enhancement may become increasingly difficult to draw. Some analysts argue that germ-line modification to eliminate abnormalities will inevitably lead to genetic enhancement.[158] In the absence of an

153. Arthur J. Dyck, "Eugenics in Historical and Ethical Perspective," in Kilner, Pentz, and Young, eds., *Genetic Ethics,* 25–26.
154. United Methodist Church, "New Developments in Genetic Science."
155. Shinn, *New Genetics,* 140.
156. Dyck, "Eugenics in Historical and Ethical Perspective," 32.
157. Troy Duster, *A Backdoor to Eugenics* (New York and London: Routledge, 1990).
158. LeRoy Walters and Nelson A. Wivel, "Germ-Line Gene Modification and Disease

objective definition of the "normal" state, the boundary between what is seen to be a correctable pathology and what is considered normal will likely shift, with the result that interventions now seemingly radical will become acceptable in the future.[159] This suggests that it will become increasingly difficult to differentiate between prevention and enhancement in genetic medicine interventions. Interventions that currently are classified as enhancements may become categorized as therapeutic. The fact that the technology for therapy and enhancement is the same is yet another factor likely to promote creeping enhancement. And, some theologies and ethics that understand humans as co-creators or created co-creators may encourage moving in this direction.

REFLECTIONS AND CONCLUSION

The 1980 letter from the three general secretaries to President Jimmy Carter quoted at the opening of this chapter pledged that the religious community would address fundamental questions related to the development of genetic engineering in a "more urgent and organized way."[160] As the literature surveyed in this chapter attests, the many efforts to grapple with the significance and implications of genetics from a faith perspective fall considerably short of being the systematic and serious treatment that would seem to be warranted. Since 1980, there have been periods of attention to genetic developments within the religious community, followed by years of seeming inattention. Involvement has rarely been sustained. After an initial burst of writing in the 1960s, there was a decade during which few theologians, ethicists, or religious communities focused on topics related to genetics. The 1980s and early 1990s were the era in which much of the currently available public theology was produced. Now, after another hiatus, there is again a wave of activity both in scholarly works and in a cluster of second-generation denominational literature.

That the community of religious thinkers working on genetic science is quite small is an ongoing problem. Only a handful of religious thinkers, mostly Protestants from mainline denominations, are dealing with the ethical implications of the genetic revolution. Many of these people play multiple roles serving on task forces, drafting denominational and ecumenical resources, and writing their own articles and books. As knowledgeable as this fraternity is—

Prevention: Some Medical and Ethical Perspectives," *Science* 262 (22 October 1993): 537.

159. Gregory Fowler, Eric T. Juengst, and Burke K. Zimmerman, "Germ-Line Gene Therapy and the Clinical Ethos of Medical Genetics," *Theoretical Medicine* 10 (1989): 151–65.

160. Letter from Three General Secretaries, in President's Commission, *Splicing Life*, 96.

and virtually all of them are Caucasian and male—they represent a relatively narrow range of religious and ethical perspectives. It is therefore difficult to overstate the importance of involving a greater diversity of religious thinkers in the considerations of these issues. There is an urgent need to engage thinkers from Jewish, Muslim, Buddhist, and Hindu backgrounds in the discussions of ethical issues related to the development of genetic science so that they can offer guidance within their own communities and develop a more authentic multireligious perspective.

It is also important to involve a greater diversity of voices within the Christian community. Few of the ethicists working on genetic science topics are feminist thinkers, process philosophers, or liberation theologians. The silence of the voices of ethicists from the global South is deafening. And, there is always a risk that a small circle of people with overlapping memberships, connections to scientists working in the field, and ongoing interaction through attendance at conferences and collaborative writing projects will develop a kind of insider perspective.

Frustration and critique in this chapter have related to the relative lack of solid work that deals with the normative dimension. Much of the effort of the religious community has been to provide background ethical analysis of the genetic revolution and to interpret its significance for people of faith. Early writings focused on the import of genetic science and the implications of the human community genetically altering nature. The next round of works explored the significance of human genetic therapy, but mostly from the perspective of assessing its meaning rather than offering specific guidelines. More recently, several resources address issues related to genetic testing and screening in order to place these choices within a faith perspective. Thus far, theology and religious ethics have rarely yielded precise and concrete directives for genetic science and the issues and choices it raises. Nevertheless, as virtually all of the work by religious thinkers notes, the genetic future is open and beckoning. Humanity will not long remain on a threshold awaiting guidelines from religious thinkers as to how to proceed.

Chapter Three

Religious Contributions to the Debate on Cloning

Like many other scientific breakthroughs, the February 1997 announcement that scientists had been able to clone a lamb from the somatic cell of a mature sheep was unexpected. Only a few religious, or for that matter secular, ethicists had considered the theological or ethical implications of either animal or human cloning. Nevertheless, the ensuing furor over the prospect of human cloning precipitated efforts to "theologize" at near breakneck speed. Media sources, both print and television, quickly acknowledged that the prospect of human cloning had significant religious implications and turned to religious thinkers for analysis and commentary. In early March, the president of the United States issued a statement describing cloning as a matter of morality and spirituality and requested that the newly formed National Bioethics Advisory Commission (NBAC), an eighteen-member, independent body of experts, study the issue and provide public policy recommendations within ninety days. Within four months of the initial cloning announcement, a wide range of theologians, religious thinkers, and secular ethicists had formulated at least preliminary thoughts about the ethical implications of human cloning; NBAC had drafted its report (one chapter of which considers religious perspectives); at least five denominations had developed statements or resolutions on cloning; and legislation based on NBAC's recommendations was forwarded to Congress. These events constitute the closest approximation of a public dialogue on the ethical and theological dimensions of a scientific or technological innovation and therefore offer an instructive case study. This chapter will review the terms of the debate on human cloning focusing on the initial reactions.

CROSSING A SCIENTIFIC FRONTIER

On 23 February 1997, the world discovered that science had crossed yet another frontier. Ian Wilmut, hitherto an unknown Scottish scientist from a small livestock research institute near Edinburgh, announced that his team of embryologists had successfully cloned a lamb from a mature sheep. To do so, they had taken cultured udder cells from a six-year-old sheep and starved them so that most of the genes would withdraw into an inactive phase. The DNA was then placed into the egg of another ewe, whose own DNA had been removed. Stimulated with an electrical charge, the cell fused. The cell's nucleus then took over coaxing the inactivated DNA to go back to an earlier stage of its development when it was totipotent or undifferentiated. Once this occurred, the egg divided and grew like a normally fertilized egg. After further development within a laboratory culture, the embryo was placed in the womb of a third sheep for gestation. Wilmut claimed that tests done after the birth of the lamb, which had occurred some seven months before the press conference, verified that it was a "delayed genetic twin," that is, a genetically identical copy of the animal that had provided the DNA.[1]

While science-fiction writers had long anticipated an era of cloning that would enable scientists to copy existing persons, the received scientific wisdom prior to Wilmut's announcement was that a mammal could not be reproduced asexually from an adult animal. Scientists had regularly engaged in cloning but of a very different type, making duplicates of isolated cells or genes for medical application such as insulin for diabetics. Beginning in 1986, researchers also began to produce genetically identical animals—sheep, cows, mice, and pigs— from embryos. This process of "artificial twinning," known as blastomere separation, splits two- to eight-celled embryos soon after they have been formed by the union of an egg and a sperm and before the cells have begun to differentiate.[2] Like virtually all reproductive technologies, blastomere separation raises ethical and theological issues, particularly if it were to be applied to humans. (The brief discussion that took place will be discussed later in the chapter.) Nevertheless, because the clones that result from this process are the products of a sexual union, they are more analogous to natural multiple births.

---

1. Michael Specter with Gina Kolata, "After Decades and Many Missteps, Cloning Success," *New York Times,* 3 March 1997, A1, 20–21; I. Wilmut et al., "Viable Offspring Derived from Fetal and Adult Mammalian Cells," *Nature* 385 (27 February 1997): 310–13.
2. Caird E. Rexroad, Jr., Research Leader, U.S. Department of Agriculture (statement before House of Representatives Committee on Science, Subcommittee on Technology, 5 March 1997).

Shortly after Wilmut's announcement, researchers at the Oregon Regional Primate Research Center disclosed that they had recently cloned two rhesus monkeys through splitting the cells of an early multicelled embryo,[3] underscoring the possibilities for human applications of this technique. However, with public attention already focused on Dolly, there was little public commentary about the implications of this development.

Dolly, the name Wilmut gave to the cloned lamb, was the first fully developed and apparently normal mammal to be born using genetic material taken from a mature animal through the technique of "somatic cell nuclear transfer." In contrast with clones produced through artificial twinning, Dolly contains the genetic material of only one parent. Her creation therefore marked the apparent ability, at least for some mammals under some circumstances, to replace sexual procreation with asexual replication. Somatic cell nuclear transfer also facilitates the insertion of new genes into the genome of an offspring. Indeed, Polly, the name assigned to Wilmut's second lamb clone, this time produced from fetal skin cells rather than the differentiated cells from a mature sheep, was genetically engineered to include a human gene.[4]

The significance of this event can be gauged from the fact that *Science* magazine recognized this achievement as science's most stunning breakthrough of 1997.[5] NBAC termed this accomplishment as marking "yet another milestone in our ability to control, refine, and amplify the forces of nature."[6] Beyond the cloning of a mammal, the feat of Wilmut's team had been to reprogram a mature cell to return to the nondifferentiated (totipotent) state of an early multicelled embryo. His team's ability to "reprogram" an adult cell provided evidence that cell differentiation and specialization into specific types of tissue (bone, muscle, organ) is reversible under some circumstances. This finding has significant potential for understanding cellular development. It also may provide new approaches to treating diseases like cancer that result from abnormal cell development patterns.

It took seventeen months to be able to prove to other scientists' full satisfaction that Dolly was indeed a clone produced from a mature cell and for scientists to be able to replicate the experiment. After some initial and then increasing doubts as to whether Dolly had been cloned from an adult cell,

---

3. M. Susan Smith, Director, Oregon Regional Primate Research Center, Oregon Health Sciences University (statement before House of Representatives Committee on Science, Subcommittee on Technology, 5 March 1997).

4. Gina Kolata, "Some Scientists Ask: How Do We Know Dolly Is a Clone?" *New York Times,* 29 July 1997, C3.

5. "Editorial," *Science* 278 (19 December 1997): 2029.

6. NBAC, *Cloning Human Beings: Report and Recommendations* (Rockville, Md.: NBAC, 1997), 1.

Wilmut's team and a second independent group conducted more rigorous forensic examinations to evaluate Dolly's origins. Reports showing that Dolly's DNA fingerprints matched the donor ewe but not those of other members of the herd, were published in July 1998. In the same issue of *Nature,* a Japanese team announced it had successfully cloned two calves. Repeating Wilmut's procedure, the team had fused oviduct cells from one cow with enucleated eggs from another. DNA testing confirmed that the calves are offspring of the oviduct cell donor. Yet another team of scientists at the University of Hawaii, Honolulu, described experiments that had yielded fifty cloned mice through a variation of the technique used by Wilmut. Like Wilmut, the University of Hawaii team took nuclei from adult cells and fused them into eggs whose own nuclei had been removed, but unlike Wilmut, they did not subject the eggs to an electrical pulse to fuse the cells and prompt the egg's activation. Instead they triggered the egg development by placing them in a culture medium containing strontium to stimulate the release of calcium from the eggs' internal stores, and thereby simulate the signal that tells fertilized eggs to start dividing.[7] A few months later in December 1998, scientists in Japan reported cloning eight copies of a single cow. Moreover, in contrast with the high wastage involved in Dolly's creation—one success out of 277 tries—the Japanese team had a far higher success rate, suggesting that cloning might be as efficacious for animal husbandry as *in vitro* fertilization.[8]

If it were to be scientifically feasible to apply this technology to humans, it would enable the progenitors, whoever they might be, to select the genetic makeup of a child by reproducing the genetic structure of another person. It would give new meaning to the desire to "have a child just like myself." For example, an adult, even a male adult, could decide to produce a child who would be a genetic copy of himself or herself. Presumably, since it requires only one cell to copy, it might even be possible to clone a particular person without receiving permission to do so, or in some circumstances to resurrect someone shortly after death. While the technology provides significant cause for concern, it could also have some beneficial applications in the repertoire of reproductive technologies. It could, for example, enable a couple in which one or both partners had genetic problems to produce a child with a healthy genome. It could as well potentially assist someone who was infertile to have a genetically related offspring. The cloning of three mammalian species suggests

---

7. Elizabeth Pennisi, "Cloned Mice Provide Company for Dolly," *Science* 281 (24 July 1998): 495–96; T. Wakayama et al., "Letter to Nature," *Nature* 394 (23 July 1998): 369, accessed from *Nature's* Web site.

8. Gina Kolata, "Japanese Scientists Clone a Cow, Making Eight Copies," *New York Times,* 9 December 1998, A1.

that human cloning may also be achievable. Indeed, several scientists heralded these developments with a prediction that the birth of a cloned person is inevitable, perhaps in the not-too-distant future.[9] Whether science proceeds with human cloning, and under what kinds of circumstances and constraints, now appears to be an ethical, religious, and legal decision.

INITIAL RESPONSE TO THE ANNOUNCEMENT

The announcement of the cloning of a lamb from a mature sheep generated a media frenzy. Dolly became an instant celebrity with her picture adorning the front pages of many newspapers. Commentators seized on the possibility of applying Wilmut's technique to humans and creating carbon copies of particular persons—and all of this, as one cell biologist quipped, without the need for men.[10] Some articles took on an apocalyptic tone evoking what one analyst described as "a major outbreak of the Frankenstein Syndrome."[11] With more imagination than fact, writers envisioned a nightmarish futuristic world in which science fiction comes to life: the dead are brought back to life; political leaders, including evil geniuses like Hitler, are duplicated from fragments of cells; and people fill the world with twins of themselves.

This sensationalized media coverage, when combined with the public's poor understanding of the science of cloning, provoked considerable apprehension. Like many other scientific breakthroughs, cloning engendered an emotional reaction as the public contemplated something startling and seemingly unnatural. Some of these fears were based on misunderstandings or speculative applications of cloning. One source of misgivings was the erroneous belief that cloning could result in the almost instantaneous production of a fully grown mature person. The "yuck factor" frequently reflected a simplistic notion of genetic determinism that ignored the complex interaction among genetic inheritance, the physical and cultural environment, and the process of learning. Some opponents apparently assumed that it was now possible to produce an exact copy, although younger, of a mature person. Others anticipated that nuclear transplantation cloning could re-create exemplary or evil people, either living or dead.[12]

9. David Soler, "News and Views," *Nature* 394 (23 July 1998): 315, accessed from *Nature's* Web site; Rick Weiss, "Scientists Clone Adult Lab Mice: Process May Hurry Human Application," *Washington Post,* 23 July 1998, A1, 27.

10. Gina Kolata, "With Cloning of a Sheep, the Ethical Ground Shifts," *New York Times,* 24 February 1997, A1.

11. Abigail Trafford, "Fear of Cloning and the Ewe To-Do," *Washington Post,* 11 March 1997, Z06 (http://newslibrary.krmediastream.com/cgi).

12. NBAC, *Cloning Human Beings,* 2.

Nevertheless, it would be wrong to attribute the public's opposition to cloning, measured at 94 percent of the population by one early survey,[13] as just an expression of ignorance or irrational unease with scientific progress. Clearly, as will be indicated later in this chapter, the negative reaction to the potential application of cloning to humans also derives from legitimate concerns raised by informed and reasoned ethical analysis. Human cloning does raise significant ethical and theological questions. And the fact that some people do not understand the mechanics of cloning or cannot adequately explain why they find cloning offensive does not necessarily mean that their moral intuitions are irrational or wrong.

Some commentators sought to dispel the panic and the queasiness, along with the simplistic notions of genetic determinism, evoked by the prospect of human cloning. Researchers and ethicists informed the public that human genetic inheritance should be conceptualized more as a set of changeable potentialities than as a precise and fixed blueprint. Others underscored that humans, more than any other species, are the product of a constant interplay between nature (genes) and nurture (environment).[14] Scientists emphasized that cloning a human being would be more like producing a delayed identical twin than creating a replica or carbon copy of a person, and, just like identical twins, a cloned person would still be unique.[15] In another opinion piece, a neurologist wrote that a brain cannot be cloned and that even genetically identical twins are born with different neural tangles and therefore divergent predilections.[16]

Within two weeks of Wilmut's announcement, President Bill Clinton issued an executive order banning the use of federal funds for human cloning and requested that non-federally funded researchers respect a voluntary moratorium. (Other countries, including Britain, Denmark, Germany, the Netherlands, and Spain, had previously banned human cloning.) The president also asked the recently established NBAC for an advisory opinion regarding the ethical and legal issues raised by the cloning discovery and recommendations on potential initiatives to prevent its abuse. In an accompanying statement, the president underscored, "any discovery that touches upon human creation is not simply

13. Wendy L. McGoodwin, Executive Director, Council for Responsible Genetics, and Philip L. Bereano, Professor, University of Washington, "Position Statement on Cloning," 10 March 1997, e-mail transmission.

14. Jessica Matthews, "Post-Clone Consciousness," *Washington Post,* 3 March 1997, A21.

15. Robert Wachbroit, "Should We Cut This Out?: Human Cloning Isn't as Scary as It Sounds," *Washington Post,* 2 March 1997, C1.

16. George Johnson, "Don't Worry. A Brain Still Can't Be Cloned," *New York Times,* 2 March 1997, A1.

a matter of scientific inquiry, it is a matter of morality and spirituality as well."[17] In his view, cloning raised deep concerns, affecting cherished concepts of faith and humanity. The president stated his belief thus: "Each human life is unique, born of a miracle that reaches beyond laboratory science" and therefore "we must respect this profound gift and resist the temptation to replicate ourselves."[18]

Along with the apocalyptic scenarios, much of the initial discussion and commentary revolved around whether cloning, particularly human cloning, should be regulated or outlawed and, if so, whether a ban would be feasible to enforce.[19] Seeking to preempt the issue, members of Congress introduced bills to outlaw human cloning. Several state legislators soon followed their example. By June, bills were pending in thirteen states that variously would ban the use of governmental funds for any research using cloned cells, or tissue for cloning an entire individual; prohibit cloning an entire individual, regardless of the funding source; or disallow any research using cloned cells or tissue.[20] The Subcommittee on Technology of the House of Representatives Committee on Science and the Senate Labor and Human Resources Committee rushed to organize hearings, as did the NBAC.

Scientists, when queried about the ethical and theological implications of the new technology, were generally reluctant to comment or minimize the problems. When pressed about human applications, Wilmut, who had been a member of the Church of Scotland committee on science and technology that had drafted a policy statement raising ethical and theological objections to human cloning,[21] responded, "There is no reason in principle why you couldn't do it . . . [but] all of us would find that offensive."[22] On the other side of the issue, one group of prominent scientists, scholars, and public personalities issued a statement in May 1997 disparaging arguments that cloning, like other novel technologies, raises significant ethical and theological concerns. Anticipating that NBAC might issue recommendations restricting cloning research and

17. "Remarks by the President on Cloning," White House Office of the Press Secretary, 4 March 1997.
18. Ibid.
19. "Human Cloning Requires a Moratorium, Not a Ban," *Nature* 386 (6 March 1997): 1; Kirkpatrick Sale, "Ban Cloning? Not a Chance," *New York Times,* 7 March 1997, A27.
20. NBAC, *Cloning Human Beings,* 104.
21. Society, Religion and Technology Project, Board of National Mission, Church of Scotland, "Cloning Animals and Humans: A Supplementary Report to the 1997 General Assembly," 30 May 1997, e-mail transmission.
22. Quoted in Daniel Callahan, "A Step Too Far," *New York Times,* 26 February 1997, A23.

applications, the statement argued that discoveries by the physical, biological, and behavioral scientists have contributed to enormous improvements in human welfare. It also dismissed "ancient theological scruples" as irrelevant, nothing more than a Luddite effort to turn back the clock.[23]

While few scientists adopted the statement's inflammatory rhetoric, many were outspoken advocates of protecting the right to continue research related to human cloning, and at least some scientists opposed legislation or regulations that would permanently foreclose human applications of cloning technologies. Responding to the unprecedented media coverage, *Nature* magazine printed an editorial stating that the arguments in favor of human cloning need to be heard and advocating that human cloning requires a moratorium, not a ban.[24] Most scientists who came forward urged legislators not to act hastily in curtailing or regulating research into cloning because it might prematurely cut off potentially valuable work.[25] Harold Varmus, director of the National Institutes of Health (NIH), spoke out against proposed legislation that would categorically prohibit human cloning on the grounds that, despite the initial flurry of negative reactions, society might decide that human cloning is acceptable in some situations.[26] A few scientists and journals even suggested that any hint of a limit on scientific inquiry would be equivalent to pandering to popular prejudice and irrational fear.[27] One ethicist may have spoken for many in the scientific community when she told NBAC that to ban an entire line of research because of possible unethical applications would be unwarranted and prejudicial.[28]

For the most part, though, scientists preferred to anticipate the beneficial commercial applications of cloning to agriculture, research on genetics, and medicine.[29] In its submission to the NBAC, the Biotechnology Industry Association (Bio) envisioned that nuclear transfer technology could enhance the development of transgenic animals for a variety of purposes, including

23. "Statement in Defense of Cloning and the Integrity of Scientific Research," Chronicle of Higher Education Web site (20 May 1997), http://chronicle. com/che-data/focus.dir/data,dir /0520.97/cloning.html
24. "Human Cloning Requires a Moratorium."
25. Frank Buni, "Experts Urge No Hasty Curbs on Science of Cloning," *New York Times,* 14 March 1997, B2.
26. Rick Weiss, "Human Clone Ban Opposed by NIH Chief," *Washington Post,* 6 March 1997, A1, 6.
27. "Hello, Dolly," *Economist,* 1 March 1997, 17–8; Peter Steinfels, "Beliefs," *New York Times,* 8 March 1997, A15.
28. Dr. Ruth Macklin, Testimony to the NBAC, 14 March 1997 (Washington, D.C.: Eberlin Reporting Service), 28.
29. "Mammalian Cloning Debate Heats Up," *Science* 275 (21 March 1997): 1733.

animal models for testing, organ transplantation, and production of medicine in animal milk. Bio also argued that scientific constraints meant that there was little immediate risk of the application of cloning techniques for developing an entire human being in the near future.[30] Others stressed the potential therapeutic applications, particularly in the area of assisted reproduction.[31]

A few scientific voices were raised on the other side of the issue. In 1994, the World Medical Association, alarmed about reports of artificial twinning experiments on human embryos, issued a statement that respect for the dignity of the human being and protection of his or her integrity as a unique and original being forbids the cloning of embryos.[32] In March 1997, the World Health Organization released a statement condemning human cloning as "ethically unacceptable" and contrary to some of the basic principles governing medically assisted procreation.[33] Jeremy Rifkin, president of the Foundation on Economic Trends and ever an opponent of biotechnology, weighed in with an admonition that "human cloning represents a turning point for civilization" and an impassioned appeal to "say no to playing God."[34] Another opinion piece, written by a professor of biochemistry of the University of Maryland School of Medicine, stressed the potential benefits but also acknowledged that cloning challenges the essence of Judeo-Christian theology upon which much of Western thought and tradition are based. He therefore urged that scientists accept indefinite research restrictions so as to enable society to have the time to digest the enormous ramifications of this technology.[35] The Council for Responsible Genetics, a group of scientists and ethicists, issued a position statement calling for a worldwide ban on human cloning and wider public debate about biotechnology. Their paper also advocated that Congress pass legislation to prohibit the cloning of humans through either embryo splitting or nuclear transfer. While the council acknowledged that DNA is not destiny and that to be human is not the simple summation of genetic, biochemical, or physiological processes, its opposition to cloning stemmed from concern that acceptance

30. Biotechnology Industry Organization, "Bio's Recommendations for the National Bioethics Advisory Commission Regarding the Implications of Cloning Technology"; the statement was forwarded to NBAC on 1 April 1 1997; a xeroxed copy was made available to this author on 24 April 1997.
31. NBAC, *Cloning Human Beings,* 29–32.
32. World Medical Association, "Statement on the Cloning of Human Embryos," 138th Council Session, Sydney, Australia, April 1994; xeroxed copy of the text was faxed to this author by staff of the World Medical Association.
33. "WHO Chief Defends Use of Animal Models," *Nature* 386 (20 March 1997): 204.
34. Jeremy Rifkin, "Say No to Playing God," *USA Today,* 25 February 1997, A14.
35. Adil Shamoo, "The Ethical Import of Creation," *The Sun,* 2 March 1997, F1, 7.

of human cloning would make possible a virtually unlimited set of eugenic "improvements" from a culturally defined and arbitrary starting point. Going beyond opposition to human cloning, the council also argued that the application of cloning to nonhuman animals would result in a dangerous loss of diversity and an erosion of the respect for life.[36]

Sensing that cloning had significant religious as well as ethical implications, the media quickly contacted a wide range of ethicists and theologians to interview them. After years of ignoring or trivializing religious views on a range of issues related to science and technology, the media cultivated religious thinkers, inviting them to submit opinion pieces and printing their perspectives on the front pages of national newspapers and journals. Theology by sound bite became a new form of commentary. Just as President Clinton had acknowledged that cloning raised moral and spiritual issues, the *Wall Street Journal,* not usually a source of theological concern or analysis, opined, "might there not be a reason, a good reason, why God made everyone since Eden look slightly different? Perhaps He was trying to tell us something, and perhaps, even though we are so smart that we now think we can make men or women in our image, perhaps for starters, we should listen."[37] When the House Science Subcommittee and NBAC held hearings on cloning, they invited ethicists and theologians reflecting a wide range of religious backgrounds to give testimony. NBAC heard from seven representatives of the religious community representing the Jewish, Protestant, Muslim, and Roman Catholic communities, and one of the six chapters in its report considers religious perspectives.[38]

Institutional church responses were not long in coming. Vatican officials quickly called for a worldwide ban on all human cloning, arguing that the creation of human life outside marriage goes against God's plan. A second statement by the director of the Institute of Bioethics at the Catholic University in Rome, released by the Vatican, indicated that animal cloning experiments were justified only when there are serious and important reasons for the benefit of humanity or for the benefit of the animals themselves.[39] Southern Baptist and United Methodist religious leaders in the United States soon followed suit opposing human cloning experiments and applications.[40] The Church of Scotland had a standing expert working group on the ethical issues of genet-

36. McGoodwin and Bereano, "Position Statement."

37. "Listening to the Lamb," *Wall Street Journal,* 25 February 1997, A22.

38. NBAC, *Cloning Human Beings,* chapter 3, 39–62.

39. "Vatican Calls for Ban on Human Cloning," *Washington Post,* 27 February 1997, A28.

40. "News: To Clone or Not to Clone?" *Christian Century* 114 (19 March 1997): 286; "Resolution on Genetic Technology and Cloning," *Southern Baptist Convention Annual 1997,* 95–96.

ic engineering, one of whose members was Ian Wilmut, as well as a Web site article on the ethics of cloning written by the director of the Church of Scotland's Society, Religion and Technology Project. On 22 May 1997, the Church of Scotland General Assembly passed a series of motions reaffirming "their belief in the basic dignity and uniqueness of each human being under God" and urging "Her Majesty's Government to press for a comprehensive international treaty to ban it [human cloning] worldwide."[41] The UCC issued a statement opposing human cloning but accepting continued research on human pre-embryos to coincide with the dissemination of NBAC recommendations and then adopted a resolution based on the statement at its July General Synod.[42]

Yet by December, some nine months after Wilmut's announcement, the uproar over cloning had subsided. As one science writer commented, the NBAC report, once eagerly anticipated, when issued was met by near silence. When President Clinton put forward legislation, much along the lines of NBAC recommendations, he couldn't find a legislator to sponsor it.[43] A front-page article in the *New York Times* reported that scientists had become sanguine about the notion of cloning a human being and that a handful of fertility centers were conducting experiments with human eggs to lay the groundwork for cloning. Only one state, California, had enacted a law making cloning illegal, and congressional interest, let alone momentum, for legislation appeared to be abating. As Lori Andrews, a law professor and expert on legal issues of reproduction, claimed, the passage from "horrified negation" to cloning to very slow but steady acceptance was taking place.[44]

Only one month later, a new outburst of anticloning indignation occurred when National Public Radio reported that Richard Seed, an obscure physicist, was trying to raise money to establish a facility to clone humans. Seed, who claimed he had the ability and the scientific team to undertake cloning, said that his reason for doing so was to fulfill God's intention for man. He also anticipated that "cloning and the reprogramming of DNA is the first serious step in coming to one with God."[45] In response, President Clinton again called for legislation to block human cloning both in his weekly radio speech and then

41. The General Assembly of the Church of Scotland, "Motions on Animal and Human Cloning," voted 22 May 1997, e-mail transmission on 30 May 1997.
42. I was a member of the task force that drafted the statement. It was initially released to the press on 9 June 1997.
43. Joanne Silberner, "Seeding the Cloning Debate," *The Hastings Center Report* 24 (March/April 1998): 5.
44. Gina Kolata, "On Cloning Humans, 'Never' Turns Swiftly into 'Why Not?'" *New York Times,* 2 December 1997, A1, 24.
45. Silberner, "Seeding the Cloning Debate," 5.

in his State of the Union address. The Food and Drug Administration announced that it had jurisdiction over cloning, implying it would not be willing to provide authorization to go ahead. Conservative members of Congress sought to seize the initiative and fast-track an anticloning bill. Because the proposed legislation was vaguely worded, it threatened, perhaps inadvertently, to prohibit many types of biomedical research as well as human cloning. Biomedical and scientific organizations quickly mobilized to counter such broad restrictions on cloning tissue and cells. As part of this campaign, the American Society of Cell Biology distributed a letter signed by twenty-seven Nobelists that declared there was "a broad consensus" in the scientific community to block human cloning through a voluntary moratorium rather than formal legislation. If anticloning legislation were to be passed, the letter recommended that it should apply only to the creation of human beings, and not to cells, tissue, or animals.

In July 1998, when scientists announced they had successfully cloned laboratory mice and calves, the United States had yet to hold a meaningful debate on the issue of human cloning. None of the various bills proposing to restrict or prohibit human cloning had been brought to the floor of Congress. Once issued, the NBAC report was largely ignored. After their initial outpouring of commentary and criticism, the religious community became almost silent. The first and only book-length treatment of religious perspectives, a collection of essays entitled *Human Cloning: Religious Responses,* was published in 1997[46] but there has been little published since. And, despite the significance of the new developments in cloning, other than a few newspaper articles, the mass media did not seem very interested.

SECULAR ETHICAL PERSPECTIVES ON CLONING

Just as somatic cell nuclear transfer technology builds scientifically on previous research and accomplishments in the field of genetic engineering, secular and religious ethicists had a body of ethical work upon which they could potentially draw. Some of the issues raised in reference to human cloning reprise earlier discussions of innovations in technologically assisted reproduction and genetic engineering. Moreover, ethicists briefly considered the ethics of cloning three times in the past. Nevertheless, ethical analysis of cloning is marked more by discontinuities than by an attempt to build upon previous discussions.

46. Ronald Cole-Turner, ed., *Human Cloning: Religious Responses* (Louisville: Westminster/John Knox Press, 1997).

The first consideration of cloning occurred more than thirty years ago. In 1966, the Nobel laureate Joshua Lederberg, then a professor of genetics and biology at Stanford University, published a series of articles and columns in which he proposed that clonal reproduction might be a good way to control the direction of human evolution and improve the species. Whether or not Lederberg was actually advocating this course of action, his "trial balloon" prompted several responses, including those by Leon Kass, then a young biochemist at NIH, and two theologians, Paul Ramsey and Joseph Fletcher. Fletcher, who was then a utilitarian, celebrated technology and potential human mastery over nature, arguing that the criterion for the acceptability of cloning, as well as for any reproductive technology, was whether it maximized happiness.[47] Kass and Ramsey both opposed cloning, particularly in the eugenic guise that Lederberg appeared to be advocating. In his book *Fabricated Man: The Ethics of Genetic Control,*[48] Ramsey considered cloning, like other assisted reproductive technologies, to be an assault on the nature of human parenthood by severing the link between sexuality, love, and procreation (87). If and when human cloning were to become technically feasible, he anticipated there would be mishaps, particularly since Lederberg was contemplating experiments of mixing human and animal genes, and Ramsey also worried about what to do with these monstrosities (78). Perhaps the most serious ethical question for Ramsey was whether we were, or would ever be, wise enough to embark on a successful self-modification program without such efforts leading instead to suicide of the species (123–30). Despite these salvos, the subject of cloning was soon dropped.

In the late 1970s, David Rorvik published a book entitled *In His Image: The Cloning of a Man* in which he claimed that a wealthy businessman had been successfully cloned through nuclear transplantation. The brief debate that the book engendered revolved around three sets of issues: First, why would anyone want to clone humans? Second, would cloning negatively affect individual identity and uniqueness, and our perception of human value? Third, would cloning have a detrimental effect on our ethical framework and social fabric? Before these questions could be thoroughly discussed, prominent biologists testifying at a 1978 congressional hearing on cloning dismissed the technical fea-

---

47. Allen D. Verhey, "Cloning: Revisiting an Old Debate," *Kennedy Institute of Ethics Journal* 4 (September 1994): 229–31.

48. Paul Ramsey, *Fabricated Man: The Ethics of Genetic Control* (New Haven and London: Yale University Press, 1970). Ramsey reviews Lederberg's initial article on 62–64 and Kass's letter to the editor of the *Washington Post,* in response to one of Lederberg's columns, is printed on 101–3.

sibility of cloning in the manner described by Rorvik.[49] Again the matter was dropped.

Despite the advances in animal cloning described above, ethicists did not again turn their attention to cloning until it became known in 1993 that researchers at George Washington University Hospital in Washington, D.C., had conducted cloning experiments on human pre-embryos. Working with seventeen pre-embryos or blastomeres of between two and eight cells, all of which were abnormal and therefore had no chance of developing into a fetus, they separated them into forty-eight embryos. The embryos began developing, but none passed thirty cells.[50] Again there was a brief flurry of activity, with debates about cloning on editorial pages, *Nightline,* and *Larry King Live* and articles in *Time* and *Newsweek.* The Roman Catholic Church expressed vigorous opposition to the procedure, terming it "a step into a tunnel of madness," and the United Methodist Church called for an executive order banning cloning in all federally financed institutions. However, the issue had soon faded from public consciousness.[51]

As with many biomedical developments, in-depth ethical analysis came later. A few Catholic moral theologians explored the implications of blastomere separation on human beings, and two thinkers, John Robertson and Richard McCormick, debated the ethical appropriateness of this technology in the pages of *The Hastings Center Report.*[52] The National Advisory Board on Ethics in Reproduction (NABER), a body of professionals from the disciplines of medicine, reproductive sciences, bioethics, theology, and law, sponsored a forum to generate further discussion of the issue, contributions from which were published in an issue of the *Kennedy Institute of Ethics Journal.*[53] Despite the diversity of perspectives among its membership, NABER was able to formulate a policy statement on the creation of multiple embryos through blastomere separation which posits that embryo splitting is ethically permissible if the resulting embryos are not damaged or destroyed in the process.[54] Most

49. National Advisory Board on Ethics in Reproduction, "Report on Human Cloning through Embryo Splitting: An Amber Light," *Kennedy Institute of Ethics Journal* 4, Cynthia B. Cohen, ed. (September 1994): 251–82.

50. "Clone Hype," *Newsweek,* 8 November 1993, 60.

51. Recounted in John A. Robertson, "The Question of Human Cloning," *The Hastings Center Report* 24 (March/April 1994): 6–7.

52. Robertson, "The Question of Human Cloning" and Richard A. McCormick, S.J., "Blastomere Separation: Some Concerns," *The Hastings Center Report* 24 (March/April 1994): 6–14, 14–16.

53. Cohen, ed., *Kennedy Institute of Ethics Journal* 4 (September 1994).

54. National Advisory Board on Ethics in Reproduction, "Embryo Splitting: An Amber Light," 266.

NABER members also supported the clinical applications of embryo splitting to improve the chances of initiating pregnancy in individuals undergoing *in vitro* fertilization by increasing the number of embryos for implantation.[55] But, most religious thinkers did not express much interest in the topic.

Secular ethicists presented a wide range of perspectives in written opinion pieces and testimonials at the hearings on cloning organized by Senate and House committees and the NBAC. As in earlier debates of cloning and other biomedical issues, Leon Kass took on his usual prophetic mantle while Ruth Macklin and John Robertson sought to uphold the freedom of scientific inquiry in the seeming face of an irrational public fear of the new. Yet it would be wrong to characterize any of the ethicists as simply resurrecting and rehashing old arguments. The prospect of human cloning through somatic cell nuclear transfer involves several novel developments, the most significant being the replacement of sexual procreation with asexual replication and the ability to produce a copy of an existing genome. Moreover, the significance and complexity of the issues related to the appropriate scope and limits of human intervention into our own future and its implications for human dignity and freedom suggest that the debate on cloning will be neither the first nor the last words ethicists will write on these topics.

Kass, currently a physician and ethicist teaching at the University of Chicago, urged NBAC to recommend a sweeping ban on human cloning warning that it "represents something radically new" that presents an unacceptable threat to human identity and individuality. According to Kass, cloning, would represent a major step into making human beings a man-made thing, a kind of technological product.[56] Like some of the religious critics of cloning, Kass was particularly concerned about the effect of "making" rather than "begetting" children from family relationships. In contrast with those who disparaged the public's opposition to human cloning, Kass defended "the wisdom of repugnance." He argued that this visceral reaction to the prospect of cloning human beings does not stem from the strangeness or novelty of the undertaking. Rather, "we intuit and feel, immediately and without argument, the violation of things that we rightfully hold dear. In this age in which everything is held to be permissible so long as it is freely done, repugnance may be the only voice left that speaks up to defend the central core of our humanity."[57] Kass, easily the most prophetic of ethical voices in the dialogue, attributed the

---

55. Ibid., 267.

56. Dr. Leon R. Kass, Testimony to the National Bioethics Advisory Committee, 14 March 1997 (Washington, D.C.: Eberlin Reporting Service), 108.

57. Dr. Leon R. Kass, "The Wisdom of Repugnance: Why We Should Ban the Cloning of Humans," *New Republic,* 2 June 1997, 20.

complacency of some of his professional colleagues when confronting the new biology to a kind of reductionism—the tendency to grind down large questions of morals into small questions of procedure. He diagnosed our society as enchanted and enslaved by the glamour of a technology that had stripped away our "awe and wonder before the deep mysteries of nature and life." He warned, however, that the stakes in the decision on cloning are very high: "We are faced with having to decide nothing less than whether human procreation is going to remain human, whether children are going to be made rather than begotten, whether it is a good thing, humanly speaking, to say yes in principle to the road which leads (at best) to the dehumanized rationality of a Brave New World."[58]

In sharp contrast with Kass's views, Ruth Macklin, a professor of bioethics at Albert Einstein College of Medicine, argued that there was no reason for society to panic at the prospect of cloning, or for that matter to ban it. Disparaging the concerns of those who opposed cloning, Macklin claimed that much of the ethical opposition seemed to grow out of "an unthinking disgust—a sort of 'yuk factor.'"[59] While Macklin acknowledged that many theologians contend that to clone a human would violate human dignity, she disagreed. According to Macklin, "It is not at all clear why the deliberate creation of an individual who is genetically identical to another living being but separated in time would violate anyone's rights."[60] If a cloned person shared the same rights as other persons, then she did not foresee that there would be problems. As for the fears that cloning engendered, she said that evidence, not mere surmise, should be required to conclude that the psychological burdens of knowing that one was cloned would outweigh the benefits of life itself. In her testimony before NBAC, Macklin underscored that the ethics of cloning must be judged not by the way in which parents bring a child into existence but by the manner in which they treat and nurture the resulting child. As a strong advocate of the freedom of scientific inquiry, Macklin's view was that it would be prejudicial to ban an entire line of research because of possible unethical applications.[61]

Like Macklin, John Robertson, a professor at the University of Texas Law School, opposed instituting a ban on human cloning. According to Robertson such a ban would be both imprudent and unjustified—imprudent because it would preclude good uses and unjustified because he did not find arguments

58. Ibid., 18.

59. Ruth Macklin, "Human Cloning? Don't Just Say No," *U.S. News and World Report,* 10 March 1997, 64.

60. Dr. Ruth Macklin, Testimony to the NBAC, 14 March 1997 (Washington, D.C.: Eberlin Reporting Service), 98.

61. Ibid., 100–101.

about potential harms compelling. Robertson argued that far from anything new, human cloning was little different from existing assisted reproductive technologies being widely used. He identified several potential beneficial uses for couples undergoing *in vitro* fertilization and for genetic selection or eugenic purposes to assure production of a child with a healthy genome. Partly because Robertson was comfortable with the prospect of parents having designer children whose genome they chose, he argued that it is very difficult to show actual harm to offspring, families, or society from human cloning. He acknowledged that the concerns raised might be a reason not to federally fund human cloning research. Nevertheless, he contended that particular moral or religious notions of how conception should occur and how children should be chosen and born should not override freedom of procreative choice or serve as a basis for banning beneficial applications.[62]

PERSPECTIVES OF MORAL THEOLOGIANS AND OFFICIAL RELIGIOUS BODIES

Like secular ethicists, religious communities and moral theologians offered a wide range of perspectives on the implications of human cloning. None were framed in the prophetic opposition of Leon Kass's rhetoric or articulated the basically unqualified support of John Robertson and Ruth Macklin, however. Although virtually all religious ethicists and theologians considered some aspect of cloning or its applications problematic, their comments generally lacked an apocalyptic tone and the phrase "playing God" was notably absent. Ironically, theologians involved in the debate seemed less inclined to refer to the potential of cloning impinging on divine prerogatives and exceeding appropriate limitations of human activity than some secular commentators. Their general hesitation to employ "God language" attested to the view of many theologians and religious ethicists that human cloning raised ethical rather than theological issues. It may also have reflected a conscious effort to use nonreligious terminology and terms of reference to address a secular audience. It is important to underscore that, regardless of their analyses of the theological and ethical implications of human cloning or their policy recommendations, religious thinkers, virtually without exception, asserted that if humans were ever cloned, the resulting person would have the inherent value, dignity, and moral status common to all of humanity and should be vested with the same civil rights and protections. The statement of the United Methodist Church typifies these affirmations: "As Christians, we affirm that all human

62. Dr. John Robertson, Testimony to the NBAC, 14 March 1997 (Washington, D.C.: Eberlin Reporting Service), 81–97.

beings, regardless of the method of reproduction, are children of God and bear the Image of God."[63]

With some simplification, the religious positions on cloning may be divided into three categories. The first encompasses the churches, official bodies, and individual theologians who oppose cloning, particularly human cloning, on fundamental theological grounds. The Roman Catholic Church's claims that human cloning is unnatural, contrary to the divine plan, and fundamentally unethical represent a strong example. The Rev. Dr. Albert Moraczewski, testifying to NBAC on behalf of the National Conference of Catholic Bishops, emphasized that the cloning of human beings would violate the inherent dignity of human beings conferred by the resurrection of Jesus Christ and its promise of union with the divine life for a joy-filled eternity. According to Moraczewski, cloning would violate human dignity by exceeding the delegated dominion given to the human race, by jeopardizing the personal and unique identity of each individual, and by providing an opportunity for genetic manipulation of the nuclear genome, perhaps with eugenic intent. He also rejected this technology because cloning implicitly involves the assertion of a right over another person.[64]

Another group of positions anticipates NBAC's recommendations in grounding opposition at least partially in the lack of safety of the technology and the unpredictability of the consequences of cloning—psychological, social, and technical. Many of these also have ethical concerns. A statement drafted by the Genetics Working Group of the UCC, subsequently adopted by its July 1997 General Synod, constitutes one such example.[65] The text of the resolution emphasizes that the current state of the technique of nuclear transfer cloning is far too imprecise to meet the minimal expectations of safety that are required for human applications. It also expresses the concern that in a society inclined toward a simplistic notion of "genetic determinism," a child produced by cloning may have an overwhelming burden of expectations that would be incompatible with the freedom necessary for each person to develop an individual identity. The UCC text concludes that it is beneficial for children to have two adults' genetic resources recombined to form a unique

63. General Board of Church and Society of the United Methodist Church, "Statement from the United Methodist Genetic Science Task Force," 9 May 1997, faxed copy made available on 20 May 1997.

64. Rev. Dr. Albert Moraczewski, Testimony to the NBAC, 13 March 1997 (Washington, D.C.: Eberlin Reporting Service), 185–92.

65. UCC, "Resolution on the Cloning of Mammalian Species to the 21st General Synod of the UCC," Columbus, Ohio, 3–8 July 1997." The text approved by the General Synod was faxed to this author, who served on the committee that drafted the statement from which the resolution was derived.

genotype that is tied to both parents. The United Methodist Genetic Science Task Force statement, issued in early May, offers another variant on this position. Like the UCC, the United Methodists argue for a ban on the intentional production of genetically identical humans and human embryos. Unlike the UCC, the United Methodists also support a ban on therapeutic, medical, and research procedures that generate waste embryos.[66] In contrast with the Catholic and Methodist statements, the UCC resolution does not object categorically to human pre-embryo research that produces and studies cloned human pre-embryos through the fourteenth day of fetal development, provided the research is well justified in terms of its objectives, shows proper respect for the pre-embryos, and does not implant them.[67]

The third category of religious positions consists of the ethicists who, despite their ethical concerns, have a qualified acceptance of cloning. Generally, thinkers in this group do not consider the act of human cloning to violate theological affirmations or to be intrinsically unethical but instead are inclined to evaluate the consequences. Lutheran theologian Ted Peters, for example, claims that no sound theological arguments have been offered that cloning violates an alleged God-given identity. Nevertheless, he is concerned that cloning may pose a risk to the dignity of children by accelerating the tendency to commodify newborn children. He therefore concludes that cloning, while not intrinsically unethical, might be unwise. While he does not believe that the risks warrant a total ban on human cloning, he does support a temporary ban so as to be able to sort out the safety and ethical issues.[68]

Interestingly, several of the religious thinkers with a qualified acceptance of human cloning were Jewish and Muslim. Because many of those in this group assumed that some form of human cloning is inevitable, they believe that it is better to attempt careful regulation than a total ban. For example, Rabbi Elliot Dorff, from the University of Judaism in Los Angeles, explained that technology in the Jewish tradition is morally neutral and gains moral valence depending upon the uses to which it is put. His testimony outlined a series of ethical issues related to human cloning: cloning could exacerbate some of the socioeconomic divisions within our society, diminish the sense of sacredness in human beings, and/or lead to eugenic applications. He also enumerated a number of theological issues that cloning raises, among them whether cloning technology goes beyond the human mandate to improve the world to usurp

---

66. General Board of Church and Society, "Statement from United Methodist Task Force."

67. UCC, "Cloning Mammalian Species."

68. Ted Peters, "Cloning Shock: A Theological Reaction," *CTNS Bulletin* 17 (Spring 1997): 1–9.

God's role, whether it transgresses the sacred nature of being created in the image of God, and whether cloning would promote self-idolization. Nevertheless, he concluded that human cloning should be allowed, explaining, "It seems to me that once the genie is out of the bottle you cannot really put it back in again and that if you do not—if we do not—allow human cloning under some restrictions . . . it will happen anyway without those restrictions."[69] When he was questioned as to what types of limitations would be appropriate, he responded that only the most egregious uses ought to be banned, such as using clones for purposes of artificial organ transplants and then destroying the clone.[70]

The testimony of Rabbi Moshe Tendler to NBAC offers another variant on this conditional acceptance. Dr. Tendler, who is both a biologist and a Talmudic scholar and holds a chair in Jewish Medical Ethics at Yeshiva University in New York, identified two problems with cloning. First, in Jewish law generational distinctiveness is quite critical, and a clone, who is not clearly either a sibling or child, would create an inversion of generations and wreak havoc on inheritance laws. Second, the sanctity of life places great emphasis on nonmaleficence, and human cloning poses great risks of abnormality. Despite these reservations, Tendler, like Dr. Dorff, recommends that cloning be regulated rather than prohibited under rules so specific that the restrictions do not interfere with embryo research that may contribute to the mastery of genetic disease and valuable cancer research. In contrast with Dorff, Tendler's position is that cloning for implantation purposes should be prohibited except in the most restrictive and exceptional circumstances.[71] Tendler cited two such situations in which cloning would be morally acceptable: the cloning of an individual such as a survivor of the Holocaust, who was sterile and the last of a genetic line, and the cloning of a child to supply a replacement organ for transplantation to save the first child's life, provided that the cloned child would be wanted and loved.[72]

As yet another variant on this third group of positions, several theologians suggest it would be better to concentrate efforts on determining what should

69. Dr. Elliot Dorff, Testimony to the NBAC, 14 March 1997 (Washington, D.C.: Eberlin Reporting Service), 5–16.

70. Ibid., 9.

71. Dr. Moshe Tendler, Testimony to the NBAC, 14 March 1997 (Washington, D.C.: Eberlin Reporting Service), 17–28.

72. Rabbi Tendler put forward these examples when he participated on a panel discussion at the AAAS Forum on Cloning, 25 June 1997, in Washington, D.C., reported in Vincent Kiernan, "The Morality of Cloning Humans: Theologians and Philosophers Offer Provocative Arguments," *Chronicle of Higher Education* (18 July 1997): A13–14.

be done with cloning rather than opposing its application. This recommendation reflects both pragmatic considerations and a sense that the application of cloning, not the technology, is the most significant moral issue. Like many other commentators, Nancey Murphy, a Protestant philosopher of religion, assumes it will be very difficult to prevent cloning from being carried out in private research facilities. Therefore, for her the "main thing to worry about is whether our culture has its priorities well enough thought out" to make appropriate choices.[73] The central moral and spiritual issues for Lutheran theologian Philip Hefner are not whether we clone, but why we clone, what interests cloning serves, and the moral status of those interests. As an example of the need to consider the consequences of individual cases, Hefner contrasts the moral implications of a wealthy person cloning an offspring as a potential source of transplantable body parts with a childless couple who resort to cloning as an alternative to *in vitro* fertilization or adoption.[74]

Several articles in a newsletter published by the Program for Ethics, Science, and the Environment at Oregon State University indicate that some Buddhist, Hindu, and Native American thinkers would tend to be in this third category as well. Ronald Nakasone, a Buddhist priest who teaches at the Pacific School of Religion, begins with the assumption that cloning is in the human future and that the critical issue is how it will expand our notion of humanity and our moral parameters. Given the Buddhist conception of interdependence, that we rise and fall together as one living body, his concern is that cloned persons be treated with the dignity, respect, and gratitude accorded to those who are born naturally.[75] Another Buddhist thinker, Damien Keown, believes there is nothing immoral in principle in the technique for cloning, but concludes that "there is no clear reason for doing it unless you want to use the clone for the kind of things you would not normally do to a human subject."[76] He cautions that regulation would be unlikely to work once the genie was out of the bottle. Three articles representing a Hindu perspective respond to the prospect of cloning in terms of its likely impact on spiritual progress, particularly whether cloning will affect the well-being of the soul in its journey from life to life.[77]

73. Gustav Niebuhr, "Suddenly, Religious Ethicists Face a Quandary on Cloning," *New York Times,* 1 March 1997, A10.

74. Philip Hefner, "Cloning as Quintessential Human Act," e-mail transmission, 13 March 1997.

75. Ronald Y. Nakasone, "The Opportunity of Cloning," *Reflections* (May 1997): 6–7.

76. Damien Keown, "Is the Genie Out of the Bottle?" *Reflections* (May 1997): 8.

77. Sri Eknath Easwaran, "Brave New World," Acharya Palaniswami, "For the President, Mr. Bill Clinton," and Arvind Sharma, "When It Comes to Karma," *Reflections* (May 1997): 8–11.

ETHICAL AND THEOLOGICAL BUILDING BLOCKS

The manner in which thinkers select, weigh, develop, and apply fundamental conceptual building blocks plays an important role in structuring their evaluation of the ethical implications of particular scientific and technological innovations. To do justice to the complexity of the task, this process of operationalizing abstract theological concepts requires a multifaceted and multidisciplinary dialogue between the science and the theology. However, the pace of the debate and pressures for something akin to sound-bite theology often precluded that kind of careful, in-depth work, especially during the first few months of discussion about human cloning. Most of the religious participants put forward their views at short notice and in public settings rather than academic journals, with the result that their presentations were more truncated and less theologically developed than writings for a professional audience. A few theologians attempted to raise fundamental theological issues—for example, linking responses to cloning to the meaning of human existence[78]—but this was very much the exception.

Religious thinkers put forward a series of concerns about the ethical implications of cloning: the risks to human dignity for both the cloned person and the rest of society, the potential effects of cloning on identity and individuality, the disruptive impact of cloning on procreation and the family, and questions about whether cloning exceeded the limits of appropriate human intervention. The manner in which moral theologians dealt with these topics and the relative weight assigned to them played an important role in shaping their perspectives on cloning. Many of these issues had been raised with reference to other scientific and technological developments and will therefore be discussed in other chapters. The remainder of this section will provide a brief overview of these areas of concern as expressed in the cloning debate.

The Effects of Cloning on Human Dignity
One of the most central theological affirmations across religious traditions is that all persons as children of God have intrinsic dignity and value. Many religious thinkers, even those who were more receptive to the possibility of human cloning, expressed views that human cloning would violate this dignity. Despite these concerns, there was complete consensus that any child produced through cloning would be a full human being, created in the image of God, with a unique spirit or soul.[79] No theologians suggested that cloning would deprive

78. Hefner, "Cloning as Quintessential Human Act."
79. See, for example, "Souls Can't Be Cloned, Pope's Panel Says," *USA Today*, 25 June 1997.

a child of a full relationship with God. In a secular society, the intrinsic dignity and worth of all persons is expressed through and protected by universal human rights. Several of the statements by official religious bodies insisted that a cloned child as a full human being would be entitled to all human and civil rights,[80] but these appear to be more of an affirmation of the moral status of a cloned human being than a serious fear that cloned persons will not be accorded full legal status and protections.

Concerns about the implications of cloning for human dignity appear to have two primary bases: the manner in which cloned persons are likely to be treated by other members of society and the possibilities that cloning will contribute to a general devaluing and commodification of human life. Whatever the motivations of the progenitor, there was apprehension that treating human life as a product to be manipulated and manufactured would diminish a sense of the sacredness of life. Members of the religious community also shared NBAC's caution that efforts to produce a child through somatic cell nuclear transfer would amount to experimenting on human beings to perfect a new technology. The question was asked more than once, what will happen to the failures, to the bad results? Even religious communities that accept abortion are disturbed by the prospect of creating waste embryos for experimental purposes and then discarding them.[81] Several of those who testified before NBAC seem to be haunted by the specter of persons cloning themselves or relatives to have a ready source of "spare parts," that is, organs available for transplant, and then destroying the clone.[82]

There was considerable apprehension that a cloned child would be treated as less than a fully equal and unique person. Even if a cloned human being were to be accorded all the legal rights and protections afforded to others, it might be difficult for its creators or a society to accept its humanity and dignity.[83] These fears were deepened by the sense that modern society is increasingly subscribing to the myth of genetic determinism. An essay by David Byers speculates that knowing someone is a clone rather than natural born would create a new class distinction and form of discrimination. He muses that since people in our society tend to view twins and triplets as interesting anomalies,

---

80. See, for example, UCC, "Cloning Mammalian Species," and Dorff, Testimony, 5.
81. General Board of Church and Society, "Statement from United Methodist Task Force."
82. Dorff, Discussion after Testimony, 29–30.
83. Sondra Ely Wheeler, "Moral and Theological Issues in Human Cloning," statement delivered at the AAAS Forum on Cloning, typescript of text made available to this author, who was a coorganizer of the event.

they would likely consider clones as freaks.[84] And, given the overwhelming publicity other early examples of technological innovation have attracted (such as Louise Brown, the first child resulting from in vitro fertilization), it is unlikely that clones would escape attention and notoriety.

Religious opponents also anticipated that objectification and commodification, both of which represent a serious violation of human dignity, would be a likely outcome of cloning. The concept of human dignity requires that a person always be treated as an end and never as a means. In religious language, "We are, as far as we know, the only creature God created for its own sake, not to satisfy some other creature's wants and needs. Each human being has inherent dignity as a child of God, free to pursue his or her eternal destiny in relationship to the divine. At this most fundamental level, cloning is unacceptable because clones would be human beings created, at least in part, to fulfill the will of another human being."[85] The likely motivations of someone who would resort to cloning, whether the cloning is an expression of vanity, an effort to replace another person, or a need for a compatible donor for a transplant, suggest that the cloned child is likely to be treated as an object or a means to achieve a particular end. As several religious thinkers noted, when a man and a woman decide to have a child, they may hope for the perfect child, but to attempt to produce a designer child with a particular genome for certain ends is to go far beyond these aspirations.[86]

Commodification by definition implies treating persons as commodities, as things that can be exchanged, bought, or sold in the marketplace. Reflecting on this issue, Dorff cautions that commodification will deny "the sacred character of human life depicted in the Jewish tradition, transforming it instead to fungible commodities on the human marketplace to be judged by a given person's worth to others."[87] As Lisa Sowle Cahill, a Catholic moral theologian, noted in her testimony to NBAC, there are particular risks in a society infused by the profit motive that economic incentives will control decisions about cloning human beings. She expressed concern that the dominance of the market makes it more likely that persons will be used as a means to the ends of those with more status, more privilege, and more power. Therefore, she appealed to NBAC to make decisions on a broader basis than self-interest and

---

84. David M. Byers, "An Absence of Love," in Ronald Cole-Turner, ed., *Human Cloning: Religious Responses* (Louisville: Westminster/John Knox Press, 1997), 73–75.
85. Ibid., 70.
86. Ted Peters, "Cloning Shock: A Theological Response," in Cole-Turner, ed., *Human Cloning,* 21.
87. Dorff, Testimony, 5.

self-determination in order to prevent economic incentives from determining when human individuals will be cloned.[88]

Risks to Human Identity and Individuality

Religious concerns about the risks of cloning to human identity and individuality focus primarily on the psychological burden on persons created through cloning rather than on whether a cloned person would be a unique individual. Although cloning by definition involves the deliberate duplication of the genome of an existing person, religious thinkers participating in the cloning debate rejected a simple genetic determinism. Most of the religious participants recognized that each person is a unique expression of the interplay between genes and environment and therefore a clone would not simply be a carbon copy of the person from which his or her genetic structure was obtained. That a person created through cloning will be unique in many ways, however, does not preclude the fact that it will doubtless be harder for a clone to establish his or her own identity and for the clone's creator to respect his or her individuality.[89]

Does a shared genetic heritage necessarily bequeath identity problems? In the discussion about cloning, several analysts compared a clone with a homozygous or identical twin to make the point that a shared genome does not automatically create identity problems. But, as several religious thinkers noted, a genetic clone would face a quite different set of conditions than those that natural identical twins confront. In the case of homozygous twins, "neither one is the source or maker of the other."[90] Nor does one twin represent a blueprint or set of expectations for the other. The genetic twins created through somatic cell nuclear transfer technology would likely be years apart in age, perhaps a full generation or more. Thus the cloned child would live under a horizon already mapped out by its twin.

Given this situation, several religious thinkers argued that children who are produced through cloning are likely to suffer from an overwhelming burden of expectation that would interfere with the freedom necessary to develop a full sense of individuality and personhood. In other words, a cloned child would be deprived of a right to an open future.[91] The UCC's resolution

---

88. Lisa Sowle Cahill, Testimony to the NBAC, 13 March 1997 (Washington, D.C.: Eberlin Reporting Service), 178.

89. Dorff, Testimony, 7.

90. Dr. Albert Moraczewski, Testimony to the NBAC, 13 March 1997 (Washington, D.C.: Eberlin Reporting Service), 185.

91. Joel Feinberg, "The Child's Right to an Open Future," in W. Aiken and H. LaFollette, eds., *Whose Child? Children's Rights, Parental Authority, and State Power* (Totowa, N.J.: Rowman and Littlefield, 1980), cited in NBAC, *Cloning Human Beings,* 67.

explains: "Prior knowledge [of what a cloned child's genes could become] would create a weight of expectation against which such a child would have to define his or her own identity. Precisely because 'genetic determinism' is so widespread in contemporary culture, this weight of expectation would likely be inconsistent with the freedom necessary for each person to develop an individual identity."[92]

There was also some concern that cloning could jeopardize the sense of unique identity of the person whose genome was cloned. Catholic social teaching describes the biological nature of every person, as well as the spirit, as constituent of the personal identity and absolute unique singularity of that individual throughout the course of his or her life. In his testimony on behalf of the U.S. Catholic Conference, Albert Moraczewski asked whether an adult who was cloned would tend to see his or her own biological, psychological, and social development in the developing clone.[93] Would the life of a cloned child be comparable in some ways to watching a rerun of one's own life with a few of the details changed? And, given the temptations of all parents to shape their child in their own image, would cloning, by enabling a person to reproduce without having to go outside of himself or herself, pose special risks of trying to create another person in one's own image, a form of self-idolization?[94]

The Implications of Cloning for Procreation and Family Relationships
In the early days of biotechnology, Paul Ramsey argued against human cloning, as well as the use of other reproductive technologies (artificial donor insemination) because such technologies separate the unitive and procreative ends of human sexuality and transform "procreation" into "reproduction." The Vatican's 1987 *Instruction on Respect for Human Life*[95] rejected human cloning (specifically artificial twinning or blastomere separation) on much the same grounds. It states that human cloning is contrary to the moral law because it contravenes the dignity of human procreation and the conjugal union.[96] Commentaries of several of the Catholic theologians on cloning reflect this concern.

Many of the most ardent and articulate voices in the cloning debate, putting forward what might be termed an ontology of human sexuality and sexual

92. UCC, "Cloning Mammalian Species."
93. Moraczewski, Testimony, 186.
94. Dorff, Testimony, 9.
95. Congregation for the Doctrine of the Faith, "Instruction on Respect for Human Life in Its Origin and on the Dignity of Life (Donum Vitae)," 1987, reproduced in Kevin D. O'Rourke, O.P., J.C.D., S.T.M., and Philip Boyle, *Medical Ethics: Sources of Catholic Teaching*, 2d ed. (Washington, D.C.: Georgetown University Press, 1993).
96. Ramsey, *Fabricated Man*, 32–59.

reproduction, were liberals and feminists, and not conservatives. Leon Kass argued that cloning was a major violation of deep biological truths about our identity and human condition and that it contravened "our given nature as embodied, gendered, and engendering beings—and of the social relations built on this natural ground."[97] Believing that procreation is a more complete activity because it engages us bodily, erotically, and spiritually, as well as rationally, Kass anticipated that the severing of procreation from sex, love, and intimacy would be inherently dehumanizing.[98] Sondra Wheeler, a Methodist ethicist, raised concerns about the genuinely revolutionary character of a technology that proposes to replace procreation with asexual replication and thereby impoverish a fundamental human relation. She characterized cloning as "the most decisive, deliberate and complete severance of the traditional unitive and procreative goods of sex imaginable, for they are not accidentally separated from one another for the sake of bypassing a faulty natural mechanism. Instead in cloning the sexual character of the transmission of human life is abrogated altogether, and with it the heretofore given fact that every person is the embodiment of a connection between persons, however fleeting or flawed or mediated that connection may have been."[99]

Given the central role of the family in some religious traditions as a divinely ordained institution for the bearing and nurturing of children, it is not surprising that there was considerable concern that cloning could undermine the integrity of the family. Both the Jewish and the Islamic experts who testified before NBAC mentioned the risks of cloning for lineage and intergenerational relationships. Changed roles (father, mother, and child) and relationships (spousal, parental, filial) could create confusion about who has what responsibilities to whom between and among the generations.[100] Lisa Sowle Cahill testified before NBAC that "the child who is truly the child of a single parent is a genuine revolution in human history, and his or her advent should be viewed with immense caution." She went on to note that the "biological relation between parents and children is a symbol of reproductive, social, and domestic partnership with great personal and social significance." For that reason she concluded, "Cloning is a violation of the essential reality of human family and of the nature of the social related individual within it."[101]

Not all religious thinkers agreed, however, that cloning represents a fundamental challenge to family relationships. Nancy Duff, ostensibly representing

97 Kass, "Wisdom of Repugnance," 20.
98. Ibid., 22.
99. Wheeler, "Moral and Theological Issues in Human Cloning."
100. NBAC, *Cloning Human Beings*, 54.
101. Cahill, Testimony, 158.

a generic Protestant perspective (if such a position exists) before NBAC, concurred with giving top priority to children's interests in an assessment of
human cloning. She argued, however, that "the idea that it would undermine
the relationships between men and women or the basic family unit is not . . .
morally or theologically convincing."[102]

Appropriate Limits to Human Intervention into the Creation
When the possibility of cloning human beings was first posed, Paul Ramsey
responded with the maxim, "Men ought not to play God before they learn to
be men, and after they have learned to be men they will not play God."[103] To
avoid abdication before the relentless advancement of biological and medical
technology, Ramsey proffered the view in his book *Fabricated Man* that "the
sine qua non of any morality at all, of any future for humanism, must be the
premise that there may be a number of things that we can do that ought not
be done" (151). Nevertheless, he did not offer a clear boundary to determine
what ought and ought not be done or what amounts to playing human and
playing God. Although he himself raised the question as to whether any articulate meaning can be given to the term "playing God" as a negative, critical
norm, he did not specify ethical principles or moral rules to give shape to
responsible action in the medical-technological context (142–43). Instead, he
reviewed critically the perspective of various theological and scientific advocates of genetic engineering and expressed concern that the genetic manipulation and alteration of human parenthood would result in the functional
equivalent of species suicide, that is, the death of the human species as we know
it and its replacement by a species of life deemed to be more desirable
(151–52). For Ramsey, the refabrication of the individual through biology also
added up to "man's limitless dominion over man," or, to put it another way,
"Who will be the Creator and who the creatures?" (152).

     Thirty years later, some of Ramsey's concerns echoed through the com-
ments of other religious commentators on cloning. Stanley Hauerwas, a
Methodist theologian, questioned whether cloning represents a drive to be our
own creators.[104] Sondra Wheeler was troubled that the project of cloning a
child demonstrates lack of respect for the otherness of the child: "It removes a
physical substratum and sign of what Jews and Christians and many other theists believe: that our children are not us, are not even ours, but ultimately

102. Nancy Duff was so quoted in NBAC, *Cloning Human Beings,* 54.
103. Ramsey, *Fabricated Man,* 138.
104. Gina Kolata, "With Cloning of a Sheep, the Ethical Ground Shifts," *New York Times,*
24 February 1997, A1, 15.

belong to God."[105] Several theologians were not so much concerned that cloning was playing God in a conventional sense but that it implied a type of control that no person should have over another human being. Nancy Duff cautioned that the attempt to create a more perfect humanity or a human made in one's own image raises the specter of sinful pride and/or having a power over other human beings appropriate only for God.[106] In a similar vein, Moshe Tendler warned that "whenever man has shown mastery over man, it has always meant the enslavement of man."[107]

In contrast, other theologians pointed to the difficulty of determining whether the prospect of human cloning crosses some as yet undefined boundary between actions appropriate for God and humankind. Elliot Dorff noted that in Jewish tradition humanity is the partner of God in the ongoing act of creation and that this concept has been actively and aggressively applied in trying to provide medical care. Nevertheless, he queried where the boundary was between implementing this mandate or going beyond it and indeed playing God.[108] Likewise, Lisa Sowle Cahill cautioned that using religious language and phrases like "playing God" without carefully relating them to human and scientific realities can be obfuscating and alienating. To her, the real questions are not whether humans have or lack any God-given or natural right to intervene in the processes of life but what constitutes appropriate intervention.[109] But neither she nor any other religious thinker illuminated that boundary.

Perhaps the most affirmative response about human cloning falling within the acceptable parameters of human initiative came from Philip Hefner, who had previously developed the concept of the human being as created co-creator. As created co-creators, we are, on the one hand, shaped by cosmic and biological prehistory and dependent on the creative grace of God and, on the other, we are able to use our freedom and power to alter the course of historical and perhaps even evolutionary events.[110] For Hefner the issue is not whether we appropriately participate with God in the ongoing creative process but how we do so, how we understand our destiny and the future toward which we are being drawn by God's will. In this context he argued that, despite all the talk about playing God, the problem with regard to cloning is that we

105. Wheeler, "Moral and Theological Issues in Human Cloning."
106. Nancy Duff, "Clone with Caution," *Washington Post,* 2 March 1997, C1, 5.
107. Niebuhr, "Suddenly, Religious Ethicists Face a Quandary on Cloning," A10.
108. Dorff, Testimony, 6.
109. Cahill, Testimony, 156.
110. Philip Hefner, "The Evolution of the Created Co-Creator," in Ted Peters, ed., *Cosmos as Creation: Theology and Science in Consonance* (Nashville: Abingdon Press, 1989), 211–34; Philip Hefner, *The Human Factor: Evolution, Culture, and Religion* (Minneapolis: Fortress Press, 1993), 27–51.

have no clear ideas about what that entails. According to Hefner, the most significant revelation deriving from Dolly will be what it reveals about ourselves. In cloning we are addressing ourselves and attempting to understand the basic nature of the human person. "We are about to enter once again into the whole question of what human life is all about and how it should be conducted— cloning has simply raised the stakes in this discussion."[111]

RECOMMENDATIONS FROM NBAC

In early June 1997, some one hundred days after receiving its mandate from the president, NBAC issued its report and recommendations, *Cloning Human Beings.* Given the tight time line assigned to the commission, the report is a considerable accomplishment. It consists of six well-reasoned chapters written with the assistance of a series of commissioned papers reviewing the literature. The report covers the science, religious perspectives, ethical considerations, and legal and policy issues as a basis for formulating its conclusions and recommendations. Nevertheless, as might be anticipated, the report does bear the marks of the severe time pressures under which NBAC functioned. Perhaps the most serious deficiency is the inability to come to terms decisively with ethical concerns other than safety issues.

The central conclusion of the report is that the use of somatic cell nuclear transfer technology to create a child would be a premature experiment because it would expose the developing child to unacceptable risks:

> The Commission concludes at this time it is morally unacceptable for anyone in the public or private sector, whether in a research or clinical setting, to attempt to create a child using somatic cell nuclear transfer cloning. We have reached a consensus on this point because current scientific information indicates that this technique is not safe to use in humans at this time. Indeed, we believe it would violate important ethical obligations were clinicians or researchers to attempt to create a child using these particular technologies, which are likely to involve unacceptable risks to the fetus and/or potential child. Moreover, in addition to safety concerns many other serious ethical issues have been identified, which require much more widespread and careful public deliberation before this technology may be used.[112]

NBAC understood the challenge to public policy formation as finding ways to support the beneficial applications of somatic cell nuclear transfer technology while guarding against potential questionable uses (107). It did so

111. Hefner, "Cloning as Quintessential Human Act."
112. NBAC, *Cloning Human Beings,* 108.

through a series of proposed compromises. The commission recommended a continuation of the moratorium on the use of federal funding in support of any attempt to create a child by somatic cell nuclear transfer, reinforced by federal legislation that would prohibit such efforts in both research and clinical settings. If enacted, this action would constitute the first regulatory restriction on the application of reproductive technologies in the private sector. Balancing this proposal, the commission concluded that the regulatory or legislative action undertaken to effect this prohibition should be narrowly and carefully written so as not to interfere with other important areas of scientific research and should have a sunset clause to ensure that Congress review the issue after a specified time period (three to five years was mentioned) to decide whether the prohibition was still needed (108–9). NBAC's studied silence on the intentional creation of human embryos through cloning for research purposes leaves open the possibility of undertaking this research as long as the clinic or laboratory does not receive federal funding. And, quite apart from the substance of their recommendations, this situation would significantly complicate the possibility of enforcing a ban on the creation of clones for implantation. NBAC also recommended that the United States government should cooperate with other countries and international organizations to coordinate common aspects of their respective policies on the cloning of human beings. Finally, to promote a meaningful public discussion of the issues that human cloning raises, the commission underscored the need for federal departments and agencies concerned with science to support opportunities to provide information and education to the public in the area of genetics and other developments in the biomedical sciences, particularly as these affect important cultural practices, values, and beliefs (110).

Within the time period allotted to its deliberations, and possibly because of divisions among its members, NBAC was either unable or unwilling to deal with the substance of the ethical and theological issues that human cloning raises. The substantive chapters on religious perspectives and ethical considerations review a range of positions, seemingly finding little to choose among them. Concerns about compromising human dignity and personhood are balanced against claims for reproductive liberty and freedom of scientific inquiry. Time and again the report emphasizes the pluralism in American society and the fact that no single set of approaches balances conflicting values in ways that can gain universal acceptance. It also notes the absence of an agreed upon methodology in moral philosophy or bioethics for resolving disputes among competing ethical theories (93). Almost like a mantra, the report reminds readers, "Religious positions on human cloning are pluralistic in their premises, modes of argument, and conclusions" (39, 107). NBAC acknowledges fears of many of the experts who provided testimony that the widespread practice of cloning could undermine the very meaning of being human as well as weaken important social values or open the door to a form of eugenics. But it merely comments that members "could not come to a common evaluation of these objections, as they are partly speculative, partly theological, and partly based on particular values or world views that are commonly, but nonetheless not universally, shared by all Americans" (93).

Given the problems in reaching consensus on how to assess moral and theological concerns, the commission bases its recommendations solely on the argument that the cloned child would be exposed to unacceptable risks and labels other ethical concerns as "speculative"—a very inadequate choice of terms. According to the text, "More speculative psychological harms to the child, and effects on the moral, religious, and cultural values of society, may be enough to justify continued prohibitions in the future, but more time is needed for discussion and evaluation of these concerns" (108). The dilemma is whether our nation will ever be able to hold a meaningful public debate on this subject. Despite all of the limitations under which NBAC operated, it seems unlikely that anybody will be able to devote even a comparable level of time and attention to the ethical implications of human cloning.

RELIGIOUS ETHICS IN A SECULAR SOCIETY

The cloning debate highlights the dilemma of determining the appropriate role of religious concerns in public policy formulation in a secular society. This section deals with some of the things learned from the cloning debate as to the potential contribution of religious ethics to societal decisions about the applications of new technologies.

1. Is it possible to have a meaningful public discussion in the United States about the ethical and theological implications of new technologies?
Time and again, particularly in the past thirty years, the United States has repeated a cycle reminiscent of the dynamics of the human cloning debate. Quite unexpectedly, or at least seemingly so to those who do not follow scientific developments, scientists announce a discovery. The media covers the story, albeit with as much sensationalism as possible. The public then responds to the announcement with surprise and consternation. A few ethicists and official religious bodies formulate positions, but often well after the controversy has passed. Eventually, most people cautiously accept the new technology, some because there seemingly is no choice and others because they overcome their initial negative reaction.

The NBAC report reviews many such instances of this cycle of discovery, reaction, and cautious acceptance. Artificial insemination by donor, considered to be a form of adultery fifty years ago, has become a widely accepted practice in the treatment of infertility. Prenatal diagnosis (introduced in the late 1960s) and *in vitro* fertilization (first available in 1978) similarly evoked consternation and then general acceptance. When recombinant DNA research was initiated, scientists, as well as the public, had concerns about safety and the unintended release of genetically altered organisms into the environment.[113]

Does this history attest to an irrational fear of the new and seemingly unnatural, aggravated by a lack of scientific understanding, in some instances bordering on total scientific illiteracy, and fueled by sensationalized media coverage? Several proponents of human cloning claimed that this was the grounding of the overwhelming public opposition to human cloning. If this is so, it does not bode well for the prospects of having any type of meaningful public discourse and consideration of the ethical implications of science and technology. Or, as Leon Kass argued, is something more profound at stake? Kass attributed this reaction to cloning to "the wisdom of repugnance," an intuition that specific discoveries and technologies violate things we rightfully hold dear.[114]

Without debating these alternative perspectives, it is important to point out that, typically, scientific discoveries are introduced without any meaningful effort to evaluate their ethical implications and are adopted, particularly in the private sector, with little, if any, public debate or effort to formulate guidelines or regulations. That scientific advances engender an emotional reaction, often fueled by the "yuck factor," as people contemplate something startling and seemingly unnatural, is not surprising. The absence of thoughtful and reasoned analysis in the media, or serious consideration of the ethical or theological issues, or even a sustained public debate, makes it difficult to educate or engage the public. Fundamentally, the United States has never tried to hold a serious public discussion as the basis for policy making on issues resulting from scientific developments and discoveries. The relatively brief flurry of media attention, congressional hearings, and the NBAC deliberations on human cloning are the closest we have come, at least on biotechnology.

Furthermore, the NBAC itself was not established until 1996 and had only one predecessor body, the 1980–82 President's Commission for the Study of Ethical Problems in Medicine and Biomedical and Behavioral Research. Congress has been reluctant to deal with biomedical and biotechnology issues. Human embryo research has constituted an exception, but the manner in which it was handled, imposing a ban on the use of federal funds through inserting language in appropriation bills, hardly provides a useful model. In several instances (one of which is gene patents, addressed in the next chapter), critical issues have

---

113. Ibid., 4–6.
114. Kass, "Wisdom of Repugnance," 20.

by default gone to the courts to decide on the basis of a narrow legal standard, and as a former chair of the National Advisory Board on Ethics in Reproduction observed about the brief embryo twinning controversy, "reporters phoning ethicists for comment and ethicists appearing on talk shows does not a debate make."[115]

Under these circumstances it is understandable that ethicists, official religious bodies, and policy makers underscore the need for further public discussion before proceeding with experiments in human cloning. In advance of NBAC's recommendations, the United Methodist statement urged widespread discussion of issues related to cloning by the general public, as well as by experts in agricultural and biological science, public policy, ethics, theology, law, and medicine, including genetics and genetic counseling. The statement contains a useful list of issues to address in the course of these public deliberations.[116] As noted above, NBAC called for a serious effort by the government to educate the public and then involve it in a national debate about the appropriateness of engaging in human cloning. To that end, it recommended that national and state legislation regulating human cloning research and application have a three- to five-year sunset clause.[117] Given the United States' history with biomedical issues, though, it seems unlikely that this set of recommendations will be fully implemented.

2. Is it possible to anticipate scientific discoveries and develop a meaningful dialogue in advance of breakthroughs?
Typically, pathbreaking scientific and technological developments occur without serious societal anticipation and ethical forethought. Even when professional ethicists address these topics, it is difficult to sustain a meaningful dialogue, especially when the technology seems far-fetched or likely to need a long period of development. Human cloning provides a relevant case study of the difficulties because there were missed opportunities for ethical reflection in advance of the most recent scientific developments. As noted, three decades ago, at the dawn of bioethics as a discipline, Joshua Lederberg, a Nobel prize–winning geneticist, floated arguments to support human cloning and Paul Ramsey and other medical ethicists responded to Lederberg opposing the experiment on ethical grounds. In the late 1970s, there was again some discussion of cloning, but scientists dismissed these discussions as irrelevant, noth-

115. Albert Jonsen was so quoted in Cynthia B. Cohen, "Future Directions for Human Cloning by Embryo Splitting: After the Hullabaloo," *Kennedy Institute of Ethics Journal* 4 (September 1994): 188.
116. General Board of Church and Society, "Statement from United Methodist Task Force."
117. NBAC, *Cloning Human Beings*, 108–10.

ing more than idle speculation about impossible things and likely to bring science into disrepute.[118] Ethicists, apparently believing that human cloning was more a province of science fiction than scientific likelihood, more of a plot device for a Frankenstein-style movie about mad scientists than a serious subject for ethical discourse, did not pursue the topic even when animal cloning through embryo splitting became a regular occurrence. The report of the 1993 experiments on defective human pre-embryos at George Washington University engendered brief commentary, but the topic was not pursued and soon vanished from attention.

Why is there such an inability or reluctance to deal with scientific developments until the future becomes the present and a discovery is announced demanding some type of response? Peter Steinfels, a writer on religion, suggests that at least some failures to ethically anticipate the direction of scientific research reflect the reluctance of ethicists to criticize science. According to Steinfels, ethicists generally defer to the claims of scientists that science should be critiqued with caution because discoveries are endangered by an irrational fear of the new.[119] It is noteworthy that at least one commentary written by a religious ethicist on cloning harks back to Galileo's persecution by the church because he supported the Copernican view that the earth moves around the sun. Nancy Duff warns that if the church supports a total ban on all cloning it may be seen to be shackling reason and science to protect faith. While she acknowledges the human capacity to misuse scientific accomplishments, she recommends that the church not call for a moratorium on all such research, but instead help forge a responsible path for the new technology.[120]

Will the experience with cloning engender a meaningful effort to anticipate related genetic and biomedical developments and begin ethical reflection at an earlier point in time? Only time will tell. It does not require a crystal ball to identify some of these dilemmas that are in the offing. One example that may be no more than three to five years in the future will be the capacity to undertake human germ-line intervention to engineer heritable changes in the human genome. Nevertheless, despite evidence that the research is progressing quickly and calls for public discussion, the silence is thus far deafening.

3. Is the dominance of technology (technological imperative) inevitable?
In the midst of the debate on cloning, commentator Kirkpatrick Sale wrote an opinion piece for the the *New York Times* that was critical of cloning but anticipated that the juggernaut of science could not be stopped. The article foresaw

118. Kolata, "With Cloning of a Sheep," A15.
119. Steinfels, "Beliefs."
120. Duff, "Clone with Caution," C5.

that human cloning would go forward despite President Clinton's decision to ban the use of federal money for research on cloning humans and the likelihood that Congress would pass legislation to prohibit all attempts and human cloning. Sale, an occasional critic of science and technology, argued that if the cloning of human embryos is possible, it will happen. According to Sale, technological possibilities are irresistible in a culture built on the myth of human power and the cult of progress. He reasoned that a society which not only permits but also commodifies reproductive technologies is unlikely to have the will to defy the relentless forward motion of science. "The history of science is the history of the dominance of technology, establishing its own definitions and boundaries, over settled human societies and ordered human perceptions."[121]

Certainly, some scientists argue that scientific research should not be held to ethical standards of evaluation. Responding to the backlash from the news in 1993 that research at George Washington University had successfully cloned human embryos, John Robertson asserted that universities would fail in their missions if they blocked controversial research just because national guidelines for dealing with ethical complexities have not yet been written. According to Robertson, "Researchers have a right to conduct research that they find to be of medical or scientific interest. . . . [They] should not stop research because it is ethically controversial, because it will bring bad publicity, or because guidelines are lacking."[122] Robertson reiterated this position in his 1997 testimony before NBAC.[123]

The NBAC report, however, qualifies the freedom of scientific inquiry. While it notes that the scientific community has enjoyed a great deal of autonomy in directing and regulating its research agency, the report also points out that regulation of science has become part of the landscape since mid-century, particularly for those who receive federal funds. It bases the legitimacy of doing so on the ethical concerns about the potential dangers, particularly in the biological sciences, of the research and its consequences:

> Because science is both a public and social enterprise and its application can have profound impact, society recognizes that the freedom of scientific inquiry is not an absolute right and scientists are expected to conduct their research according to widely held ethical principles. There are times when limits on scientific freedom must be imposed, even if such limits are perceived as an impediment by an individual scientist.[124]

121. Kirkpatrick Sale, "Ban Cloning? Not a Chance," *New York Times,* 7 March 1997, A27.
122. John A. Robertson, "Point of View," *Chronicle of Higher Education* (24 November 1993): A40.
123. Robertson, Testimony, 81–97.
124. NBAC, *Cloning Human Beings,* 6.

Nevertheless, its presumption in favor of the freedom of scientific inquiry motivates NBAC to set some narrow boundaries on the ethical constraints on science. The report emphasizes that limits on freedom of inquiry must be carefully formulated and satisfy certain conditions—that the criteria emerge from the careful balancing of costs and benefits, that there is continuing public discourse, and that the limitations be open to reconsideration in the light of new information and understanding.[125] Clearly, NBAC attempted to follow its own guidelines in developing its policy recommendations on human cloning. It sought to balance the safety and well-being of a potential clone and the wider society with the freedom to continue with research. Only time will disclose whether NBAC's recommendation of a temporary ban, with a review in three to five years, is a feasible option, or, if it were to be adopted, whether it would be a meaningful bulwark against the juggernaut of science and technology.

4. What is the appropriate role of the religious community in making national policy on sensitive bioethical issues?
As noted, the religious community participated in the debate about cloning in a quite visible and unprecedented manner. Representatives of the religious community were invited to testify before NBAC. The views of religious scholars and the statements of official religious bodies were given considerable publicity. As might be anticipated, some individuals and groups objected to the role of the religious community. According to a May 1997 "Statement in Defense of Cloning and the Integrity of Scientific Research," issued by a group of scientists and scholars,

> The immediate question raised by the current debate over cloning is, therefore, whether advocates of supernatural or spiritual agendas have truly meaningful qualifications to contribute to that debate. Surely everyone has the right to be heard. But we believe that the danger is very real that research with enormous potential benefits may be suppressed solely because it conflicts with some people's religious beliefs. It is important to recognize that similar religious objections were once raised against autopsies, anesthesia, artificial insemination, and the entire genetic revolution of our day—yet enormous benefits have accrued from each of these developments. Views of human nature rooted in humanity's tribal past ought not to be our primary criterion for making moral decisions about cloning. . . . The potential benefits of cloning may be so immense that it would be a tragedy if ancient theological scruples should it lead to a Luddite rejection of cloning.[126]

125. Ibid., 6–7.
126. "Statement in Defense of Cloning."

NBAC's justification of why it chose to consider religious perspectives on human cloning provides a powerful rejoinder to the claims that "ancient theological scruples" have no appropriate role in the formulation of public policy on sensitive biomedical issues. Acknowledging that the United States Constitution prohibits the establishment of policies solely motivated by religious belief, the commission explains its decision to invite testimony and solicit papers from leading scholars of a variety of religious traditions as follows: "NBAC felt this was especially important because religious traditions shape the moral views of many U.S. citizens and religious teachings over the centuries have provided an important source of ideas and inspiration."[127] It goes on to state that, "although in a pluralistic society particular religious views cannot be determinative for public policy decisions that bind everyone, policy makers should understand and show respect for diverse moral ideas regarding the acceptability of cloning human beings."[128]

Moreover, the May 1997 "Statement in Defense of Cloning" itself reveals a form of irrational prejudice, antireligious sentiment. The reasoned analysis and concerns articulated by the various religious participants in the brief human cloning debate hardly constitute outbursts from some distant tribal past. Some scientists' refusal to respect people of faith and to take their concerns seriously constitutes at least as serious a problem as lingering antiscience attitudes among members of the religious community. Extreme claims on behalf of scientific truth may also reflect an assumption that Science (with a capital "S") constitutes the only reliable source of ultimate explanation as well as the best hope of human happiness and well-being.[129] Proponents of this view, sometimes referred to as scientism, are making more than an epistemological assertion about the characteristics of inquiry and knowledge. They are also putting forward a metaphysical or ontological claim about the characteristics of reality that casts science as an alternative religion.[130]

ETHICAL FORMATION
FROM A RELIGIOUS PERSPECTIVE

Cloning provides a useful case study of issues related to the dilemmas of engaging in religious ethics at the frontiers of science. Some of these are briefly reviewed in this section.

127. NBAC, *Cloning Human Beings,* 7.
128. Ibid.
129. Steinfels, "Beliefs."
130. Ian Barbour, *Religion in an Age of Science: The Gifford Lectures,* vol. 1 (New York: HarperSanFrancisco, 1990), 5.

1. Who represents or speaks for particular religious traditions and on what basis?
Almost immediately after Wilmut's announcement, the media and then NBAC
solicited the views of the religious community. At that time, however, none of
the major religious communities had explicit policy covering animal or human
cloning and efforts to apply traditional theological concepts and formulations
to cloning require a considerable level of interpretation and discretion. NBAC
appears in the main to have relied on its member networks of contacts, sup-
plemented by academics who had published opinion pieces in newspapers. Of
the seven religious representatives invited to testify, only one, Albert
Moraczewski, claimed to represent a church body, in his case the National
Conference of Catholic Bishops. For the most part, therefore, the religious
thinkers involved in the initial phase of debate about cloning presented their
own theological perspectives and approaches, but in the heat of the moment
this distinction was not always made clear. NBAC's labeling of various theologians in such broad categories as "Protestant" certainly did not illuminate
anything other than the range of views within these broad religious groupings.

Of the participants in the NBAC hearings, Aziz Sachedina, a bioethicist at
the University of Virginia, was most explicit that he was not and could not present a position speaking on behalf of his tradition. Dr. Sachedina explained that
in the absence of a central institution in Islam resembling the Vatican there was
a plurality of ethical views based on independent research and interpretation
of legal scholars on many issues. He was also more forthcoming about the
complexities and limitations of applying scripture and traditional legal formulations to cloning than many of his colleagues. Dr. Sachedina acknowledged
that Islam originated within a Semitic tribal culture fundamentally different
from contemporary society. He pointed out that the Qu'ran and the Islamic
tradition even lack a universally accepted definition for an embryo. Nor do
these sources anticipate the modern biological data about the beginning of life
from the moment of impregnation.[131]

Two denominations, the United Methodist Church and the UCC, convened task forces to develop policy positions. The United Methodist Genetic
Science Task Force is composed of church members closely connected with
biotechnology and ethics fields, having backgrounds in microbiology, virolo-
gy, neurology, ethics, Christian ministry, and law. It was initially established
several years earlier to draft a policy statement on genetics. Like the United
Methodist Church, the UCC has a long history of grappling with the ethical
implications of advances in genetic engineering. After the announcement of
the cloning of Dolly, church leaders decided to turn to an adhoc committee

131. Dr. Aziz Sachedina, Testimony to the NBAC, 14 March 1997 (Washington, D.C.:
Eberlin Reporting Service), 56–64.

on genetics appointed by one of its national agencies to develop a denominational statement. Originally intended to coincide with the release of the
NBAC report, the statement then became the basis of a resolution adopted several weeks later by the General Synod.[132]

2. To what extent do traditional confessional distinctions shape positions on cloning?
A careful examination of the work of particular ethicists and theologians clearly indicates that something more complex is happening than the mechanical
application of traditional dogmas. In the unlikely circumstances that there
might be inclinations in this direction, few moral theologians would find much
of direct relevance to cloning in their traditions. As Albert Moraczewski noted
in his testimony to NBAC, "Neither sacred Scripture nor the Catholic
Church's moral tradition have explicitly and fully treated this issue."[133]
Obviously, most religious thinkers do not begin with a tabula rasa.
Nevertheless, given the unprecedented character of somatic cell nuclear
cloning, as well as the other issues explored in this volume, moral theologians
generally have considerable latitude as to how they interpret and dialogue
with their tradition. Even when the process of conceptual development reflects
historical doctrinal and methodological perspectives, the relationship is rarely
linear. An examination of the contributions on cloning by various religious
thinkers underscores that religious affiliation may impose certain boundaries
and offer methodological approaches and ethical and theological themes, but
it rarely determines the content, the emphasis, or the conclusions drawn by
theologians and ethicists.

That traditional confessional boundaries do not necessarily predetermine
ethical reasoning can be shown by comparing the views on cloning of particular religious ethicists. To be more specific, both Elliot Dorff and Moshe
Tendler ostensibly gave voice to a shared Jewish tradition, and they concurred
about many things. Nevertheless, their differences in seeking to interpret the
relevance of the Jewish heritage to this issue are striking. Both made use of biblical passages, Dorff to argue that the Jewish tradition recognizes humanity as
the partner of God in the ongoing act of creation,[134] and Tendler to caution that
biblical literature stresses limits equating humanity to a guest in someone's
home who can enjoy but not rearrange the house.[135] Dorff was concerned that
cloning may diminish the sense of sacredness in a human being and cheapen
life[136] while Tendler argued that cloning would not impact significantly the

132. As noted earlier, I served as a member of the committee.
133. Moraczewski, Testimony, 186.
134. Dorff, Testimony, 6.
135. Tendler, Testimony, 18.
136. Dorff, Testimony, 9.

sanctity of life.[137] Although both drew conclusions that the Jewish tradition permitted cloning, at least under some circumstances, the Chief Rabbi of Israel issued a blanket prohibition against any research in cloning.[138]

Differences in interpretation and evaluations about the implications of cloning were even more striking among three Lutheran theologians who participated in the cloning debate. Much as Paul Ramsey argued thirty years earlier, Gilbert Meilaender, a professor at Valparaiso University, found cloning problematic because it would sever the connection between marriage and begetting children. According to Meilaender, the Bible presents a normative view that sexual differentiation is ordered toward the creation of offspring and that children should be conceived within the marital union. Meilaender also emphasized that humans do not have the freedom to make and remake ourselves.[139] In contrast with Meilaender's position, Philip Hefner wrote about cloning against the horizon of the human person as created co-creators, creatures of nature who themselves intentionally enter into the process of creating nature."[140] Ted Peters, a third Lutheran theologian connected with the Berkeley-based Center for Theology and the Natural Sciences, argued that cloning did not pose any fundamental theological problems and dismissed fears that cloning would compromise human identity and violate human dignity. Rather than banning cloning, he advocated for the acceptance of an ethical framework: "God loves each of us, regardless of our genetic makeup, as we should do likewise."[141]

Although Lisa Cahill and Albert Moraczewski share a Roman Catholic background, in their testimonies before NBAC they offered very different perspectives on cloning. Here Moracziewz spoke for the National Conference of Catholic Bishops and therefore was grounded in the church's official teachings. As in her writings, Cahill drew on the Catholic natural law tradition as modified by a feminist perspective. Undoubtedly her considerable experience with and expertise on reproductive technologies also helped shape her position on

137. Tendler, Discussion after Testimony, 39.
138. Ibid., 40.
139. Dr. Gilbert Meilaender, Testimony to the NBAC, 13 March 1997 (Washington, D.C.: Eberlin Reporting Service), 220–31.
140. Hefner, "Cloning as Quintessential Human Act."
141. Ted Peters made these remarks at the AAAS Forum on Cloning. This statement also appears in several of his publications, including most recently his article "Love and Dignity: Against Children Becoming Commodities," in Roger A. Willer, ed., *Genetic Testing and Screening: Critical Engagement at the Intersection of Faith and Science* (Minneapolis: Kirk House Publishers for the Evangelical Lutheran Church in America, 1998), 129.

cloning. While Moraczewski's testimony reiterated official church teachings on marriage and sexuality and attempted to apply them to the new issue of cloning, Cahill never mentioned Catholic doctrine. Instead she chose to focus on two issues—the need for NBAC to resist the technological imperative and related market forces, and the importance of going beyond autonomy and informed consent when engaging in moral reflection on cloning. When she dealt with the issue of the family, it was to note the cross-cultural variety and the importance of the biological relationship between parents and children as a symbol of repro-ductive, domestic, and social partnership. Commenting on the possibility cloning presented for reproduction without any male contribution, Cahill acknowledged that at one level her feminist instincts were attracted to this pos-sibility, but she was inclined to believe it would not be to the advantage of human responsibility for the next generation.[142]

3. Given the diversity of positions among religious thinkers, are there any characteris-tics that set religious ethicists apart from secular ethicists?
This query relates back to the complex and difficult question of defining the nature of religious ethics at the frontiers of science. Are there specific approach-es, themes, or criteria that distinguish religious and secular ethicists? As already noted, the use of explicitly theological formulations or "God language" was generally absent from the discussion of the implications of human cloning, like-ly because of the public fora in which it took place. Of the seven religious par-ticipants who testified before NBAC, only Meilaender utilized a consistently biblical and theological frame of reference, and another, Moraczewski, partial-ly so. Others referred to biblical and religious traditions, but frequently did so in secular terms. Even the issue of appropriate limits of human intervention lacked the usual epithets of "playing God." In directing their comments at a secular constituency, the religious thinkers became relevant to the considera-tion of public policy issues at the expense of further conceptual development of religious ethics at the frontiers of science.

The NBAC report sets its chapter on religious perspectives within the framework of emphasizing differences: "Religious positions on cloning are pluralistic in their premises, modes of argument, and conclusions."[143] Nevertheless, NBAC also notes that several major themes are prominent in Jewish, Roman Catholic, Protestant, and Islamic positions, among them responsible human dominion over nature, human dignity and destiny, procre-ation, and family life.[144] The fact that religious thinkers address these topics does

142. Cahill, Testimony, 181.
143. NBAC, *Cloning Human Beings,* 39.
144. Ibid.

not, of course, mean that they agree either in their conceptual understanding or their application to cloning. That there are significant differences in the positions of religious thinkers, both within and between various traditions and in the official statements issued by the religious bodies that participated in the cloning debate, is apparent from the preceding discussion in this chapter.

Although the religious community certainly did not speak with one voice in the cloning debate, there were important shared themes and affinities. In general, religious thinkers were more inclined than secular thinkers to view the cloning debate through a wider lens than an individualist frame of reference, to be concerned with justice dimensions of the issues, to have a strong sense of the sacredness and value of the human person, and to assign potential concerns more weight than possible benefits. It is also noteworthy that several of the religious ethicists and official church bodies expressed strong reservations about unlimited animal cloning.

That religious ethicists tend to go beyond an individualistic perspective may reflect a sense of connectedness to a community as well as a link theologically to a tradition and ultimately to the divine. Several religious communities work explicitly from a framework that emphasizes the importance of the community and the common good. The legacy of Catholic social teaching was very apparent in Cahill's eloquent appeal to NBAC to go beyond the confines of the principles of autonomy, individuality, and individual freedom typically used in our society as the basis of social policy. She advocated considering other social goods, particularly the interdependence of all in the society we create for ourselves and or children. Like many other religious thinkers, Cahill's frame of reference was the character of a good society and what we can do concretely to move in the appropriate direction.[145] Similarly, Sachedina stated that the central ethical question for Islam was how cloning might affect interhuman or interpersonal relationships. He asked whether human advancement in biotechnology-created relationships would jeopardize the very foundation of human community.[146]

Justice traditions within the religious community were also apparent in the commentaries on cloning. Like Dorff, several of the religious commentators were concerned about the implications of cloning on socioeconomic divisions within our society.[147] The UCC resolution specifically mentions the denomination's commitment to justice and views cloning through this lens: "When the world groans with hunger, when children are stunted from chronic malnutrition, when people die of famine by the thousands every day—when this

145. Cahill, Testimony, 176.
146. Sachedina, Testimony, 56–64.
147. Dorff, Testimony, 5.

is the reality of the world in which we live, the development of any more technologies to suit the desires of those who are relatively privileged, secure, and comfortable seems to fly in the face of fundamental claims of justice."[148] In her testimony to NBAC, Duff urged that if we proceed with research into human cloning we be mindful of those who are most likely to be exploited. She specifically mentioned the importance of protecting women, racial and ethnic minorities, prisoners, and the poor against exploitation.[149] The statement from the United Methodist Genetic Science Task Force has very similar language.[150]

As discussed above, religious commitment to the sanctity and sacredness of life is expressed in their concerns with the implications of cloning for human dignity. While both religious and secular ethicists evince a commitment to human dignity, the religious approach differs. Secular thinkers were more likely to conceptualize human dignity negatively in terms of the absence of constraints on autonomy, the lack of interference in reproductive choices, and the freedom for particular individuals to choose lifestyle options. In contrast, religious thinkers tend to have a much broader concept of human dignity that goes beyond autonomy with a more positive construction. In an interchange during a question-and-answer period, Cahill and Moraczewski explained that autonomy was an important value but certainly not sufficient as a grounding for a moral life or the basis of a full understanding of the human reality of parenthood, being a child and being a family.[151] Far from human dignity necessarily being enhanced by the absence of constraints, Dorff cautioned that self-idolization is a significant danger in cloning because a person can be reproduced without having to go outside of him- or herself. Emphasizing the importance of mortality and finitude in curbing human arrogance, Dorff reminded NBAC that Adam and Eve were not allowed to eat of the tree of life and become immortal.[152]

In the brief debate on cloning, most religious thinkers evinced what might be described as a presumption of caution that placed greater priority on potential problems than on the possible benefits resulting from human cloning. The difference in emphasis is considerable when comparing the religious approach with the comments of some secular thinkers. Ruth Macklin, for example,

148. UCC, "Cloning Mammalian Species."
149. Nancy Duff, Testimony to the NBAC, 13 March 1997 (Washington, D.C.: Eberlin Reporting Service), 239.
150. General Board of Church and Society, "Statement from United Methodist Task Force."
151. Lisa Cahill and Albert Moraczewski, Discussion after Testimony to NBAC, 13 March 1997 (Washington, D.C.: Eberlin Reporting Service), 193–95.
152. Dorff, Testimony, 5.

argued that it would be premature to close off research opportunities on the grounds that only a few people are likely to reap benefits and claimed that it would be prejudicial to ban an entire line of research because of possible unethical applications.[153] In contrast, religious thinkers tended to be more mindful of those who were likely to be harmed than those who were likely to benefit, seeking to protect important societal values even if it required constraints on science and technology. The United Methodist Genetic Science Task Force statement captures this presumption of caution in a comprehensive list of questions:

- Is there a compelling argument for human cloning? Are there clear enough benefits to outweigh the risks?

- Is human cloning the only or best way to arrive at these benefits?

- Is human cloning in the best interest of those affected—particularly children, women, families, and parents?

- How do we exercise stewardship in the allocation of scarce resources? Would money and human effort be better spent on other forms of research?

- How can societies effectively implement, enforce, and maintain cloning guidelines and regulations nationally and globally? What measures can be taken to discourage the misuse of these technologies and the exploitation of human beings?[154]

Despite the tendency of some commentators to cast the cloning debate in narrow terms, several religious thinkers and communities insisted that those "faithful to their Judeo-Christian religious heritage should not only be concerned about the well-being of humanity, but about the welfare of all of God's creatures."[155] The UCC statement addresses the cloning of mammalian species, not just humans. It expresses concern that "the use of nuclear transfer cloning, together with other genetic and reproductive technologies, will contribute to a diminished regard for nonhuman species"[156] and laments the utilitarian attitude that nonhuman species have no inherent dignity or significance beyond their usefulness to human beings. A press release issued on behalf of the Church of Scotland distinguishes between the acceptable use of nuclear transfer technology in the limited context of research and the unacceptable mass cloning

153. Macklin, Testimony, 99.
154. General Board of Church and Society, "Statement from United Methodist Task Force."
155. Duff, "Clone with Caution," C5.
156. UCC, "Cloning Mammalian Species."

of animals for production purposes.[157] Both the Church of Scotland and the UCC attempt to balance respect to each creature as valuable in its own right with taking advantage of the benefits of animal cloning. The UCC does compromise. It states that the use of nuclear transfer cloning in research on non-human mammalian species is morally and theologically permissible provided that "animals be treated humanely and that needless suffering is avoided," but it does not specifically exclude development of cloned animals as pharmaceutical factories or convenient sources of donor organs for human patients.[158]

CONCLUSION

"There is something far worse than theological disagreement, and that is theological silence," Ronald Cole-Turner comments in his preface to *Human Cloning: Religious Responses,* the one book presenting religious perspectives on cloning. He goes on to say, "For our society to make its way blithely into the practice of human cloning without having heard the concerns of Christians would be a great failure on the part of the church."[159] This chapter testifies to the important contribution the entire religious community made to the discussion of human cloning. Religious thinkers who contributed to the discussion of the prospects of human cloning frequently raised broader and more significant issues than many of the secular commentators. In a conversation with this author, a member of NBAC acknowledged his appreciation for the testimony and perspectives of the religious community for just this reason.[160] Despite their many differences in specifics and the rationale for arguing them, the various religious thinkers whose views were discussed here shared a strong commitment to moral and theological analysis of the implications of technological development, and to bringing science under the guidance of ethical choice. In a society where risk-benefit analysis tends to be the currency of public policy analysis, the religious community offered an alternative vision based on principles of human dignity and worth. In contrast with those who claimed that decisions about cloning should be left solely to the individual, moral theologians argued that societal well-being goes beyond questions of private ethics to wider issues of public decision making and morality.

157. Dr. Donald Bruce, Director of the Society, Religion and Technology Project of the Church of Scotland, "Cloning Animals and Humans—A Church of Scotland View," 25 February 1997, e-mail transmission.
158. UCC, "Cloning Mammalian Species."
159. Ronald Cole-Turner, "Preface," in Cole-Turner, ed., *Human Cloning,* xii.
160. Conversation with Tom Murray, 24 September 1997.

Ronald Cole-Turner further comments in his preface, "If there are lasting objections to cloning, they will be religious."[161] How compelling, then, were the religious analyses of cloning? In an essay written for a 1998 collection of essays on cloning by secular ethicists, Jan Heller concludes that arguments put forward thus far by Christian ethicists and moral theologians are not sustainable. According to Heller, who was trained as a moral theologian, objections to human cloning made under the category of responsible human dominion over nature fail to clarify whether human cloning should be regarded as an appropriate expression of the image of God in humans or as an inappropriate expression of human hubris. Objections made under the theme of human dignity do not indicate what it is about cloning humans that violates their dignity. Finally, he argues, that objections made under the category of procreation and families do not specify adequately how human cloning will significantly undermine the identity formation of clones or the relational and social qualities of family life. Heller characterizes the Christian contributions to date as "moral intuitions seeking reasons or grounds."[162] Given his analysis, Heller recommends that more work be done by Christians to specify the reasoning used in moving from core religious symbols to moral judgments about particular actions as a grounding for providing more meaningful content to their evaluation of the implications of cloning.

Heller is unduly harsh in his critique of religious objections to cloning. Nevertheless, he is correct that religious analyses of cloning were preliminary at best and require further development. Like many other genetically based developments, cloning raises fundamental questions about what it means to humans and the human role in the creation. While the religious community has a long history of reflection on theological anthropology, the abstract philosophical content of this tradition tends not to be directly relevant to cloning or other issues raised by contemporary science. That is to say, it is not simply a matter of identifying relevant theological and ethical concepts and applying them to the questions posed by cloning. Nor do traditional confessional formulations and dogmas provide a satisfactory grounding for responding to the issues raised by late–twentieth-century science and technology. None of the traditions involved in the cloning debate could simply reapply past deliberations on human nature, human distinctiveness, and the human role in creation to answer the unprecedented dilemmas posed by the prospects of human

---

161. Cole-Turner, "Preface," in Cole-Turner, ed., *Human Cloning*, xiii.
162. Jan Christian Heller, "Religiously Based Objections to Human Cloning: Are They Sustainable?" in James M. Humer and Robert F. Almeder, eds., *Human Cloning* (Totowa, N.J.: Humana Press, 1998), 174.

cloning. Thus, I would go beyond Heller's appeal to specify the arguments used in moving from core religious symbols to moral judgments about particular actions. The prospect of human cloning reveals the need to rethink and redevelop our theological anthropology to be consonant with contemporary scientific understandings and issues.

Chapter Four

The Patenting of Life

On 18 May 1995, the titular leaders of more than eighty religious faiths and denominations held a press conference to announce their opposition to the patenting of genetically engineered animals and human genes, cells, and organs. They launched the Joint Appeal Against Human and Animal Patenting, a coalition organized by the General Board of Church and Society of the United Methodist Church and Jeremy Rifkin's Foundation on Economic Trends that brought together representatives of mainline Protestant denominations and Catholic, evangelical, charismatic, and Orthodox churches with Jewish, Muslim, Buddhist, and Hindu leaders. Each of the signatories subscribed to the text of a brief statement:

> We, the undersigned religious leaders, oppose the patenting of human and animal life forms. We are disturbed by the U.S. Patent Office's recent decision to patent human body parts and several genetically engineered animals. We believe that humans and animals are creations of God, not humans, and as such should not be patented as human inventions.[1]

An accompanying press release indicated that the signatories, described as "the broadest ever assembled on a science and technology issue," planned a nationwide educational campaign in the nation's churches, synagogues, mosques, and temples to raise critical theological concerns about the patenting of life.[2]

---

1. General Board of Church and Society of the United Methodist Church, "Joint Appeal Against Human and Animal Patenting" (press conference announcement, Washington, D.C., 17 May 1995).
2. Ibid.

RESPONSES TO THE JOINT APPEAL

Characteristically and erroneously, the media response to the announcement portrayed the initiative as yet one more battle in the ongoing war between religion and science. *USA Today,* for example, headlined it as "Today's Debate: Genetics Versus Religion."[3] The *New York Times* described the press conference as "a passionate new battle over religion and science."[4] While this slant may make for more exciting media coverage, it misrepresents the nature of the relationship between the two communities as well as the purpose of the Joint Appeal. As theologian Ronald Cole-Turner commented in a perspective published in *Science* magazine,

> Recent scholarship is showing that the "warfare between science and religion" is turning out to be mostly myth, kept alive by those who want to push these two great human endeavors—the need to focus in communities on our deepest moral and spiritual yearnings, and the longing to understand the natural world of which we are a part—into opposing camps. The fact is that many religious leaders have seen science as a means to achieve the goals of religion, namely, to help and to heal. Religion gives science its purpose, and science gives religion its eyes and its hands.[5]

Far from being Luddites opposed to scientific advances, many of the faith communions whose leadership endorsed the statement, particularly the Christian mainline denominations, have policy statements that detail the potential benefits of genetic engineering and recognize the need to provide financial incentives for product development. As noted in chapter 2, official denominational statements on genetic engineering generally have a positive and hopeful attitude toward genetic science. The 1992 United Methodist Church resolution, "New Developments in Genetic Science," for example, states that "genetic techniques have enormous potential for enhancing creation and human life when they are applied to environmental, agricultural, and medical problems."[6] A National Council of Churches of Christ statement, written in 1986, specifically mentions that "scientists, investors, and managers who provide the knowledge and capital necessary for biotechnological devel-

---

3. "Today's Debate: Genetics Versus Religion," *USA Today,* 19 May 1995, 12A, cited in Ronald Cole-Turner, "Religion and Gene Patenting," *Science* 270 (6 October 1995): 52.

4. "Religious Leaders Prepare to Fight Patents on Genes," *New York Times,* 13 May 1995, A1.

5. Cole-Turner, "Religion and Gene Patenting," 52.

6. "New Developments in Genetic Science," *The Book of Resolutions of the United Methodist Church* (Nashville: United Methodist Publishing House, 1992), 332–34.

opment and marketing deserve fair compensation for their ingenuity, work, and willingness to incur economic risks."[7]

Rather than express an antitechnology position, this opposition to patenting reflects a religiously grounded conviction that biological patents constitute a threat to the dignity and sanctity of life. These views, while voiced sporadically, have a history in the religious community. The 1980 letter written by three general secretaries of the National Council of Churches, the Synagogue Council of America, and the U.S. Catholic Conference to President Jimmy Carter about the development of genetic engineering stated that control of life-forms by any individual or group poses a potential threat to humanity.[8] It was sent only a few days after the Supreme Court ruling permitting the patenting of new life-forms and may have been prompted by it. Two years later, a WCC report entitled *Manipulating Life* also expressed concern about the patenting of microorganisms.[9] In 1989, another WCC publication, *Biotechnology: Its Challenges to the Churches and the World,* recommended that animal life-forms not be patented: "The patenting of life encodes into law a reductionist conception of life which seeks to remove any distinction between living and nonliving things. . . . This mechanistic view directly contradicts the sacramental, interrelated view of life intrinsic to a theology of the integrity of creation."[10]

Nevertheless, at the time of the Joint Appeal few of the participating communions had an explicit policy on patenting. Of those that did, in 1984 the General Conference of the United Methodist Church declared genes to be part of the common heritage of all peoples. A report of the Genetic Science Task Force of the United Methodist Church adopted by the 1992 General Conference states the following:

> The position taken by the church in 1984 is consistent with our understanding of the sanctity of God's creation and God's ownership of life. Therefore, exclusive ownership rights of genes as a means of making genetic technologies accessible raises serious theological concerns. While patents on organisms themselves are opposed, process patents, wherein the method for engineering a new organism is patented, provide a means of economic

7. National Council of Churches of Christ in the U.S.A., "Genetic Science for Human Benefit" (New York: Office of Research and Evaluation, adopted by the Governing Board 22 May 1986).

8. "A Letter to the President of the United States," *Panel on Bioethical Concerns, National Council of Churches, Genetic Engineering: Social and Ethical Consequences* (New York: Pilgrim Press, 1984), App. A.

9. WCC Church and Society, *Manipulating Life: Ethical Issues in Genetic Engineering* (Geneva: WCC, 1982), 19.

10. WCC Church and Society, *Biotechnology: Its Challenges to the Churches and the World* (Geneva: WCC, 1989), 22.

return on investment while avoiding exclusive ownership of the organism, and can be supported. We urge that genes and genetically modified organisms (human, plant, animal) be held as common resources and not be exclusively controlled, or patented. We support improvements in the procedures for granting patents on processes and techniques as a way to reward new developments in this area.[11]

In June 1995, a month after the Joint Appeal, the Southern Baptist Convention adopted a resolution that requested "an immediate moratorium on the patenting of animal and human tissues and genetic sequences until a full and complete discussion has occurred."[12] Pope John Paul II had commented in a 1994 statement to the plenary session of the Pontifical Academy of Science Appeal, "We rejoice that numerous researchers have refused to allow discoveries made about the [human] genome to be patented. Since the human body is not an object that can be disposed of at will, the results of research should be made available to the whole scientific community and cannot be the property of a small group,"[13] but the Vatican had not adopted an official position on genetic patenting.

Apparently some members of the 1995 religious coalition assumed that it is possible to have the potential benefits of genetic engineering without the moral and theological problems associated with genetic patents. Rabbi David Saperstein, Director of the Religious Action Center, explained at the Joint Appeal briefing:

> I am not here today to deny the immeasurable benefits of genetic engineering. However, the biotech industry would be able to continue discovering these marvels of science without the patenting process. Numerous products have already been created, manufactured, and marketed without patents. The only undeniable benefit of issuing patents for genetically engineered life forms is the monopolization of profits by the invested industries.[14]

Similarly, C. Ben Mitchell, an ethicist at the Southern Baptist Theological Seminary in Louisville who serves as a consultant on biomedical and life issues

---

11. "New Developments in Genetic Science," 332–33.

12. Southern Baptist Convention, Committee on Resolutions, "On the Patenting of Animal and Human Genes," adopted by the Southern Baptist Convention meeting in Atlanta, June 1995, *Southern Baptist Convention Annual 1995,* 91–92.

13. The statement is reprinted in "The Human Person Must Be the Beginning Subject and Goal of All Scientific Research," *L'Ossservatore Romano* (9 November 1994): 15–16, cited in William B. Friend, Bishop of Shreveport, Louisiana, "An Introduction to Genes and Patents," *Law and Human Genetics Review* 3 (1995): 246.

14. David Saperstein, Press Release issued by the Religious Action Center of Reformed Judaism, 18 May 1995.

for the Southern Baptist Christian Life Commission, explained that the goal of the Joint Appeal as this: It was intended "to initiate a discussion about ways to preserve the therapeutic goals of genetic intervention without collapsing the important noneconomic values of living organisms into crass market values." He went on to note that "a blind frenzy of patenting is far more dangerous than a strict prohibition."[15]

It is important to note that the fault lines on the issue of genetic patenting run through the religious, scientific, and business communities. That there are advocates and opponents of patenting in all three communities was very apparent in the four meetings of a dialogue group on genetic patenting convened by the Program of Dialogue on Science, Ethics, and Religion at AAAS. (I am the director of this program and served as the coorganizer of the AAAS Dialogue Group on Genetic Patenting.) As part of the dialogue process, fifteen participants submitted position papers, an analysis of which attests to the considerable internal divisions in each of the groups. On the question of patenting human genes, six persons, including three representatives of the religious community, two scientists, and one secular ethicist, opposed any form of patenting of human DNA, but the grounds on which they did so differ considerably. Three of the statements, one representative each of the religious, scientific, and corporate communities, appeared to unconditionally support or find no objection to patenting human DNA or gene fragments. Four others, a secular ethicist, two scientists, and two industry representatives, conditionally accepted gene patenting if it met specific criteria, the most common being that the proposed patent specifies a function or use. The positions were just as diverse and complicated on the patenting of a living nonhuman organism. The third topic, the patenting of human tissues, cells, and organs, came closer to eliciting a consensus based on opposition to this form of patenting.[16] Of the three groupings in the dialogue, representatives of the religious community had the greatest problem with, and the most emotional reaction to, their disagreements.

Although nearly two hundred religious leaders signed the Joint Appeal, the position taken in that statement does not reflect a consensus within the religious community, not even within the faith communions represented. In fact, some of the strongest criticisms of the Joint Appeal have come from members of the religious community, even (and sometimes particularly) from staff, ethicists, and theologians in the faith communions whose leaders endorsed the statement. With the exception of the Methodist bishops, the religious leaders who signed

15. C. Ben Mitchell, "Brave New World of Biopatents," in *Patenting of Biological Entities: Proceedings of the ITEST Workshop, October 1996* (St. Louis: ITEST Faith/Science Press, 1996), 24.
16. I prepared an analysis of the positions for the March 1997 session of the dialogue group.

the statement were not representing the official positions or policies of their respective communions. Moreover, many of the signatories did not consult relevant experts and interested parties in their communities before doing so, probably because of the tight time line. One indication of the complexity of the situation is that the U.S. Catholic Conference declined to support the statement. Ninety-one Roman Catholic bishops became signatories, however.

Negative responses to the Joint Appeal in the religious community reflected a variety of considerations. Many critics feared that the statement would once again convey the impression that the religious community was anti-science. Others were reluctant to be associated with Jeremy Rifkin, a longtime opponent of biotechnology. While religious activists engaged in social justice ministries may be comfortable working with Rifkin, others are critical of his views and strategies. A press release issued by the Center for Theology and the Natural Sciences, for example, characterized Rifkin as "the Pied Piper for the Coalition Against Life Patents" and an irresponsible activist with a penchant for hoodwinking and "borrowing baptism from the prestige of honored religious leaders" for his own causes.[17] It should be noted that Rifkin had twice before put together a coalition of religious leaders to support his campaigns. In 1983, Rifkin persuaded fifty religious leaders to sign a resolution opposed to "efforts to engineer specific genetic traits into the germline of the human species";[18] human germ-line alteration was then a very distant prospect and several of the faith communities represented had official positions expressing caution rather than an absolute prohibition. In 1987 Rifkin again collected signatures from religious leaders for a statement opposing the patenting of genetically altered animals.[19] Several theologians also find Rifkin's underlying worldview suspect, characterizing him as a vitalist with a very different perspective on the genetic patenting issue than theists. According to these critics, theism, unlike vitalism, believes that only God is sacred, not the creation.[20] Additionally, a book written by the policy director of Rifkin's Foundation on Economic Trends, *The Human Body Shop*,[21] which apparently played a major role in inspiring the Joint Appeal, has been criticized as sensationalizing and misrepresenting the current situation.[22]

17. Center for Theology and the Natural Sciences, Press Release, 18 May 1995.
18. Richard Stone, "Religious Leaders Oppose Patenting Genes and Animals," *Science* 268 (26 May 1995): 1126.
19. Ibid.
20. Cole-Turner, "Religion and Gene Patenting," and Center for Theology and the Natural Sciences, Press Release.
21. Andrew Kimbrell, *The Human Body Shop: The Engineering and Marketing of Life* (New York: HarperCollins Publishers, 1993).
22. Center for Theology and the Natural Sciences, Press Release.

This chapter analyzes the debate about human genetic patenting, focusing on the discussions and disagreements within the religious community to illuminate some of the conceptual and methodological dilemmas and to assess the requirements for public theology. Resources comprise written sources and my own participation in various forums on gene patenting organized by the AAAS Program of Dialogue on Science, Ethics, and Religion and the Hastings Center. It should be noted that only a small portion of the growing literature dealing with human genetic patenting is specifically religious or theological in character. Most publications dealing with this topic, particularly those published before the Joint Appeal was issued, were written by lawyers and secular philosophers. The Joint Appeal statement can be characterized as more of a public policy declaration than a work of ethical or theological analysis. Subsequent to the Joint Appeal, a small body of theological commentary was written both by critics and by Joint Appeal participants to justify their position. Two dialogues on this subject, a workshop organized by ITEST (Institute for Theological Encounter with Science and Technology) and an eighteen-month dialogue group convened by AAAS, commissioned papers and resulted in publications. The ITEST resource, *Patenting of Biological Entities: Proceedings of the ITEST Workshop*,[23] includes the text of its papers along with the responses of several participants. The AAAS-sponsored book, *Perspectives on Gene Patenting: Religion, Science, and Industry in Dialogue*,[24] which was edited by this author, is a collection of seventeen essays by participants in the AAAS dialogue. Given these limitations, the work on genetic patenting by religious thinkers can be appropriately described as a theology in process.

THE LEGAL FRAMEWORK

Prior to 1980, some two hundred years of legal doctrine conceptualized life-forms as "products of nature" rather than a human invention and therefore ineligible for patent protection. To be eligible for patent protection in the United States, a patent application has to meet three criteria established by Congress: novelty, utility, and nonobviousness. As interpreted by the United States Patent and Trademark Office (PTO), to be "novel" an invention must not have been known and available to the public at the time of the application. "Utility" refers to usefulness. To qualify, a proposed patent must specify concrete function, service, or purpose. "Nonobviousness" has a technical definition: an invention

23. *Patenting of Biological Entities: Proceedings of the ITEST Workshop, October 1996* (St. Louis: ITEST Faith/Science Press, 1997).
24. Audrey R. Chapman, ed., *Perspectives on Genetic Patenting: Religion, Science, and Industry in Dialogue* (Washington, D.C.: AAAS, 1999).

cannot obtain a patent if the differences between its subject matter and the prior art are such that "the subject matter as a whole would have been obvious at the time the invention was made to a person having ordinary skill in the art to which said subject matter pertains."[25] For two centuries, biological entities were not considered to fulfill these three criteria. In fact, until 1980 the PTO did not issue patents for living organisms, but only for compositions containing living things, such as a waste disposal system containing bacteria.

These legal standards were overturned by a landmark 1980 United States Supreme Court decision. In *Diamond v. Chakrabarty* the Court ruled, in a narrow 5–4 decision, that a genetically modified strain of bacteria capable of degrading components of crude oil and thus useful in cleaning up oil spills was patentable as a new and useful manufacture or composition of matter. Although Ananda Chakrabarty, a microbiologist then working at General Electric, had acknowledged that he used commonplace methods to exchange genetic material between bacteria, the Court held that "his discovery is not nature's handiwork but his own" and "the result of human ingenuity and research."[26] While the decision affirmed that phenomena of nature in their natural state are not patentable, the Court identified a major exception: goods that have been transformed from their natural state through human intervention. According to the Court, Congress intended that "anything under the sun that is made by man" be patentable subject matter.[27] In making this decision, the Court was apparently motivated by the goal of stimulating the economy through inventive activity and assumed that the refusal to accord patent rights in genetically engineered organisms would slow down the pace of research in this field.[28]

After the 1980 Supreme Court decision, the PTO began to grant new kinds of biotechnology patents. These changes in patent policy coincided with a movement to privatize commercial development of discoveries arising from federally supported research. Utility patents on newly developed plant varieties were soon accepted and went well beyond the limited protection that had been available.[29] Some of these patents were so broadly conceived that they covered all seeds and plants of a particular species that were genetically engineered in any manner.[30] Then a 1987 PTO announcement extended patent eligibility to

25. 35 United States Code, Sec. 103.

26. Cited in Mark Sagoff, "Patenting Genetic Resources" (paper prepared for the AAAS Dialogue Group on Genetic Patenting, 1996), 13.

27. *Diamond v. Chakrabarty,* 477 US 303 (1980).

28. E. Richard Gold, *Body Parts: Property Rights and the Ownership of Human Biological Materials* (Washington, D.C.: Georgetown University Press, 1996), 81–83.

29. Mark Sagoff, "Animals as Inventions: Biotechnology and Intellectual Property Rights," *Philosophy and Public Policy* 16 (Winter 1996): 18.

30. Ned Hettinger, "Patenting Life: Biotechnology, Intellectual Property, and Environmental Ethics," *Environmental Affairs* 22 (1995): 269–71, 276.

"nonnaturally occurring nonhuman multicellular living organisms, including animals."[31] The following year a Harvard University biologist received a patent for a mouse that had been genetically altered so as to be susceptible to breast cancer and thereby able to serve as an animal model for studying human cancers. This "Harvard oncomouse" became the first animal to be considered an invention. Between 1988 and 1996, the PTO granted at least nine additional patents for genetically engineered animals.[32]

The origins of the current debate on human genetic patenting can be traced to the establishment of the HGP, with its goal of mapping and sequencing the human genome. Spurred by grants from the project, researchers began to uncover DNA sequences in human genetic material that code for particular proteins with specific functions. In June 1991, well before any of the significant issues regarding intellectual property rights or applications of the research and discoveries funded through the HGP were thoroughly debated, let alone resolved, NIH filed a patent application on 350 human gene fragments that had been identified by one of its scientists. Despite strong internal opposition to patenting, specifically by James Watson, then the director of the HGP, NIH submitted a second patent application in February 1992, this time on an additional 2,375 gene fragments, and it later filed a third application for another 4,000. The PTO turned down NIH's initial patent application on the grounds that the gene fragments were neither novel nor useful in themselves. It also found NIH's proposed invention obvious. In one of the ironies of this debate, a new NIH director reversed the agency's position, deciding not to appeal the PTO decision. NIH eventually issued a statement advocating that its grantees desist from seeking patents on human gene sequences.

In May 1998, John Doll, the director of the PTO section that handles biotechnology patents, sought to provide a clarification of its policy on the patenting of DNA. Two of the points he made are particularly important. To respond to criticisms that the PTO accepted patents on discoveries of naturally occurring sequences and organisms, Doll distinguished between naturally occurring DNA sequences and isolated and purified forms. According to Doll, the former still does not qualify for patents under United States law. A patent application stating that the DNA sequences in question are isolated and purified manufactures, compositions of matter, part of a recombinant molecule, or part of a vector, however, would meet the requirement of being distinguished from its natural state and thereby constitute patentable subject matter. Doll justified the patenting of DNA fragments on the grounds that, even if these gene

31. Ibid., 269.
32. Sagoff, "Animals as Inventions," 15.

fragments do not directly identify genes, they may be extremely useful and thus satisfy the utility requirement.[33] This is a much watered-down standard of utility.

By the time of the Joint Appeal, patent agencies around the world had been awarding patents based on DNA, including human genetic material and cell lines, for nearly fifteen years. In February 1998, the PTO reported that it has received more than 5,000 patent applications based on whole genes since 1980 and granted more than 1,500 of them. A study conducted by a science policy group found that the patent offices of the United States, Europe, and Japan issued 1,175 patents on human DNA sequences (partial rather than whole genes) between 1981 and 1995. In mid-1997 the PTO had at least 350 patent applications pending, covering more than 500,000 gene sequences.[34]

Some of the granted patent applications were especially controversial. A well-known example is the University of California at Los Angeles's patent of a potentially lucrative cell line produced from a spleen removed from a leukemia patient, a Seattle businessman named John Moore. The case attracted attention because Moore sued the University of California, seeking to share in the commercial potential of the pharmaceuticals produced from his cell line. Despite that fact that Moore had explicitly refused to sign a consent form giving away his rights to the cell line and anything else derived from the research, the California Supreme Court ruled that Moore had no ownership interests in these cells after they had been removed from his body.[35] Another controversy was set off when NIH filed and received a patent on cell lines from blood samples taken from two individuals, one a member of the Hagahai tribe in Papua New Guinea and the other from the Solomon Islands—groups known to sometimes have an unusual resistance to leukemia. Scientists and policy advocates in several nations in the global South lodged protests, as many viewed the patent as an exploitation of their national genomic resources by avaricious scientists from economically privileged countries. Eventually, in 1996 NIH filed a disclaimer forfeiting all of the United States government's past and future rights under the patents.[36]

---

33. John J. Doll, "The Patenting of DNA," *Science* 280 (1 May 1980): 689–90.
34. Elliot Marshall, "Companies Rush to Patent DNA," *Science* 275 (7 February 1997): 780–81.
35. Beth Burrows, "Second Thoughts about U.S. Patent No. 4,438,032," *GeneWATCH* 10 (October 1996): 4–7; Hettinger, "Patenting Life," 271.
36. Rural Advancement Foundation International, "Hagahai All Patent," *GeneWATCH* 10 (February 1997): 6.

ISSUES IDENTIFIED IN THE SECULAR DEBATE

Initial opposition to human gene patenting within the scientific community focused on two issues. First, because the work on which the patent applications were based did not provide knowledge of the function of the relevant gene sequences, patenting of gene fragments was viewed, at best, as premature. The second source of opposition related to the anticipated negative effects that patenting would have on research and therapeutic applications of the knowledge generated by the HGP.[37] The statement on the patenting of DNA sequences issued by the Human Genome Organisation (HUGO), the international research consortium coordinating and enhancing efforts in genome research, reflects these concerns. According to the statement, HUGO is concerned that

> the patenting of partial and uncharacterized cDNA sequences will reward those who make routine discoveries but penalize those who determine biological function or application. Such an outcome would impede the development of diagnostics and therapeutics, which is clearly not in the public interest. HUGO is also dedicated to the early release of genome information, thus accelerating widespread investigation of functional aspects of genes.[38]

The scientific community is still divided over whether granting patents for DNA sequences will foster or deter research. Some scientists, particularly those affiliated with the Council for Responsible Genetics, state that gene patents work against the tradition of shared knowledge in scientific discovery and do not foster science or help people.[39] Currently, one pharmaceutical giant, Merck, Sharpe and Dohme, which is the source of funding for a major genomic database at Washington University in Saint Louis, argues that genetic sequences should be placed in the public domain and not be subject to patenting. Others in the biotechnology industry, including SmithKline Beecham, the sponsor and owner of another of the three major gene-sequencing databases, are seeking patent protection for their sequences. Nevertheless, Merck has filed for a series of patents on transgenic animals, screening assays, and complementary DNA sequences that have specific therapeutic applications.[40]

A 1998 article raises yet another issue, namely, that the proliferation of gene patents was creating too many concurrent fragments of intellectual property

37. L. Roberts, "Genome Patent Fight Erupts," *Science* 254 (11 October 1991): 184–86.
38. The Human Genome Organisation, "HUGO Statement on Patenting of DNA Sequences" (Bethesda, Md., 1995), 1.
39. "No Patents on Life!" *GeneWATCH* 10 (Special Issue, February 1997).
40. George Poste, "The Case for Genomic Patenting," *Nature* 378 (7 December 1995): 535–36.

rights by different owners and thereby likely to create serious problems for future product development.[41] The authors, Michael Heller and Rebecca Eisenberg, both faculty members at the University of Michigan Law School, invert Garrett Hardin's well-known metaphor of the "tragedy of the commons" to claim that privatization of biomedical and genetic research is producing a "tragedy of an anticommons." Hardin's thesis, published some thirty years earlier, which was that people often overuse resources they own in common because they have no incentive to conserve them,[42] subsequently served as an intellectual justification for advocates of privatizing common property. Heller and Eisenberg argue that privatization can solve one tragedy but in the process produce another, the underutilization of scarce resources, because too many owners can block each other. By conferring monopolies in discoveries, patents necessarily increase prices and restrict use. According to Heller and Eisenberg, the current fragmentation in ownership will require costly future transactions to bundle licenses together before a firm will have the ability to develop new products. Faced with this situation, they anticipate that many firms will choose to invest resources in less-promising projects with fewer licensing obstacles and lower initial start-up costs. Because patents matter more to the pharmaceutical and biotechnology industries, they also foresee that firms in these industries will be less willing to participate in mechanisms like patent pools that can help overcome these problems. Additionally, as they point out, some researchers and developers—universities, for example—may be ill-equipped to handle multiple transactions for acquiring rights to research tools. They therefore conclude that, far from spurring investment and product development, the current situation is more likely to lead to fewer useful products for improving human health.

Various secular ethicists have also raised questions about patenting life-forms. The lack of forums for public discussion has meant that these "debates" occurred primarily in articles published in specialized academic journals, papers presented at professional meetings, and panels held during academic conferences. Given the nature of these settings, it is not surprising that few members of the religious community appear to have been involved or even aware of this work. By late 1993, four sets of concerns had emerged related to the patenting of human DNA sequences.[43] The first issue was the appropriateness of patenting human DNA sequences and other things that exist in nature. The

41. Michael A. Heller and Rebecca S. Eisenberg, "Can Patents Deter Innovation? The Anticommons in Biomedical Research," *Science* 280 (1 May 1998): 698–701.
42. Garrett Hardin, "The Tragedy of the Commons," *Science* 162 (13 December 1968): 1243.
43. Baruch Brody, "Ethical Considerations in Patenting Human DNA Sequences," commissioned by the Office of Technology Assessment (OTA). This article became the

second was the justification for recognizing intellectual property rights over material that is part of humanity's common heritage. The third was whether patenting human DNA sequences is compatible with respect for the dignity of human beings and human life. And the fourth focused on justice concerns, particularly the claim that patents place research and commercial efforts in developing nations at a significant disadvantage.[44] This section now turns to the nature of these discussions.

1. Should there be patents on life?

A significant issue, still being debated, is whether patents or other forms of intellectual property rights should be granted on living things, particularly human genetic material, even if these products are altered in some way through human intervention. As noted above, physical phenomena and products of nature were traditionally considered to be nonpatentable. Accordingly, prior to 1980 there was a general consensus that those who manipulated the powers or mechanisms in nature could not claim any intellectual property rights. A distinction was made between objects designed from simpler materials by reason of a plan or principle and objects simply discovered or produced by applying a process or instrument to natural materials or forces which were not patentable.[45] The former was considered to be an invention and therefore patentable; the latter was not.

In making its decision in the Chakrabarty case, the Supreme Court refused to deal with the central ethical question of whether life should be the subject of patents. Some of the opponents of Chakrabarty's patent claims, specifically, the briefs written for the religious and public interest communities, argued that the Court should examine the effects that patents on life would have on human dignity, human health, and the environment. Unwilling to consider noneconomic values, the Court stated that only Congress was competent to consider such factors or matters of "high policy."[46] Despite the significance of these watershed decisions to patent life—described by one ethicist as "brazen forays into unchartered moral, legal, social, and environmental territory"[47]—

basis for a chapter on ethics in the April 1994 OTA report *The Human Genome Project and Patenting DNA Sequences*. The article itself was never published. Because the status of Brody's article is unclear, citations are from the relevant chapter of the OTA report.
44. OTA, *Human Genome Project*, 4–11. The OTA report groups issues 1 and 2 under one rubric, but I think they are better treated as separate concerns.
45. Mark Sagoff, "Patenting Genetic Resources: A Survey of Normative and Conceptual Issues" (paper written for the AAAS Dialogue Group on Genetic Patenting, 1996).
46. Gold, *Body Parts*, 82–83.
47. Hettinger, "Patenting Life," 269.

there has never been a satisfactory public discussion. The Supreme Court, whose primary concern apparently was to assure economic competitiveness with other countries, did not provide a legal, ethical, or philosophical rationale for its decision. Despite the Court's efforts to shift responsibility to Congress, legislators have not wanted to address the topic of life patents. Moreover, until 1997, the United States did not have a functioning national bioethics commission that could serve as an alternative venue for a wider review, and as of the beginning of 1999 the NBAC has not taken up this issue. To date, therefore, the limited consideration that has taken place has been within narrow academic and professional circles and has focused primarily on legal precedents rather than broader ethical considerations.

In the period since the 1980 Supreme Court decision, much of the debate over the patenting of life has assumed an instrumental frame of reference, but even in a capitalist society there are commodities on which monetary exchanges are blocked, banned, or prohibited. A line of philosophical thinking stresses the moral need to protect certain items from being treated as commodities. Michael Walzer's concept of "blocked exchanges" is useful here. He notes that there are categories of items about which society has determined distribution should not be on an economic basis. His list of fourteen such blocked exchanges, or things that cannot be bought and sold, includes human beings; political power and influence; criminal justice; freedom of speech, press, religion, and assembly; exemptions from military services, jury duty, or other communally imposed work; political offices; and love and friendship.[48] He does not, however, specifically mention genes, human tissue, or body parts, possibly because the book was published in 1983.

The assumption or intuition that there are categories of things which by their very nature should not be treated as commodities has important implications for understanding the nature of property. As Paul Thompson points out, property and ownership are moral precepts encompassing philosophical beliefs as well as legal, economic, and cultural practices. He distinguishes between two basic approaches to property—an instrumental and an ontological frame of reference. An instrumental or utilitarian conception presumes that property itself is a legal fiction, an artifact of a legal code, which is validated to the extent that it is useful in promoting some more fundamental social, political, or economic end. Most advocates of genetic patenting have an instrumental or utilitarian conception of property. They justify granting patents on biological organisms on the grounds that intellectual property rights will bring individual or

48. Michael Walzer, *Spheres of Justice: A Defense of Pluralism and Equality* (New York: Basic Books, 1983), 100–103.

social benefits through promoting research and development of useful medical applications.[49]

Many of the opponents of patenting hold, at least implicitly, what Thompson defines as an ontological conception of property. In contrast with an instrumental or utilitarian perspective, an ontological approach bases property status on traits or characteristics alleged to inhere in specific objects and thereby excludes broad categories of objects from private ownership. Each of the three major forms of ontological reasoning limits property claims. Natural law philosophy stipulates that property be based on traditional practices deemed justified by their obviousness and noncontroversial nature. Labor theory confines property claims to objects that are the product of human work. There is also a broad consensus that ownership of human beings should be prohibited. In addition to excludability, ontological approaches offer two other criteria to consider whether property claims are appropriate. These are the concepts of rivalry, which is whether the use or consumption of the good by one person diminishes the availability for others, and alienability, whether a good can be dissociated from one owner and transferred to another.[50] Thompson also argues that an ontological approach provides strong grounds for rejecting most forms of intellectual property rights claims. He concludes that recombinant DNA techniques particularly challenge the natural law bias against alienating goods from previous patterns of ownership and exchange.[51]

Thompson's distinction between instrumental and ontological approaches to property helps illuminate why the two views on the appropriateness of genetic patents frequently talk past one another. Defenders of patents utilize an instrumental approach, offering a consequentialist-incentive rationale. Industry has long held that intellectual property rights are necessary incentives for major investments in research and development needed to commercialize new products that are of benefit to the public. Its representatives claim that it takes six to eight years, with an average investment of some $300 to $400 million per year, to take a discovery from invention to commercialization. They argue that, to embark on a project of this magnitude, an investor needs assurance that the corporation will be able to recoup its investment. And, a patent provides a monopoly on the marketing of the product, which affords essential protection for such an investment.[52]

49. Paul B. Thompson, "Conceptions of Property and the Biotechnology Debate," *BioScience* 45 (April 1995): 275–57.

50. Ibid., 277–81.

51. Ibid., 278.

52. This is the position put forward in the AAAS Dialogue Group on Genetic Patenting by Alan Goldhammer, of the Biotechnology Industry Corporation, and Patrick Korten, then of the Pharmaceutical Research and Manufacturers of America. See "Brave New World of Biopatents," *Science* 272 (28 June 1996): 1965.

Some opponents of patenting (and the Joint Appeal proponents are includ-ed in this category) try to have it both ways—they attempt to mix an onto-logical and an instrumental approach to property. On the one hand, they have a moral intuition that it is inappropriate to patent life-forms, particularly human tissue and DNA. Nevertheless, they concur with the utilitarian goal of facilitating research and product development and even the premise that indus-try is entitled to financial incentives and rewards. Nor are they willing to take on the industry's claim that patents stimulate investment in the research, devel-opment, and commercialization of new products and therefore contribute to the public benefit. It should be noted, though, that some of those who are con-vinced there is no persuasive reason to forbid the patenting of human genes, and others who believe that it is a settled issue, are still uneasy about the con-sequences.

2. Is it appropriate to grant intellectual property rights over humanity's common heritage?
In a 1991 letter to *Science* magazine, Hubert Currien, then the French Minister for Research and Technology, argued that "it would be prejudicial for scientists to adopt a generalized system of patenting knowledge about the human genome. A patent should not be granted for something that is part of our uni-versal heritage."[53] Ned Hettinger uses a similar line of reasoning to oppose gene patents. He claims that proper appreciation for the three-and-a-half-billion-year story of the development of life on this planet and respect for the processes of evolution and speciation preclude gene patenting. He goes on to observe that

> Just as it is presumptuous to patent laws of nature, so too it is presumptuous to patent genes, which are equally fundamental to nature. Ideally, gene-types should be treated as a common heritage to be used by all beings who may benefit from them. As previously existing, nonexclusive objects that may be used beneficially by everyone at once, no one should possess the right to monopolize gene-types with patents or to "lock up" genes through any other property arrangements.[54]

Article 1 of the Universal Declaration on the Human Genome and Human Rights adopted by the UN General Assembly in December 1998 similarly states, "The human genome underlies the fundamental unity of all members of the human family, as well as the recognition of their inherent dignity and diversity. In a symbolic sense, it is the heritage of humanity."[55]

53. Hubert Currien, "The Human Genome Project and Patents," *Science* 254 (20 December 1991): 1710.
54. Hettinger, "Patenting Life," 286.
55. Universal Declaration on the Human Genome and Human Rights, adopted by the

A paper written for the AAAS publication *Perspectives on Genetic Patenting* by Pilar Ossorio, a geneticist and lawyer, explores common heritage arguments against patenting human DNA.[56] Ossorio distinguishes between two separate legal interpretations of common heritage: the common heritage property doctrine that vests all people or nations with equal property interests and the common heritage duties doctrine based on the idea of heritage as a public or collective concern. The former reflects the interests of less-industrialized countries in attaining equal access to resources and technologies. The second derives from nationalist movements for the preservation of cultural artifacts and the promotion of national identity. This latter form of the doctrine does not so much create a property right in the common heritage as create a duty of preservation and rights of access. She concludes that the second approach may be better suited to promoting the designation of the human genome as our common heritage.[57] Ossorio does caution that such a designation would run the risk of inappropriately reifying the genome and attributing too much significance to the human DNA as an essential component of our humaneness. Moreover, the normative implications of doing so are not particularly clear. Without necessarily ruling out patenting, designating the human genome as our common heritage would qualify the right to exclude others from using the patented resource.

Those who are disturbed by the ability of an individual to claim intellectual property rights over a resource that belongs to the whole of the human community frequently propose some form of public ownership. Advocates of this position often point out that government funds have tended to play a major role in sponsoring the research that has led to these discoveries, and it is contrary to the public interest to then turn over the fruits to a single owner. Some argue that human genes, particularly the human germ line, should be considered as an asset in the common heritage of humankind and propose that it be placed under the same type of international stewardship as the planet's seabed.[58] Another variant is the claim that some genes are of sufficient potential public benefit that a commercial monopoly should be prohibited. Examples are the recent calls for compulsory licensing of patents for detection of the

United Nations General Assembly, December 1998 (http://www.unesco.org/opi/29gencon/eprince.htn).
56. Pilar N. Ossorio, "Common Heritage Arguments and the Patent of Human DNA," in Chapman, ed., *Perspectives on Genetic Patenting,* 89–110.
57. Ibid., 104.
58. These positions are cited in Eric T. Juegst, "A Global Human Resource?" in E. Agius and S. Busuttil, eds., *Germ-Line Intervention and Our Responsibilities to Future Generations* (Great Britain: Kluwer Academic Publishers, 1998): 86–87.

hepatitis C virus in the blood and the use of the BRCA-1 gene in breast cancer screening.[59]

Defenders of gene patenting respond to the common heritage argument by
claiming that private ownership of genes is no different than most private
ownership of property. According to this line of reasoning, all tangible property has some naturally occurring object as its physical basis. Private ownership of genes can be justified in a like manner to all other naturally occurring
objects. If the creation of intellectual property rights over genes unfairly
excludes those who are rendered unable to engage in research or application
of specific genes, it is possible to provide an experimental use exemption.[60]

3. Is recognition of patents compatible with respect for human dignity?
The concept of the inherent dignity of the human person is well established
in both United States and international law and provides the basis for both
international law and the rights enumerated in the Bill of Rights. The
Thirteenth Amendment to the Constitution also prohibits owning and selling
human beings. Some opponents of patenting assume that these protections
should extend to human tissue and body parts as well. A Directive on the
Legal Protection of Biotechnological Inventions approved by the European
Parliament in 1998 instructs member states that "patent law must be applied
so as to respect the fundamental principles safeguarding the dignity and integrity of the person."[61] To fulfill this principle, it excludes the human body, at any
stage of its formation or development, including germ cells and the sequence
or partial sequence of a human gene from patenting, with the caveat that any
such element isolated from the human body or otherwise produced is
patentable.[62]

Proponents of patenting, on the other hand, often distinguish between the
status of human material in the body and outside of it. Even if they recognize
a moral basis for excluding patenting of human material, they claim it does not
extend to patenting *ex vivo* DNA sequences.[63] As noted, the directive was only
meant to cover parts of the human body as found inside the human body. A
proposal by law professor Louis Guenin to resolve the patenting controversy

59. George Post, "The Case for Genomic Patenting," *Nature* 378 (7 December 1995):
535.
60. OTA, *Human Genome Project,* 4–11 through 4–15.
61. "Directive 98/44/EC of the European Parliament and of the Council of 6 July 1998
on the Legal Protection of Biotechnological Inventions," *Official Journal of the European
Communities,* Para.16.
62. Ibid., Paras. 16, 20, 21.
63. This is the position in *Directive* 98/44/EC of the European Parliament.

also differentiates between the moral status of human property claims on substances within and outside of the body.[64]

Some of those who object to patents on the grounds that intellectual property rights impair human dignity do so because of a commitment to preserve human genetic integrity. They anticipate that DNA sequences, once patented, might be altered either to eliminate flaws or to enhance human potential. Here the opposition to eugenics intersects with the patent debate. To respond to the need to preserve human dignity against potential eugenic alteration, the European Community directive would impose a selective ban that prohibits patenting substances and processes for producing human genetic modifications inconsistent with respect for human dignity. The directive excludes the following, without qualification, from patentability: processes for cloning human beings, processes for modifying the germ-line genetic identity of human beings, and uses of human embryos for industrial or commercial purposes.[65]

Does protecting human dignity require treating human biological materials as blocked exchanges, that is, something that cannot be commodified and thereby be owned and sold? It is relevant to note that there is a tradition, supported by philosophical and ethical thinking, of moral opposition to the ownership and sale of human parts. Beginning with the collection of blood for transfusions, measures have been taken to protect against the development of a market in human body parts and organs. There is a consensus that human organs required for transplants should be obtained through donation as a gift. It is argued that allowing an organ market to develop would place pressure on poor people to make organs available, as indeed has occurred in some countries, enabling the affluent to exploit poor and vulnerable individuals. Claims are also made that allowing a market to develop in human biological material might undermine social bonds. While individuals are sometimes paid for the collection of blood or semen, such payment, from a legal perspective, is considered to be for services rendered, and not remuneration for the commodity itself.[66]

A 1988 report by an Office of Technology Assessment (OTA) Task Force determined that while current law permits the sale of replenishing cells, such as blood and semen, the law does not endorse such transactions or characterize such transactions as involving property.[67] After considering the traditional relationships between donors and researchers in obtaining samples, the report

64. Louis M. Guenin, "Norms for Patenting Life Forms," *Theoretical Medicine* 17 (month not given, 1996): 279–314.
65. "Directive 98/44/EC," Paras. 40, 41.
66. OTA, *Human Genome Project,* 4–17 and 4–18.
67. Office of Technology Assessment (OTA), *New Developments in Biotechnology: Ownership of Human Tissues and Cells* (Philadelphia: J. B. Lippincott Co., 1988), 9.

stated that there does not appear to be movement away from the existing system of free donations of human biological materials for use in research and commerce in biotechnology.[68] On the question as to whether the human body and its parts are fit objects for commerce, that is, things that may properly be bought and sold, the report concluded that it depended on positions regarding the status of the body. The acceptability of commercialization of the human body seemed to depend primarily on whether one held a dualistic view of the separation between the body and mind or not.[69] It pointed out that all three major religious traditions in the United States—Jewish, Catholic, and Protestant—generally believe that there are limits on what human beings can do with their own bodies and those of others and therefore prefer the transfer of human biological materials as gifts.[70]

The question as to whether patenting human genes is wrong because it diminishes human dignity was the subject of a paper philosopher Baruch Brody wrote for the AAAS Dialogue Group on Genetic Patenting.[71] Brody acknowledges that it is perfectly appropriate to limit intellectual property rights in human genes when necessary to preserve human dignity, but he does not believe that most objections to human gene patenting warrant doing so. After analyzing a variety of concerns raised, he identifies only two that he considers to put forward valid criticisms. Drawing on an analysis by Judge Byk, the secretary general of the International Association of Law Ethics and Science, Brody recommends that applications to patent an entire set of genes should be rejected, if ever proposed, because of human dignity considerations. The second, related to protecting against eugenics, justifies not allowing the patenting of genetic modifications that are incompatible with human dignity. Otherwise he does not find sound reasons to reject the patenting of a specific human gene on the grounds that it is incompatible with protecting human dignity.

4. Will granting patents on life-forms disadvantage poor countries?

The 1991 letter from Hubert Currien to *Science* magazine, cited above, anticipated that patenting would have distributive justice implications because it "would increase costs and penalize low-budget research teams and countries with fragile economies."[72] These concerns mirror an ongoing debate on the implications of plant genetic engineering for the global South. Questions

68. Ibid., 13.
69. Ibid., 15, 143.
70. Ibid., 14, 137–43.
71. Baruch Brody, "Protecting Human Dignity and the Patenting of Human Genes" (paper written for the AAAS Dialogue Group on Genetic Patenting, 9 May 1997), in Chapman, ed., *Perspectives on Genetic Patenting,* 111–26.
72. Curren, "The Human Genome and Patents," 1710.

about life as intellectual property, ownership of seeds, control of plant genomes, and the appropriateness of patenting new plant varieties have been considered.[73] In addition to the concern that intellectual property rights will exacerbate economic disparity between the global North and the South, there are other equity considerations. Organizations like the Canada-based Indigenous People's Biodiversity Network and the Rural Advancement Foundation International have criticized patents as inappropriately conferring benefits on researchers from industrialized countries to the exclusion of the source or owners of the tissue in the Third World.[74] Here the debate intersects concerns raised by the Human Genome Diversity Project, a proposal to collect and store blood samples from a wide range of ethnic groups to be able to study characteristics of these groups before patterns of migration and intermarriage and eliminate differences among them. Public interest groups claim that this project infringes on the rights and beliefs of many of the targeted groups and fails to conform to appropriate procedures for informed consent.[75]

On the other side, proponents of patenting claim that neither developed nor developing countries will benefit from genetic discoveries unless incentives exist to develop commercial products.[76] Others take refuge in market theory claiming that people in developing countries can decide not to purchase patented products if they consider the cost too high. This argument, however, ignores the substantial constraint that poverty imposes.[77] Yet another approach is trying to assure that the source of the material be granted financial benefit from potential profits arising from research on their genetic endowments.[78]

THEOLOGICAL ISSUES

This section reviews the major theological issues raised by discussions of genetic patenting in the religious community. Limitations of the sources, noted in the introduction, should be kept in mind.

73. See, for example, Calestous Juma, *The Gene Hunters: Biotechnology and the Scramble for Seeds* (Princeton, N.J.: Princeton University Press, 1989), and Robert Walgate, *Miracle or Menace: Biotechnology and the Third World* (Budapest, London, Paris, Washington: Panos Institute, 1990), for two different perspectives.
74. See various articles in *GeneWATCH* 10 (October 1996).
75. Craig Benjamin, "Indigenous Peoples Barred from DNA Sampling Conference," *GeneWATCH* 10 (February 1997): 5, 18.
76. Bernadine Healy, "On Gene Patenting," *New England Journal of Medicine* 327 (1992): 664–68.
77. OTA, *New Developments in Biotechnology*, 4–24.
78. Sagoff, "Patenting Genetic Resources," 17.

God's Ownership of Life

Of all of the various concerns put forward by religious opponents of patenting, the insistence that "humans and animals are creations of God, not humans, and as such should not be patented as human inventions"[79] is central. The 1984 United Methodist resolution, cited above, bases its position on genetic patenting on the sanctity of God's creation and God's ownership of life. Distributed with the text of the Joint Appeal, a statement by Kenneth Carder, Resident Methodist Bishop of the Nashville Area and then chair of the denomination's Genetic Science Task Force, reiterates that genetic science and technologies "raise fundamental questions about the nature and purpose of life and the meaning and implication of the sovereignty of the Creator God."[80] Richard Land, president of the Southern Baptist Convention's Christian Life Commission and another leader in the Joint Appeal campaign, claims that granting patents on genes or organisms "represents the usurpation of the ownership rights of the Sovereign of the universe."[81] An article by Richard Land and C. Ben Mitchell, written after the Joint Appeal, describes human beings as preowned and belonging to the sovereign Creator.[82]

Mitchell explains his theology of patenting in greater detail in another article written for the AAAS Dialogue Group on Genetic Patenting.[83] The article makes a careful distinction between the role of God, the true Inventor of every living creature, and the contribution of the scientist, who at best reorganizes or manipulates some of the genes. According to Mitchell, the oncomouse was not a human creation. Scientists involved merely inserted an oncogene into the mouse. The very notion that life can be a human invention reveals scientific and legislative hubris. It also constitutes a blatant form of scientific and philosophical naturalism that should be repugnant to any theist. Moreover, patenting biological materials as the stuff of human artifice risks obscuring the revelation of God in the created order. Patenting human beings or human body parts (genes, cells, cell lines, and other tissues) is doubly problematic because it also violates human dignity. Mitchell claims—without clarifying the basis—that

79. General Board of Church and Society, "Joint Appeal Against Human and Animal Patenting."

80. Bishop Kenneth L. Carder, "Statement on Patenting of Genes" (letter issued by the General Board on Church and Society of the United Methodist Church, 18 May 1995).

81. Stone, "Religious Leaders Oppose Patenting."

82. Richard D. Land and C. Ben Mitchell, "Brave New Biopatents," *First Things: A Monthly Journal of Religion and Public Life* (May 1996): 21.

83. C. Ben Mitchell, "A Southern Baptist Looks at Patenting Life" (paper written for the AAAS Dialogue Group on Genetic Patenting and presented 13 March 1997). A slightly revised version of the paper is published in Chapman, ed., *Perspectives on Genetic Patenting*, 167–86.

"the right to own one part of a human being is ceteris paribus the right to own all the parts of a human being."[84] As an extension of this reasoning, he opines that the ability to patent human genes amounts to a form of slavery or subjugation contrary to Thirteenth Amendment protections.

This line of reasoning seems problematic in several regards. It seems to be based on a novel and untraditional concept of God's role as owner of the creation, discussed below. It also appears to reflect a preevolutionary view of the world that assumes that the nature and purpose of all species were clearly fixed by God at their moment of creation. This static conception of nature is quite out of keeping with modern science and, for that matter, the dynamic and fluid understanding of the interplay between God, evolution, and human initiative put forward by many contemporary theologians. While Land and Mitchell argue that patenting infringes on God's prerogatives, they refrain from dealing with the wider implications of genetic engineering. As theologian Ronald Cole-Turner comments, the religious affirmation that God is the creator has traditionally meant that God defines the purpose of all creatures, species, and individuals. Given this belief, the action of producing a transgenic animal to redefine its purpose, for example, the oncomouse engineered to develop cancer neoplasms, would seem to be a more serious infringement on God's claims (or evolution) than patenting, which at most can exclude others from also taking the action.[85] Therefore, if the Joint Appeal's theological arguments were compelling, it would require the religious community to go beyond biological patenting and to oppose genetic engineering and all commercialization of biology. The religious community is not on record as doing so. To the contrary, as noted in chapter 2, most religious bodies are favorably inclined toward genetic engineering.

Does affirming God as sovereign creator preclude recognition of some, but not all, forms of intellectual property rights? Is the claim that God is the exclusive owner of life consistent with traditional theological affirmations? Virtually all theists, including those on both sides of this debate, acknowledge God as the creator and, in some sense, the ultimate owner of the universe. The theme that creation is the Lord's and humans are but the stewards caring for the earth and its inhabitants appears in many passages of the Old Testament and figures prominently in various forms of contemporary environmental theology. According to Rabbi Daniel Swartz, the premise that "you and what you possess are God's (Avot 3:7)" underlies most of Talmudic thinking about

---

84. Ibid., 178.
85. Ronald Cole-Turner, "Theological Perspectives on the Status of DNA: A Contribution to the Debate over Genetic Patenting," in Chapman, ed., *Perspectives on Genetic Patenting*, 153.

the environment.[86] Or, as this foundational belief is also often stated: "God owns everything in the world: we are but tenants in the garden meant to till and to tend, to serve and to guard."[87] Stewardship obligations have obvious implications for property ownership and use. Yet these affirmations are usually interpreted to vest humanity with the responsibility to respect and conserve nature, and in the case of the sabbatical year and the Jubilee, to allow the land to lie fallow, not to exclude human property ownership.[88] In the biblical period, God's ultimate ownership of the creation did not even prevent the ownership of other human beings, despite the acknowledgment that persons were created in the image of God.

Cole-Turner offers an understanding of God's ownership that varies significantly with the theology of the Joint Appeal and one that seems more consistent with mainstream Christian theologies. Cole-Turner takes issue with the position of the Joint Appeal. His view is that God's ownership right does not entail exclusion or domination, but instead the right to define the purpose and value of each creature, as well as to define the moral relationship among creatures.[89] He also points out that God's "ownership" differs considerably from human conceptions based on property relationships.

> God owns all things, not in an exclusive sense, but precisely in the opposite way, that is, to give all the goodness of creation as gifts to be shared by all creatures. God's ownership of all things is best understood as God's reserving the right to define their purpose, value, and relationship to other creatures. God owns the land, not to exclude creatures from it, but to give it for their right use and to set the limits of proper use and care. For example, we are not to leave others destitute or deny habitat to other species. Human beings may own individual animals and plants, and these or their products may be bought, sold, and used for food. That is, we may own these things as long as God's prior claim of ownership is acknowledged, which is to say, as long as we own them in a way that is consistent with God's definition of their purpose. . . . God's ownership does not exclude but relativizes and qualifies human ownership.[90]

86. Daniel Swartz, "Jews, Jewish Texts, and Nature: A Brief History," in Roger S. Gottlieb, *This Sacred Earth: Religion, Nature, Environment* (New York and London: Routledge, 1996), 488.

87. Ibid.

88. For theologies of stewardship see Douglas John Hall, *The Steward: A Biblical Symbol Comes of Age* (New York: Friendship Press, 1983) and *Imaging God: Dominion as Stewardship* (Grand Rapids, Mich.: Wm. B. Eerdmans Publishing Co. and New York: Friendship Press, 1986).

89. Cole-Turner, "Theological Perspectives on the Status of DNA," 152–55.

90. Ibid., 152.

Cole-Turner argues that there should be no theological objection to biological patents as long as individuals and corporations exercise their intellectual property rights in a way that is consistent with the purposes God defines.

Theologian Ted Peters, another critic, questions how theologically and factually sound it is to draw a sharp distinction between divine creation and products of human invention. As he points out, it is often difficult to delineate the boundaries, particularly in regard to the many instances in which humans alter what exists in nature. Therefore Peters finds the Joint Appeal theology objectionable because it separates divine from human creativity and does not recognize sufficiently the various forms of God's ongoing creativity in the creation. Building on Philip Hefner's concept of the human being as God's created co-creator, Peters suggests that one might include not only evolutionary history but also the evolutionary development of the human genome as a testimony to divine creativity. One implication would be that human intelligence and creativity, one mark of which is the ability of the human being to alter itself, would be understood as a vehicle through which the divine acts in creation. Peters concludes, "It is misleading to argue that technological intervention into the cell line of a life form, even a human life form, lies outside the realm of God's creation."[91]

Dignity and Worth of Human Life
In making the claim that patenting human DNA and tissue demeans human life and human dignity, the religious community echoes concerns raised in the secular community. Moreover, given the commitment to the value of the human person in Western religious tradition, a concern with the implications of patents on human dignity is understandable. Both Christianity and Judaism conceptualize the human person as the *imago Dei,* a representation of a divine creator. The affirmation of humanity as the image of God plays an important role in the thinking of at least some of the opponents of patenting.[92]

Nevertheless, the affirmation of humanity as the image of God does not in and of itself provide a clear grounding for opposing patenting of altered human tissue or DNA fragments. One of the complexities in discussions of this issue is that conceptions and interpretations of the phrase "image of God" have differed dramatically. Theologian Douglas John Hall has shown that through the centuries commentators have had a conspicuous tendency to identify those traits or gifts that are valued by their particular culture as the central meaning of the phrase.[93] Moreover, the acknowledgment of human dignity and even the

91. Ted Peters, "Should We Patent God's Creation?" *Dialog* 35 (Spring 1996): 122.
92. Land and Mitchell, "Brave New Biopatents," 20–21.
93. Hall, *Imaging God,* 88–112.

sacredness of persons have not precluded religious acceptance of slavery, the death penalty, war, or unspeakable forms of abuse and torture.

Even if the premise is accepted that human sacredness is incompatible with the patenting of whole human beings, body parts, and organs, it may not hold that this restriction also applies to gene fragments and altered human cells when they are outside of the body. As noted above, Brody's paper, written from a secular philosophical perspective, concluded that patenting gene fragments, single genes, or even connected sequences of human genes did not infringe on human dignity. He did, however, take issue with any attempts to patent an entire person's genome or to use patenting for eugenic purposes.[94] Land and Mitchell acknowledge that a single human gene or cell line is not a human being, but by virtue of being undeniably human, they believe that a human gene or cell line warrants different treatment than all nonhuman genes or cell lines. The image of God pervades the human person in all its parts, they claim, and furthermore the right to own any part of a human being "must not be transferred from the Creator to the creature."[95]

Their reasoning, however, fails to make clear why this is so. How do they or others define the specific content of the *imago Dei* and link it to the patenting issue? If God's ultimate ownership is affirmed, why can't this ownership be shared? Presumably an individual holds some kind of proprietary rights over his or her body. Why specifically should God's role as creator preclude some form of property rights over fragments of a human cell or DNA when outside of the body? How can claims of the distinctiveness and sacredness of human DNA be justified when human beings share up to 98 percent of their DNA with other forms of life, particularly chimpanzees? Given the centrality of this argument to the theology of the Joint Appeal, it deserves a much clearer and more developed exposition.

Ted Peters deals with some of these issues in a paper written for the AAAS dialogue group. His view is that the patenting of a portion of DNA does not threaten any individual person's dignity because the concept of intrinsic worth applies to the person as a whole, not to any parts or knowledge of parts. Peters opposes the rush to patent human DNA, but on other grounds. He acknowledges that DNA sequences deserve a certain level of respect due to the vital role they play in sustaining life and contributing to our identity. In contrast with Land and Mitchell, he argues, though, that DNA is general knowledge of the physiological makeup of humans. Peters also underscores that human identity is not determined solely by genetics. "Each of us is more than our genome, and dignity applies to who we are as a whole human being."[96]

94. Brody, "Protecting Human Dignity," 111–26.
95. Land and Mitchell, "Brave New Biopatents," 20–21.
96. Peters, "DNA and Dignity," 134.

A related theme in the religious critique is that patenting demeans life by commodifying it. A statement by Bishop Kenneth Carder warns, "The patenting of genes, the building blocks of life, tends to reduce it to its economic worth." His statement continues with the observation that "the conflict is between reverence for life and exploitation of life, life valued for its marketability and life valued as an intrinsic gift."[97] Using more colorful language, Land was quoted in newspapers as saying, "Marketing human life is a form of genetic slavery. Instead of whole persons being marched in shackles to the market block, human cell lines and gene sequences are labeled, patented and sold to the highest bidders."[98] These concerns are widely shared in the religious community. Even critics of the Joint Appeal process and theology resonate with Carder's warning that patenting will transform life into a commodity whose value will be determined by commercial considerations. Peters, for example, acknowledges that the relationship between the dignity of living beings and the patenting of intellectual knowledge is a delicate one. He goes on to state that "the Joint Appeal may have done the public a service by alerting us once again to the danger of commercializing life."[99]

Will patenting of human DNA and tissues promote commodification? Margaret Jane Radin, a legal theorist, defines commodification as the social process by which something previously valued in a noneconomic manner comes to be understood as a commodity, that is, the appropriate subject of free market transactions. According to Radin, commodification "assimilates personal attributes, relations, and desired states of affairs to the realm of objects by assuming that all human attributes are possessions bearing a value characterizable in monetary terms and by implying that all these possessions can and should be separable from persons to be exchanged through the free market."[100] She distinguishes between literal or narrow, broad or metaphorical senses of commodification. In the narrow sense commodification describes events in which material goods and economic services are literally bought and sold. Commodification also encompasses a worldview that conceives of human attributes as fungible, owned objects even where no money literally changes hands.[101] Much like the religious critics of patenting, Radin believes that the way we conceive of things matters to who we are. She concurs that a commodified view of personhood undermines a Kantian conception of the person as an end

97. Carder, "Statement on Patenting of Genes."
98. Quoted in Peters, "Should We Patent God's Creation?" 117.
99. Ibid., 123.
100. Margaret Jane Radin, *Contested Commodities: The Trouble with Trade in Sex, Children, Body Parts, and Other Things* (Cambridge, Mass., and London: Harvard University Press, 1996), 6.
101. Ibid., 12–13.

in itself.[102] Her book *Contested Commodities* offers a trenchant criticism of trade in sex, children, and body parts. Nevertheless, Radin recognizes that commodification is not an all-or-nothing process. She offers the useful concept of incomplete commodification, a situation in which only one segment of society accepts a commodified understanding. Similarly, she points out the possibilities for the coexistence of commodified and noncommodified understandings in a society or even in a single person.[103]

Mark Hanson uses Radin's categories to show how the genetic patenting debate relates to both Radin's narrow and broad conceptions of commodification.[104] On one level patents may be seen as related to the narrow sense of commodification, the actual buying and selling of material goods and economic services, because they literally enable the commercialization of and possible monetary transactions involving genes and other biological material. Religious concerns about a kind of "slippery slope" are that market rhetoric once applied to genes and tissue may be contagious and lead to further literal commodification of human beings. Nevertheless, he suspects, quite rightly, that what is really at stake in the religious objection to patenting, independent of any claims about God's ownership, is Radin's broader conception of commodification. Namely, religious opponents of patenting DNA assume that it will promote a worldview that reduces all things to commodities subject to market exchange. Here he notes the criticism of Rabbi Saperstein speaking broadly on behalf of religious critics "that patenting would lead to the most fundamental degradation of all—the turning of all nature, perhaps even humanity itself, into an ownable market commodity."[105]

The question as to whether gene patenting necessarily promotes commodification is an important one, and an issue on which two legal scholars who deal with the topic disagree. A recent study of legal decisions related to property rights and the ownership of human biological materials argues that property discourse—that is, the sum of the assumptions, conceptions, and language used by judges, lawyers, and legislators in allocating rights of control over goods—promotes economic modes of valuation. Property discourse, such as patent regimes, does so because the assumption that proprietary goods are best allocated through the market is implicit. Thus, E. Richard Gold, the author of the book *Body Parts,* argues that making any commodity, including human biological material, subject to property claims will translate its valuation into a market

102. Ibid., 92.
103. Ibid., 102–3.
104. Mark J. Hanson, "Religious Voices in Biotechnology: The Case of Gene Patenting," *The Hastings Center Report* 27 (November/December 1997): S10–11.
105. David Saperstein, "Press Release of the Religious Action Center of Reform Judaism," 18 May 1995, quoted in Hanson, "Religious Voices in Biotechnology," 15.

price. Moreover, he claims that market modes of valuation preempt other more authentic and meaningful forms of valuation, such as valuing human DNA, blood, or tissue as inherently valuable in themselves and as being instrumentally valuable in aiding human health. He therefore concludes that safeguarding noneconomic values related to the human body requires that human biological materials be treated as nonproprietary goods. To this end, he recommends constructing a method of allocating rights of control over these materials that takes both economic and noneconomic modes of valuation into account, but does not offer the specifics of such a scheme.[106] Radin's proposal about incomplete commodification suggests otherwise. She believes it is possible to have commodified and noncommodified conceptions side by side without one necessarily overriding the other. Because neither Gold nor Radin draws on extensive empirical data, however, it is difficult to evaluate their conclusions.

The Ontological and Metaphysical Status of DNA

What is the moral, ontological, and metaphysical status of DNA? Is this biological sequence of DNA, which serves as the unit of heredity and carries the information that helps to form living cells and tissues, sacred? Religious critics of patenting imply that it is. Or, is DNA merely a complex molecule deserving no more or less respect than other organic chemicals? Representatives of the biotechnology industry generally describe genes and DNA as mere chemical compounds. Several theologians critical of the Joint Appeal initiative have argued against vesting DNA, even human DNA, with a sacred status. Writing in *Science* magazine, Cole-Turner asserted that "there is no metaphysical difference between DNA and other complex chemicals. Therefore, there is no distinctly religious ground for objecting to patenting of DNA."[107] He also claims that vesting DNA with sacred status amounts to a form of vitalism. He does so on the basis that to argue for the sacredness of life amounts to a form of vitalism. According to Cole-Turner, theists believe that only God is sacred, and not God's creation.[108] I disagree with his position on the sacredness of life, as do many Christian thinkers writing on environmental topics, but then again Cole-Turner would undoubtedly label us as vitalists for doing so.

To assess the various claims and counterclaims, it is necessary to consider four distinct issues: First, what is implied by describing something as sacred? Second, is the claim that something within God's creation is sacred incompat-

106. Gold, Body Parts.
107. Cole-Turner, "Religion and Gene Patenting."
108. Cole-Turner, "Theological Perspectives on the Status of DNA," 157–63.

ible with a theistic theology? Third, is it appropriate to vest DNA with sacred status? And fourth, does the belief that DNA is sacred imply that DNA is the source of human personhood and result in a reductionist conception of human nature?

While labeling something sacred carries so much import to people of faith, it is rarely conceptualized clearly. Ronald Dworkin, a secular philosopher, links the idea of the sacred to the concept of intrinsic worth, much as Bishop Carder did in his statement. Dworkin distinguishes between three modes of valuation: instrumental value, derived from the usefulness of an object, subjective value, where value attaches only to people who happen to desire an object, and intrinsic value, which considers something as important in itself.[109] According to Dworkin, "Something is sacred or inviolable when its deliberate destruction would dishonor what ought to be honored."[110] He identifies two processes through which something becomes sacred for a given culture or person. The first is by association or designation, when the respect owed to one entity, a nation, for instance, is transferred onto a symbol, such as its flag. The second is through the history of an object and what it comes to represent or embody.

Life, particularly human life, is widely regarded in Western culture as having intrinsic worth. Virtually all adherents of the dominant Western religious traditions would most likely affirm Bishop Carder's statement, some perhaps only in reference to human persons, that "life is a sacred gift from God the Creator. As a gift from God, life has intrinsic value."[111] The fundamental principle of the dignity and intrinsic worth of each individual undergirds international human rights norms and the United States constitutional and legal systems. If Dworkin's premise that the recognition of an object's intrinsic worth confers sacred status is accepted, then there is a consensus that human life is sacred. To pursue Dworkin's reasoning a bit further, recognition of the intrinsic worth of human life comes about through two different paths, both by association and by the value it has come to represent and embody. The sanctity of human life first reflects our relationship to the Creator and the belief that human life is the highest achievement of God's creation, or in the case of non-believers, the most significant product of the process of evolution. As God's masterpiece, our status and worth are partially derived through our association with the author of life. The ideal that human life has intrinsic dignity and purpose is also rooted, like our concern for the survival of our species, in the complex creative investment each human organism represents, in the human capac-

109. Ronald Dworkin, *Life's Dominion: An Argument about Abortion, Euthanasia, and Individual Freedom* (New York: Alfred A. Knopf, 1993), 71–72.
110. Ibid., 74.
111. Carder, "Statement on Patenting of Genes."

ity for creativity, reason, and judgment, and in the empathy and communion we have with every other person.[112]

Moreover, acknowledgment of the intrinsic worth of all life, just not human life, goes far beyond those who are vitalists to many theists as well. One of the major contributions of environmental theology and ethics is to transcend the anthropocentrism inherent in modern Christian theology so as to recapture the biblical vision of the sacredness of all of life. Christian environmental theology, along with deep ecology, affirms the intrinsic worth of all life. For some theologians, particularly those who might be categorized as pantheists, respect for life is bound up with God's continuing presence in the creation. Ethicists like James Nash write about all creatures having intrinsic value as independent expressions of divine activity, with the qualification that intrinsic value does not mean equal value.[113] Even in a secular context there has been a wide acceptance of the idea of reverence for all forms of life. Dworkin, for example, points out that in our culture we tend to consider animal species, although not individual animals, as sacred and therefore worth considerable economic expense to protect from destruction at human hands or by human enterprise. He relates the concern for preservation to respect for the way animal species came into being as well as the status of the animals considered independently of that history. According to Dworkin, both religious believers who acknowledge life as a gift of a divine creator and secularists who understand life as the outcome of a random evolutionary process now consider it a mark of cosmic shame for a species to become extinct through human actions.[114]

If it is consistent with theism to consider human persons and/or life as sacred, is it appropriate also to confer sacred status to DNA? Here it is relevant to note that a recent book by Dorothy Nelkin and M. Susan Lindee, *The DNA Mystique,* documents that the gene has become "a cultural icon, a symbol, almost a magical force."[115] The authors conclude that DNA images and narratives of DNA in popular culture convey a message that they term genetic essentialism. "Genetic essentialism reduces the self to a molecular entity, equating human beings, in all their social, historical, and moral complexity, with their genes" (2). According to Nelkin and Lindee, DNA functions in many respects as a secular equivalent of the medieval Christian conception of the immortal soul. It is considered to contain the essential human self, to be the

112. Dworkin, *Life's Dominion,* 81–84.
113. James Nash, *Loving Nature: Ecological Integrity and Christian Responsibility* (Nashville: Abingdon Press, 1991), 181.
114. Ibid., 74–81.
115. Dorothy Nelkin and M. Susan Lindee, *The DNA Mystique: The Gene as a Cultural Icon* (New York: W. H. Freeman, 1995), 2.

source of individual difference, moral order, and human fate, and to promise a form of eternal life, either through progeny or through the body reconstituted by scientific manipulation of DNA (39). They locate the origins of this genetic essentialism to the metaphors geneticists and other biologists use to describe DNA, namely, the "Bible," the "Book of Man," and the "Holy Grail." Nelkin and Lindee identify three themes in the images that scientists use: the characterization of the gene as the basis of identity, an anticipation that genetic research will enhance prediction of human behavior and health, and an image of the genome as a text that will define a natural order (4). Their book raises profound questions about both genetic essentialism's implications on responsibility and accountability and whether the cultural construction of genes portends eugenic social policy.

Does the Joint Appeal theology reflect the genetic essentialism of the underlying culture, or does it derive from their theological analysis? The paucity of serious theological analysis on the nature of DNA from participants in the Joint Appeal makes it difficult to answer that question in a meaningful way. Religious critics of genetic patenting appear to vest genes with a special kind of intrinsic value, possibly even a sacred status, that makes patenting inappropriate. But their grounds for doing so are not clear.

THE JOINT APPEAL AS PUBLIC THEOLOGY

Before proceeding, it may be appropriate for me to outline briefly my own perspective on these issues. I tend to be sympathetic with the intuition that it is inappropriate to patent life-forms, but I also concur with many of the criticisms and theological analyses of critics of the Joint Appeal. As someone who has affinities to process theology, my unease with patenting reflects concerns that treating life-forms as commodities is inconsistent with their sacredness and dignity. At the same time, however, I consider patenting to be a secondary issue, more a manifestation of policies that wrongly encourage the privatization and commercialization of biology. Although I consider the 1980 Supreme Court decision and subsequent PTO policy to be a mistake, I also realize it is too late to turn back the clock. Even the European Parliament, long a holdout, has recently approved a directive that will permit the patenting of genes and genetically modified animals under specific conditions. Therefore, I am inclined to focus on modifying the patent system, specifically to limit the scope and type of patents that can be issued and to advocate for the European model of incorporating ethical criteria in making determinations of patent eligibility. Moreover, I think it is important to distinguish between categories of patenting life-forms. I am more opposed to the patenting of whole animals, human tissue, or (if they are ever at issue) human organs and body parts than I am to the patenting of DNA because I do not view gene fragments or genes, human or otherwise, as having equal moral status.

Like many other religious critics of the Joint Appeal, I also have serious problems with the manner in which the Joint Appeal campaign proceeded. While I acknowledge that the Joint Appeal raised legitimate concerns that deserve further attention, the manner in which it did so detracted from its objectives and violated key elements of the way I believe public theology should be conducted. Here it is relevant to note that my view about the requirements for public theology derives from nearly ten years of experience as a staff member in a national religious agency, the United Church Board for World Ministries, involved with the formulation of several public theology initiatives. The Joint Appeal typifies an approach to public theology of which I became increasingly critical during my tenure there.

First, I believe that public theology should proceed from a clear religious rationale and sense of priority within the religious communions who are speaking to the wider society. Opponents of patenting did provide a religious grounding, but the Joint Appeal did not build on a long-term and consistent concern with patenting issues in the religious community. As described in the opening of the chapter, groups within the religious community have raised the issue on several occasions, particularly at an ecumenical level, but then dropped it for long periods of time. At the time of the Joint Appeal, very few of the communions who participated had explicit policy on this issue. Far from there being a consensus in the religious community over patenting, many religious analysts, even those knowledgeable and concerned about genetic engineering, argue that the patenting of life-forms is peripheral to the real issues faced by the religious community.[116] Others find it strange that the Joint Appeal raised issues about patenting but not about the uses to which genetically engineered life-forms are applied. As noted, critics of the Joint Appeal disagreed fundamentally with both its position and its theological rationale.

To be able to speak for rather than to the religious community, public theology should represent the views of a strong cross section of members of a faith communion, not just its leadership. To this end, it requires systematic education and wide-ranging consultations. Although the leaders who were signatories of the Joint Appeal purported to represent their communities, it seems highly unlikely that they went through an appropriate process. Indeed, most do not appear to have even consulted staff or theologians who are knowledgeable about genetics. And, while the Methodists and eventually the Baptists had the

---

116. Robert Brungs, S.J., "Biotechnology and Patenting: A Catholic Perspective," in *Patenting of Biological Entities: Proceedings of the ITEST Workshop, October 1996* (St. Louis: ITEST Faith/Science Press, 1997), 50–51.

legitimacy of acting in accordance with denominational policy, they did not prepare their members in advance of making a public statement or apparently seek broad membership support for their initiative.

Second, to be appropriate, public theology should be timely. The Joint Appeal lacked context and therefore was problematic. Although the Joint Appeal referred to a recent PTO decision as a rationale for the statement, the press release accompanying the text of the statement cited the 1987 PTO decree which extended patentability to genetically engineered animals.[117] By the time the religious campaign against gene patents was launched, eight years had elapsed since that decree. Hundreds of patents had already been granted, with thousands more pending. Thus, the initiative certainly was not timely, and it came far too late to change fundamental policy directions. It would have made more sense for the initiative to come in 1980 or 1987 as a response to the landmark decisions to go forward with patenting life, or in 1991 after the NIH first sought patents for its human gene fragments. Certainly, if the religious community had delayed all this time, it should have come forward with far more than a poorly formulated three-sentence statement, not to mention a better explanation of why the religious community was now moving into the public arena.

What motivated the organizers to proceed in 1995? According to Jaydee Hanson, assistant general secretary of the United Methodist Board of Church and Society and a key organizer of the initiative, the campaign was originally scheduled to mark the twentieth anniversary of the Asilomar Conference, but it was delayed.[118] It seems perfectly appropriate for those working on genetic issues within the religious community to commemorate the Asilomar Conference, the event at which scientists established a voluntary moratorium on recombinant DNA research until guidelines could be established by NIH, but its direct relevance to patenting ranges from tenuous to nonexistent. When the Asilomar anniversary passed by without an event, the United Methodist Church took the initiative of contacting Rifkin and other religious groups, and Rifkin then played a key role in building the coalition. Whatever the specific impetus, the Joint Appeal needs to be viewed in the broader framework of the virtual nonexistence of a meaningful ethical discussion of genetic patenting issues in public policy forums.

The members of a Bioethics Working Group of the European Ecumenical Commission for Church and Society, a combination of scientists, ethicists, and

117. General Board of Church and Society, "Joint Appeal."
118. Jaydee Hanson, Assistant General Secretary of the United Methodist Board of Church and Society, relayed this information at the first meeting of the AAAS Dialogue Group on Genetic Patenting, December 1995.

theologians representing Protestant, Anglican, and some Orthodox churches in Europe, also issued a statement opposing patenting in March 1997, but they did so in a far more timely and appropriate manner. In 1996 the European Parliament began considering a draft patenting directive that would update the 1973 European Patent Convention. Proposals, subsequently approved in principle by the members of the European Parliament, advocated changing the existing policy and permitting the patenting of genes and genetically modified animals under specific conditions. To have religious input into the debate, the working group made a detailed submission to the European Parliament and European Ecumenical Commission in October 1996, and when it appeared that there were some misunderstandings, the working group wrote a note of clarification the following month. The text of its statement was issued publicly the following March. The Church of Scotland General Assembly then adopted a slightly shortened and simplified version of the October submission in May 1997.[119]

Third, it is important that public theology be well reasoned, informed, and understandable to persons within both the religious and the secular community. When public theology appeals to theological beliefs, even when the beliefs are not widely shared, the logical relationship between the beliefs and the conclusions should be comprehensible to believer and nonbeliever alike.[120] To be compelling, public theology should exhibit knowledge of relevant research and data related to the subject it is addressing. This is particularly relevant when the public theology relates to science and technology. Otherwise the religious voices will lack credibility. Here it is relevant to note that religious participants in the genetic patenting debate were not well informed about the specifics of patent law and this undercut their public standing. Moreover, few of them appeared to be knowledgeable about the secular literature, even the ethicists from whom they could have drawn support. This is not surprising since much of the work on this subject is specialized and published in law journals, and religious ethicists, theologians, and denominational staff members generally do not read these publications, but it is unfortunate. Further, leadership on the patenting issue debate came primarily from staff members of religious agencies with responsibility for social justice issues rather than theologians and ethicists, and social activists are less likely to read academic literature.

119. "Official Church of Scotland Motion on Patenting and Text of Talk to MPs from the Bioethics Working Group of the European Ecumenical Commission for Church and Society," made available by Donald Bruce, e-mail transmission, 30 May 1997.
120. Ronald Cole-Turner, "The Theological Status of DNA: A Contribution to the Debate over Gene Patenting" (revised version of a paper written for the AAAS Dialogue Group on Genetic Patenting, originally presented 13 March 1997).

Because the various statements by the Joint Appeal proponents did not show understanding of patent law and relevant developments, the response from industry focused on "educating" the religious community rather than acknowledging the substance of the ethical issues related to patenting.

Fourth, if public theology is directed at changing public policy, it needs to be clear about what it is advocating. The Joint Appeal was not. Its critique against patenting specific forms of life was not combined with a set of specific remedies sought. Did the coalition propose eliminating some twenty years of patent development and, if so, how did it propose to deal with the existing patents on animals and patent sequences? Some of the explanatory statements distinguished between product and process patents. Did the Joint Appeal advocate eliminating product but not process patents? Some analysts have suggested that the entire issue was over symbolism and the manner in which patent claims are ethically framed and theologically interpreted. Because Mark Sagoff, a philosopher from the University of Maryland who participated in the AAAS Dialogue Group, assumed that symbolism was the primary issue, he suggested that resolution of the controversy may depend less on finding ways around some of the problems that patents impose on research and product development and more on finding new terminology for patents that clearly does not infringe on divine prerogatives vis-à-vis the creation.[121] This may be the case, but the Joint Appeal certainly did not offer clarification of this point.

In contrast, the text of a statement from the Bioethical Working Group of the European Ecumenical Commission for Church and Society was far more specific. It combined reflections on the inappropriateness of extending the patent system to animate matter with advocating for the urgent need for a public forum to debate the ethical acceptability of biotechnical inventions. It also affirmed the importance of framing patent issues within an ethical context. And, like some of the Joint Appeal participants, the statement advocated that patent eligibility be limited to process patents.[122]

CONCLUSION AND REFLECTIONS

The May 1995 Joint Appeal statement was equivalent to waving a red flag and insisting that our society finally deal with the ethical and theological implications of conferring patents on life, particularly on human biological material. It appears, however, that the organizers were inspired more by the moral intuition that it was wrong to patent life than by careful theological or ethical

121. Sagoff, "Patenting Genetic Resources," 13–14.
122. "Press Release: Churches Challenge MEP's on Patenting Life," made available by Donald Bruce, e-mail transmission, 30 May 1997.

analysis. While they raised legitimate concerns that deserve further attention, the manner in which they proceeded detracted from their objectives. Some critics of the Joint Appeal have reacted as much to the process and the superficiality of the statement as to the substance of the issues it raises. Most likely, organizers did not anticipate the attention their initiative would receive. When they succeeded beyond their expectations, proponents were not adequately prepared to justify their grounding or to develop a religious ethic.

Much of the concern with patents infringing on God's theological status and claims appears to be symbolic. Participants in the Joint Appeal did not challenge broad categories of intellectual property rights or object in principle to providing financial incentives for investing in genomic research and product development, although some would prefer that more of the financing and benefits be in the public domain. Nor was there a consensus opposing all forms of genetic patenting. The Methodist statement, cited above, supported "process" patents on recombinant DNA techniques while opposing product or utility patents, and at least some of the other Joint Appeal members also seem comfortable with that position. Further, opponents did not attempt to link opposition to patents to a broadly ontological approach to property claims. While on one level the technical and legal issues related to patents are relevant to the debate, as far as the Joint Appeal proponents are concerned, they may also be largely beside the point

In proceeding as it did, the Joint Appeal coalition showed the possibility of developing an interreligious approach to public theology but fell far short of articulating a well-formed theology, let alone theological norms representative of a wide spectrum of religious communions. The theology of the Joint Appeal initiative, or at least that of its most vocal members, placed the critique of patents primarily within the context of God's ownership of life. Spokespersons from the Southern Baptist Convention played a central role in this development. This appears to have resulted more from accident than design, primarily because the Southern Baptist agency involved in the initiative had a professional theologian on staff. Yet, it seems unlikely that their theological perspective represents the position of the wide range of Christian denominations in the Joint Appeal coalition and even less of the other faith communities in the coalition. As evangelical fundamentalists, the Southern Baptist Convention's confession states that "the scriptures of the Old and New Testaments are authoritative in matters of faith and practice." The belief that scripture "has God for its author" with every word "written by men divinely inspired" to provide a "record of God's revelation of Himself" supports their affirmation that the text is "without any mixture of error."[123] This

123. Article I, "The Scriptures," *The Baptist Faith and Message,* adopted by the Southern Baptist Convention, 9 May 1963.

literal reading of scripture undergirds a conception of God as the creator and owner of God's world that seems out of keeping for such a multireligious coalition, some members of which are not even theists.

What can be said in defense of the Joint Appeal? As already mentioned, it did raise a valid issue about the appropriateness of patenting life-forms and its potential implications for denigrating respect for life and human dignity, albeit in an inadequate manner. Like the members of the Joint Appeal campaign, I am disturbed by the failure to have a meaningful public discussion of this issue. The courts and the patenting office are not the proper venue for making such decisions. To embark on a course of promoting commercialization and privatization of biology without a single meaningful public debate constitutes a violation of the implicit social contract between the government and the governed in a democratic society. Unfortunately, this is not the first—nor will it be the last—time that Congress abdicates its responsibility and refuses to make public policy on issues related to the development of science and technology.

Organizers of the Joint Appeal have complained that they are being held to a higher standard than either the scientific or the business communities. They argue that supporters of the current patenting regime are not subjected to a comparable level of scrutiny. A paper by John Evans, a sociologist of religion and former Methodist national staff person, concurs with this view. Like the Joint Appeal proponents, Evans makes the point that the debate thus far has not involved a balanced two-way examination.[124] It is true that supporters of the current patent regime had the advantage of the status quo on their side. Rather than debating the substance of the issues being raised, however, they took refuge in the specifics of current patent policy. Given the refusal of the courts to consider noneconomic factors in making their determinations about patentability and the manner in which the PTO has developed its criteria for applying these judgments, the fact that it is permissible to patent genes and gene fragments does not make it ethically right. Moreover, legal analysts as well as secular ethicists have raised fundamental questions as to whether current patenting regimes promote scientific research or benefit the wider public.

Evans also contends that religious critics of patenting have been disadvantaged because they are attempting to make a "prophetic" argument.[125] Utilizing ideal types put forward by James Gustafson,[126] Evans characterizes the prophetic approach as an effort to expose the roots of what is perceived to be funda-

124. John H. Evans, "The Uneven Playing Field of the Dialogue on Patenting," in Chapman, ed., *Perspectives on Genetic Patenting,* 57–74.
125. Ibid., 60–68.
126. James M. Gustafson, "Moral Discourse about Medicine: A Variety of Forms," *Journal of Medicine and Philosophy* 15 (1990): 127–30.

mentally and systematically right or wrong. In contrast, according to Evans, proponents of patenting use ethical arguments that focus on concrete acts which are clearly immediate and apply to specific circumstances. Evans is correct that critics generally confront a heavier burden than supporters of the status quo in political discussions. And, undoubtedly politicians find prophetic reasoning problematic. Nevertheless, the very difficulty of their task requires that would-be prophets conform to a high standard of reasoning. Moreover, as physician and social thinker Leon Kass has shown, it is quite feasible to be scientifically informed, ethically rigorous, and prophetic in orientation. A prophetic approach does not excuse inadequate theological preparation and imprecise ethical reasoning.

Taking Evans' two ideal types or categories of prophetic and ethical reasoning, it is relevant to raise another set of issues. Do religious thinkers have to make a choice between these two approaches or is it possible to argue on both levels? Either by intention or because of the manner in which it was drafted, the Joint Appeal was a broadside against the patenting of life that implicitly advocated for dismantling fifteen years of precedents and patents. Could the coalition have offered its critique with a more careful ethical analysis and more specific proposals without undermining the force of its prophetic critique? I believe the answer is yes. The European Ecumenical Bioethics Working Group comes closer to doing so. A more reasonable and better-reasoned initiative might have meant forgoing front-page coverage in major newspapers. And, I suspect that was the goal of Rifkin and at least some of the religious organizers.

Now that the Joint Appeal has managed to gain a measure of attention for this issue, it is incumbent to clarify a variety of issues. At least some members of the coalition believe it is fundamentally different to have intellectual property claims to categories of life than to own tangible property in land or animals. Despite the seeming obviousness of such a distinction, it needs to have a clear intellectual, and preferably theological, grounding. Their sweeping indictment of all forms of genetic patents does not distinguish sufficiently between the implications of according intellectual property rights over different categories of genetic material. Is it, for example, as much of an affront to religious sensibilities to issue patents on DNA fragments as on whole organisms? Is it as problematic to recognition of God's claims to patent single-cell animals as complex higher animals? Does it matter theologically whether the genetic resources being patented are derived from an animal or a human cell, and why or why not? Finally, what is the goal of the organizers of the Joint Appeal? Are they attempting just to initiate a discussion on possible alternatives to biopatents or to wage a campaign to end all or some product or utility patents on life? If the bottom line is symbolic, would a change in the nomenclature that clearly stripped product patents of pretensions of ownership, but accorded legal monopoly protection for product development, resolve the controversy?[127]

Discussions in the AAAS Dialogue Group suggest that some members of industry are willing to explore such a compromise. If so, what does this imply regarding the religious community's concern or lack thereof about other justice and equity issues related to patenting?

Another subject deserving of attention is a theology of property that would clarify the following issues: How does the affirmation of God as creator relate to our understanding of the basis, scope, and limits of human intellectual property rights? Is it theologically appropriate in Christianity, as well as other religious traditions, to consider God to be an owner, even as the ultimate owner of the creation, and if we do, how does this qualify the conditions and type of human ownership? What kinds of theological warrants raise problems about intellectual property rights over life-forms, and how widely are they shared within and among various religious traditions? Are all forms of intellectual property rights related to biological material and life-forms equally problematic? Do various religious traditions and contemporary theological approaches differ on this topic? Is the granting of intellectual property rights or the commercialization of biology the fundamental issue?

There is also a need to gain greater conceptual clarity about the concept of human dignity and its relationship to the affirmation of the human being as created in the image of God. What is being implied in affirming the dignity and worth of the person? Does the concept of human dignity carry fundamentally different connotations from a religious as compared with a secular perspective? How does human dignity relate to the physical body and bodily integrity? Specifically, are all tissue, DNA, and body parts vested with human dignity? Does a commitment to protecting human dignity impose restrictions on the patenting of all DNA or only the DNA of an identifiable person? Relatedly, what is the foundation of human personhood and to what extent are theological affirmations of human distinctiveness based on DNA? Does a nondualistic but nonreductionist conception of personhood vest human DNA with a sacred status? Conversely, does the conception of the indivisibility of human dignity imply a physical list conception of personhood?

Another topic deserving of treatment by religious thinkers is commodification. Both opponents of patenting and some others expressed concerns that patenting of human DNA and tissues would promote a commodified view of the person that will undermine human dignity. Yet none of those involved in the debate either explained clearly what they meant by commodification or specified how commodification diminishes human dignity. The only treatment of this topic is by legal scholars, and they disagree as to

127. Mark Sagoff proposed something similar. See Mark Sagoff, "DNA Patents: Making Ends Meet," in Chapman, ed., *Perspectives on Genetic Patenting,* 259–61.

whether property or economic discourse once applied necessarily trumps all other forms of valuation. In a society in which commercialization and privatization are rampant, many relationships and objects are becoming newly commodified. If the religious community is going to address this topic, now is the time, not fifteen or twenty years into the future.

Finally, what is the ontological, ethical, and theological status of DNA? And on what basis do various religious traditions make those determinations? Despite more than twenty years of involvement with developments in genetic science, members of the religious community have yet to clarify these issues. The nature of DNA and its policy implications were a source of ongoing debate in the AAAS genetic patenting dialogue. Yet only one religious thinker, theologian Ronald Cole-Turner, attempted to address this very important topic.[128] And, while he wrote a fine paper for the dialogue group, parts of which are referred to in this chapter, his views do not necessarily represent the full range of religious positions. Moreover, his paper is more in the vein of a response and critique than a constructive theology.

Hopefully, the next phase of the debate will feature less rhetoric and more systematic probing of these questions. To do so will require a far more rigorous effort to carry on a dialogue between theology on the one side and genetic science and patent law on the other. The credibility of the entire religious community, and not just the signatories of the Joint Appeal, may rest on doing so.

128. Cole-Turner, "The Theological Status of DNA," 149–46.

Chapter Five

Theological Reflections on Genetics and Human Nature

In 1969 James Gustafson, anticipating developments in genetic science, called for the reconceptualization of the traditional nonevolutionary, fixed, unchanging, and essentially dualistic concepts of human nature. According to Gustafson, growing capacities for intervention in the course of the development of human life exacerbated philosophical and theological questions about what is the "normatively human." He argued that the resolution of this central issue underlay the more specific and concrete ethical dilemmas posed by the field of genetics. To address the topic, he advocated formulating a theological anthropology adequate to conserve inherited biblical and philosophical insights while still responsive to the new scientific knowledge.[1]

His call for a reconceptualization of traditional theological anthropology was in many ways prescient. When Gustafson put forward this proposal at a symposium organized in conjunction with the annual meeting of the AAAS, the new science of genetics was still at an early stage of development. James Watson and Francis Crick had described the double-helix structure of DNA only sixteen years earlier. It was not until seven years after Gustafson's lecture that the discovery of restriction enzymes provided the key to undertaking genetic engineering, the procedures utilized to manipulate, replicate, and modify DNA. The inception of the HGP, a $3 billion international initiative to sequence and map the entire human genetic code, was still nineteen years in the future.

By the 1980s, various religious communities and ecumenical bodies realized that genetics research had significant ethical implications. Some of the literature

---

1. James M. Gustafson, "Genetic Engineering and the Normative View of the Human," in Preston N. Williams, *Ethical Issues in Biology and Medicine: Proceedings of a Symposium on the Identity and Dignity of Man* (Cambridge, Mass.: Schenkman Publishing Co., 1973), 46–58.

also acknowledged that developments in modern biology challenged historic Christian teachings about the dignity of human life and the way this is to be expressed.[2] Others anticipated that the new molecular science would "require rethinking our scheme of the universe and the role of humanity within it."[3] In a similar vein, yet another observed, "Developments in genetic science and technology compel our reevaluation of accepted theological/ethical issues, including determinism versus free will, the nature of sin, just distribution of resources, the status of human beings in relation to other forms of life, and the meaning of personhood."[4]

Despite these and other acknowledgments of the need to reexamine traditional concepts of theological anthropology in light of genetics, religious thinkers have tended to focus on broad themes about the meaning of genetic discoveries or consider specific ethical and social issues raised by genetic discoveries. That the work of religious ethicists on genetics has generally not proceeded from and been informed by either a reinterpretation or a reaffirmation of a conception of human nature has weakened the grounding of these efforts. The delay in developing an updated understanding of human nature and personhood consistent with genetic science reflects at least in part the complexity of this project. Nevertheless, the scope of the new knowledge gained from genetics makes the reconceptualization of theological anthropology even more important now than it was thirty years ago. Recently some ethicists and theologians have begun this task, prompted at least in part by the desire to counter interpretations of genetic findings that challenge religious conceptions of human dignity and the foundations of ethical norms.

This chapter explores work at this vital intersection of genetics and theology as it pertains to developing a theological anthropology consistent with genetic discoveries. It considers issues posed by genetic science for traditional Christian conceptions of human nature and current efforts by Christian theologians to respond. The approach of the chapter is more synthetic than analytical. While previous chapters surveyed and critically evaluated relevant literature written by religious thinkers, this one seeks to integrate work on a variety of topics so as to explore their implications for an updated theological understanding of personhood.

2. WCC Church and Society, *Manipulating Life: Ethical Issues in Genetic Engineering* (Geneva: WCC, 1982).
3. Panel on Bioethical Concerns, *Genetic Engineering: Social and Ethical Consequences,* Frank M. Harron, ed. (New York: Pilgrim Press, 1984), 20.
4. United Methodist Church, "New Developments in Genetic Science," *The Book of Resolutions of the United Methodist Church* (Nashville: United Methodist Publishing House, 1992), 329.

GENETICS, EVOLUTION, AND HUMAN NATURE

Some twenty-five hundred years ago an unknown poet looked into the heavens and wrote a hymn celebrating God's glory and the God-given dignity of human beings. His composition has come down to us as Psalm 8:

> what are human beings that you are mindful of them,
>> mortals that you care for them?
> Yet you have made them a little lower than God,
>> and crowned them with glory and honor.
> You have given them dominion over the works of your hands;
>> you have put all things under their feet,
> all sheep and oxen, and also the beasts of the field,
> the birds of the air, and the fish of the sea,
>> whatever passes along the paths of the seas.[5]

Reflecting the theology in the opening chapters of Genesis and anticipating the medieval notion of a great chain of being, this passage describes a fixed order in nature set by God at the moment of the creation. It assumes that human beings are set at the pinnacle of a natural hierarchy and given dominion over the beasts of the field, the birds of the air, and the fish within the sea. According to the author, humanity is set apart from and fundamentally different from the rest of nature by divine design. The psalm describes human persons as only "a little lower than God," and crowned "with glory and honor." These beliefs have long infused Western religious concepts of human nature.

The scientific understanding of evolution challenges this view of the creation and the place of human beings in the scheme of things. The central thesis of Charles Darwin's landmark work, *On the Origin of the Species,* is that all organisms are the product of a long, slow, random, and apparently directionless process of evolution governed by the mechanism of natural selection. These claims leave little room for a view of nature, and by extension humanity, as the product of divine purpose or intentionality. Instead, the mindless process of natural selection suggests a universe that is blind and indifferent to life and humanity. Darwin's description of a struggle for survival, in which most organisms lose out to those better adapted to their environments, conveys a notion of a universe that is cruel and weighted in favor of the strong, leaving little place for the loving and compassionate God posited by biblical theism.[6] And, evidence that modern humans are a late development, emerging through

5. Psalm 8:3-8, *The New Oxford Annotated Bible,* New Revised Standard Version (New York: Oxford University Press, 1991), 679.
6. John F. Haught, *Science and Religion: From Conflict to Conversation* (Mahwah, N.J.: Paulist Press, 1995), 47–49.

millions of years of an evolutionary process, seemingly contradicts a view of a privileged position for a humanity created intentionally in the image of God.

There has been surprisingly little systematic theological exploration of the implications of evolution for understanding human nature. While many theologians may assume an evolutionary perspective, few of them explicitly address the implications for traditional concepts and doctrines based on an immutable and fixed order of creation. There are, however, some fresh and creative expressions of theology in evolutionary terms. Process theology is one important example. A few theologians also persuasively argue that evolution does not necessarily contradict the conceptions of a loving God who is intimately related to the world. John Haught, a Roman Catholic theologian deeply influenced by process thought, understands God as the ultimate source not only of order, but more importantly of the troubling novelty, creativity, and diversity in the cosmos that shatters the settled order. He conceptualizes the role of the divine as inviting the cosmos to express itself in increasingly diverse ways.[7] Hans Kung, also a Roman Catholic theologian, writes that evolutionary theory makes possible a deeper understanding of a God who is not above or outside the world but in the midst of evolution, and a deeper understanding of humans as organically linked to the cosmos.[8] Overall, though, evolution has not received the attention it deserves from religious thinkers. And, given the significant issues that evolution raises, theologians who deal with this subject generally focus on its implications for understanding God's role and agency in the world and not on human nature.

Some of those willing to acknowledge the reality of evolution for the rest of nature are reluctant to place human beings fully within the evolutionary process. Pope John Paul II provides a key example of the latter disposition. In October 1996, the pope made headlines when in his annual message to the Pontifical Academy of Science he affirmed that biological evolution is more than an open question and accepted it as scientific fact. In doing so, however, he sought to maintain the ontological transcendence and distinctiveness of the human species. In his statement, the pope took a position that could best be characterized as modified creationism. He accepted that the human body is the product of an evolutionary process, but in keeping with tradition, stated that God directly intervenes in the creation of each person, adding the spiritual soul at the point that human reproductive cells unite.[9] The implication of this for-

---

7. Ibid., 60–71.
8. Hans Küng, *Does God Exist?* Edward Quinn, trans. (New York: Doubleday, 1980), 347.
9. Anne M. Clifford, C.S.J., "Biological Evolution and the Human Soul," in Ted Peters, ed., *Science and Religion: The New Consonance* (Boulder, Colo.: Westview Press, 1998), 163–64.

mula is that the most distinctive and significant dimensions of human nature do not emerge through evolution.

An evolutionary approach raises profound questions about the origins, role, status, and nature of human persons. As Thomas Shannon, one of a small group of theologians writing on genetics, has observed, in view of the theory of evolution, "we cannot claim that human nature is static or fixed. What our nature is now is not what it was nor is it necessarily what it will be. Given the fact of evolution we cannot claim a human nature that was created distinctly and apart from the animal kingdom."[10] Once Homo sapiens are understood to be a product of the evolutionary process, we then have to ask whether human nature is God-given or an accidental product of evolution. And, if it is the latter, what does that mean for our understanding of our relationship to the divine? If there is not a fixed order or great chain of being, what does this imply about our sense of human uniqueness and our relationship with other forms of life? And, in the great march of evolution, what will humanity become and to what extent do we or should we control our own destiny?

The revolution in genetics further underscores the need to place theological anthropology in an evolutionary perspective in two ways. The first is by providing an explanation of the manner in which random variations occur in DNA. Although it is a relatively stable molecule, on rare occasions a spontaneous change or mutation occurs when DNA replicates itself. This may occur from an error in cell division, environmental influences, such as exposure to a virus, radiation, or a chemical substance, or still other causes that are not understood. Once the mutations occur, they are passed on to succeeding generations.

The second is by showing human kinship with other forms of life, particularly the great apes. Genetic analysis has generally provided confirmation for fossil evidence regarding the human evolutionary journey and underscored how close our genetic composition is to our two closest primate relatives, bonobos and chimpanzees. According to current reconstructions of the evolutionary sequence, the ancestors of the great apes appeared approximately ten million years ago, and hominids, chimpanzees, and bonobos divided into separate evolutionary lines some five to six million years ago. The origin of Homo sapiens is now dated to be about 150,000 to 230,000 years ago.[11] In 1984, two Yale geneticists established that humans are very closely related to the chimpanzee, so much so that Charles Sibley and Jon Ahlquist argued that

10. Thomas A. Shannon, "Genetics, Ethics, and Theology: The Roman Catholic Discussion," in Ted Peters, ed., *Genetics: Genes, Religion, and Society* (Cleveland: Pilgrim Press, 1998), 170.
11. Richard Wrangham and Dale Peterson, *Demonic Males: Apes and the Origins of Human Violence* (Boston and New York: Houghton Mifflin Co., 1996), 43.

humans should be considered to be a fifth group of great apes.[12] Further genetic analysis also showed that chimpanzees and bonobos are more closely related to humans than to other great apes, such as gorillas.[13]

Philip Hefner is perhaps the theologian who has grappled the most seriously and most explicitly with the evolution of human nature. His approach to this topic, particularly in his major work, *The Human Factor*, is to sacralize the process of evolution. Describing nature as "God's great project," Hefner proposes that God works through evolutionary mechanisms. He argues that we should conceptualize the meaning and purpose of human life through the prism of the evolutionary processes from which we have emerged and the natural ecosystems of which we are a part and to which we are intended to contribute.[14] A central thesis of his writings is that human beings are products of evolution shaped by natural selection. For Hefner this understanding of evolutionary origins and heritage does not diminish the status and value of human beings.

Like several other thinkers, Hefner presents a biocultural evolutionary paradigm of Homo sapiens. He portrays human beings as two-natured creatures living at the confluence of two major streams of evolutionary information, the genetic and the cultural. He acknowledges that genetically programmed patterns drive much of human behavior, but also views culture as shaping much of what is distinctively human. Hefner defines culture as learned patterns of behavior and symbol systems that humans construct to be able to interpret the world, guide behavior, and interface with the rest of the natural world. He understands culture and information as central to human evolution, development, and successful adaptation to our niche and survival within it.[15] As he aptly points out, "genes alone do not a human being make."[16] Because Hefner considers culture to be a natural phenomenon and an evolutionary development, he does not posit a dualism between culture and nature. For him, culture "is a happening within nature. Culture belongs to nature. It is, in a metaphorical sense, nature's organ. . . . culture is nature's own process of being self-aware— of being aware of itself, of trying to understand itself and its world—and of trying to discharge fundamental processes of evolution under the condition of free choice and decision."[17]

---

12. Ibid., 29.
13. Ibid., 41.
14. Philip Hefner, *The Human Factor: Evolution, Culture, and Religion* (Minneapolis: Fortress Press, 1993), 37.
15. Philip Hefner, "Determinism, Freedom, and Moral Failure," in Peters, ed., *Genetics,* 112.
16. Philip Hefner, "The Spiritual Task of Religion in Culture: An Evolutionary Perspective," *Zygon: Journal of Religion and Science* 33 (1998): 536.
17. Ibid., 539.

His evolutionary interpretation leads to a view of religion as an information system within culture that is part of the effort of nature to understand itself
and conduct itself in freedom. Myth and ritual, for Hefner the heart of religion,
form critical components of this cultural system of information and guidance.[18] Myths and doctrines try to embrace culture, explain it, and justify it. He
posits that these are not above nature; they constitute emergent forms that
nature itself takes in its own effort to understand nature's meaning, including
the meaning of human nature. He proposes that "organizing consciousness in
viable ways for passage into the next generation is religion's contribution to the
epic of evolution."[19] Like many other thinkers who draw inspiration from science, Hefner in his book *The Human Factor* calls for the revitalization of our
myths and rituals, in tandem with scientific understandings, to make them
more appropriate for contemporary human existence.[20]

To interpret the purpose of being human, Hefner develops a theology of the
human being as God's "created co-creator." According to this proposal, God's
intention is for humanity to act in freedom "to birth the future that is most
wholesome for the nature that has birthed us" (27). He understands this future
as "not only our own genetic heritage but also the entire human community
and the evolutionary and ecological reality in which and to which we belong"
(27). His theory has three core elements. The first and most fundamental is that
"humanity has been created by God to be a created co-creator in the creation
that God has brought into being and for which God has purposes" (32). The
second thesis is that evolution constitutes God's process for bringing such a
creature into being. And third, Hefner claims that the freedom which marks the
created co-creator and its culture represents an instrumentality for enabling the
creation to participate in the intentional fulfillment of God's purposes (32).

GENETICS, HUMAN UNIQUENESS, AND IDENTITY

Traditional theological anthropology in the three monotheistic faiths begins
with the affirmation that the human person is created in the image of God. As
such, the human being has innate worth and value. Genetic research poses the
knotty question of how to reconcile this view of what it means to be human
with the discoveries of the intimate connection between genetic constitution
and human identity and behavior. Are we our genes? If not, in what ways do
we transcend our biological inheritance?

18. Hefner, *Human Factor*, 156.
19. Hefner, "Spiritual Task of Religion in Culture," 541.
20. Hefner, *Human Factor*, 278.

Assuming that the HGP will meet its objectives, what will it mean to map and sequence the full human genome? As a leading cancer biologist has commented, "For the first time, we humans are reducing ourselves down to DNA sequences.... We're not talking about how butterflies fly or trees grow: we are dealing here with the mystery of the human spirit."[21] What will it mean to reduce the dignity and mystery of the human spirit to banal biochemical sequences? Popular culture assumes that this will reveal something very fundamental about human nature. James Watson, the first director of the HGP, described its goals as nothing less than the attempt "to find out what being human is."[22] Watson also told *Time* magazine, "We used to think our fate was in our stars. Now we know, in large measure, our fate is in our genes."[23] The book *The DNA Mystique* explores what it describes as the "genetic essentialism" of our culture. "Genetic essentialism reduces the self to a molecular entity, equating human beings, in all their social, historical, and moral complexity, with their genes."[24] The authors, Dorothy Nelkin and M. Susan Lindee, claim that the gene has become "a cultural icon, a symbol, almost a magical force" (2). According to Nelkin and Lindee, DNA functions in some ways as a secular equivalent of the medieval Christian conception of the immortal soul. It is considered to contain the essential human self, to be the source of individual differences, moral order, and human fate, and to promise a form of eternal life, either through progeny or through the body reconstituted by scientific manipulation of DNA. They link the development of this genetic essentialism to the metaphors and claims that Watson and other scientists have used to garner public support and government funding for human genetics. Going beyond claims that genetic research would revolutionize approaches to human health, scientific hype has characterized the gene as the basis of human identity and described DNA as the "Bible," the "Book of Man," and the "Holy Grail." Scientists, and even more the media coverage of their discoveries, have also implied that genetic research will enhance prediction of human behavior and account for human variability (chapter 3).

Theologian Ted Peters, in *Playing God? Genetic Determinism and Human Freedom,* a work he identifies as a genre of "response theology, a form of intellectual discourse that responds theologically to issues prompted by public

---

21. Dr. Robert Weinberg, quoted in Nicholas Wade, "The Struggle to Decipher Human Genes," *New York Times,* 10 March 1998, C1.
22. Quoted in Ronald Cole-Turner, *The New Genesis: Theology and the Genetic Revolution* (Louisville: Westminster/John Knox Press, 1993), 20.
23. Quoted in Ted Peters, *Playing God? Genetic Determinism and Human Freedom* (New York and London: Routledge, 1996), 6.
24. Dorothy Nelkin and M. Susan Lindee, *The DNA Mystique: The Gene as Cultural Icon* (New York: W. H. Freeman, 1985), 2.

debate over scientific matters,"[25] explores the grounding and implications of genetic essentialism. He associates this attitude with what he terms the "gene myth," the belief that genes determine everything about us, and a belief in "puppet determinism," that there is no human self that transcends our DNA. His thesis is that these claims are unsupportable by science. "Despite DNA determinism, we as persons are still free. We are also morally responsible. That responsibility includes building a better future through genetic science, a form of human creativity expressive of the image of God imparted by the divine to the human race."[26]

What, then, does the scientific evidence reveal about the relationship between human beings and their genes? On a species level, is there a genome or set of genes that accounts for distinctive characteristics of Homo sapiens? Based on evidence to date, the scientific answer is at least provisionally no. Instead, recent genetic analysis underscores the close interrelationship of all forms of life. Most of the human genes being discovered through research sponsored by the HGP turn out to have a counterpart in the genetic structures of simpler life-forms. Therefore, studies of the tiny nematode worm, C elegans, a soil dweller not unlike the earthworm, have been able to yield basic information on human biology. The similarity and closeness is such that biologists have been able to insert the human version of a gene as a replacement for the worm's copy and have it function satisfactorily.[27] These discoveries underscore the stunning genetic affirmation of our kinship and shared evolutionary heritage with all living things. Our shared genetic code provides a scientific underpinning for the theme of the interrelatedness of all creation. Further arguments against equating human distinctiveness with DNA come from analyses that indicate a correspondence of some 98 percent of the genome between humans and chimpanzees and bonobos.[28] While humans have twenty-three pairs of chromosomes and the chimpanzee has twenty-four, if the two shorter non-human primate chromosomes are placed end to end, they strongly resemble one human chromosome.[29] Scientists have not yet identified the function of the approximately 2 percent of the genetic code that differs, but it is unlikely that

25. Peters, *Playing God?* xv.

26. Ibid., xvii.

27. Nicholas Wade, "Dainty Worm Tells Secrets of the Human Genetic Code," *New York Times,* 24 June 1997, C1, 3, 8.

28. Ian Tattersall, *The Human Odyssey: Four Million Years of Human Evolution* (New York: Prentice Hall, 1993), 42–43.

29. V. Elving Anderson, "A Genetic View of Human Nature," in Warren S. Brown, Nancey Murphy, and H. Newton Malony, eds., *Whatever Happened to the Soul? Scientific and Theological Portraits of Human Nature* (Minneapolis: Fortress Press, 1998), 51.

human uniqueness resides in these genes.[30] Geneticists suggest that specific genetic mechanisms may also be different in human beings. These include the regulatory mechanisms, the developmental timing of the way in which genes are turned on and off in different parts of the body, and/or the manner in which human genes are expressed and affect the phenotype (the observable physical trait of a genotype).[31] Nevertheless, it is unlikely that genetic factors alone can explain what it means to be human.

On a biological level, the major difference between humans and their primate cousins is in brain capacity and not in the genes. Beginning four million years ago, our brain grew three to four times in size to reach its present capacity conferring enhanced intellectual ability. Brain size alone was not the sole answer, however, because the Neanderthals may have had an even bigger brain than anatomically modern humans, but they apparently lacked a fully formed anatomical capacity for speech. A recent book by neuroscientist and evolutionary anthropologist Terrence Deacon, *The Symbolic Species: The Co-Evolution of Language and the Brain,*[32] suggests that the evolution of language was the central factor in human evolution. Deacon does not believe that this evolutionary breakthrough resulted directly and simply as a by-product of a larger, more complex brain or a specific language organ. Instead, his thesis is that symbolic thinking, itself a gradual emergent product of brain development, triggered a coevolutionary exchange between language and brains during hominid evolution (349–65). He theorizes that many of the traits distinguishing the bodies and brains of our "symbolic species," which he designates "Homo symbolicus" (340), were ultimately brought about by the evolutionary dynamic between social and biological processes. The myriad spin-offs of symbolic communication, ranging from the capacity to transmit knowledge across generations to various processes of social interaction, played an important role (350). Other paleoanthropologists, for example, Ian Tattersall, also assign the development of the unique human capacity for language and the consciousness that accompanied it a central place in the process of becoming human. According to Tattersall, "Almost all the unique cognitive attributes that so strongly characterize modern humans—and that undoubtedly also distinguished our fellow Homo sapiens who eliminated the Neanderthals—are tied up in some way with language."[33]

30. Ibid.
31. Ibid.
32. Terrence W. Deacon, *The Symbolic Species: The Co-Evolution of Language and the Brain* (New York and London: W. W. Norton and Co., 1997).
33. Ian Tattersall, *Becoming Human: Evolution and Human Uniqueness* (New York, San Diego, and London: Harcourt Brace and Co., 1998), 186.

What about the relationship between the genome and the identity, capabilities, and behavioral patterns of the individual person? In the recent debate cum media circus over the prospects of human cloning, this became more than a theoretical issue. One factor contributing to the strong reaction against cloning is the belief that reproducing a genome would be a "violation of the uniqueness of human life, which God has given to each of us and to no one else."[34] This statement assumes that individual identity requires a unique genome and that this relationship somehow reflects the divine order. It should be noted, however, that despite the profound opposition to the prospects of human cloning in the religious community, few religious communities and thinkers made such a direct correlation between the human genome and human identity. Concerns about the potential violation of human dignity and individuality focused primarily on the relationship between the agent and the clone, the manner in which cloned human beings would be treated by others, and the psychological effects that being a clone would have for the child. Rejecting genetic determinism, the religious thinkers who testified before the NBAC generally affirmed that cloning humans would "produce independent human beings with histories and influences all their own and with their own free will."[35]

What does genetic science show about the nature of the link between the human genome and human identity? That each person, with the exception of monozygotic (identical) twins, has a unique genome is true, but personality and behavior cannot be reduced to genetics. Findings from studies of identical twins reared together and apart underscore that even genetically identical people are unique. While identical twins have greater than average personality similarity, identical twins are less behaviorally alike than most people think.[36] Human development features a continuous and ongoing interaction between the organism and the environment throughout life that influences expression of genes and the development of the brain. Furthermore, there is a complex relationship between genotype and environment that influences the manner in which each makes its relative contributions to individual variability. Geneticists have discovered that a given individual may have the potential to develop different

---

34. "Cloning Animals—A Suitable Case for Concern," *Glasgow Herald,* 25 February 1997, quoted in Ted Peters, "Cloning Shock: A Theological Response," in Ronald Cole-Turner, ed., *Human Cloning: Religious Responses* (Louisville: Westminster/John Knox Press, 1997), 16.

35. This statement of Rabbi Elliot is quoted as representative of the views of the religious community in the NBAC report, *Cloning Human Beings: Report and Recommendations* (Rockville, Md.: NBAC, 1997), 50.

36. Nancy L. Segal, "Behavioral Aspects of Intergenerational Human Cloning: What Twins Tell Us," *Jurimetrics* 38 (Fall 1997): 61–66.

phenotypes (observable physical traits of the genotype), depending on their exposure to certain features in the environment. This is termed plasticity. That plasticity confers important survival benefits can be seen by comparing the stereotyped patterns of behavior in other species, as, for example, in mating situations, with the wide range of responses of humans. A second important variable in the heredity-environment interaction that geneticists label a reaction range is the array of potentials for an individual's behavioral expression depending on specific circumstances and experience.[37]

Both biology and the environment, relating dynamically, have a strong influence over the development of an individual, but a full concept of human personhood involves more than a self who is the product of interactions between biology and the environment. While it is critical that we be aware of the significant role genes and the environment play in the functioning of the human person, it is equally important that human beings not be dehumanized and reduced to these factors in ways that reduce the real contributions of human agents.[38] Human beings are also cultural beings whose language and symbolic capacities enable them to interpret and shape their contexts and choose their course of action. Perhaps most importantly, the human person and human society have an inherent capacity for ethical behavior and spiritual development. Genetic science has not eliminated the mystery of the human spirit and the apparently unique human capacity for self-transcendence.

NORMATIVE DEFINITIONS OF HUMANITY

In a paper, James Gustafson commented that developments in genetic science raise age-old questions about what is the "normatively human" in an exacerbated form. He went on to observe, "The difficulties in coming to a consensus on the normatively human are almost insuperable, yet it is my deepening conviction that some efforts must be made to overcome them."[39] In making the proposal, Gustafson apparently anticipated the possibilities of human gene therapy and believed that ethicists had better address the issue rather than leave it to others who might not have benevolent objectives. Like others favorably disposed to using the power of genetic science for healing and possibly for enhancing human beings, Gustafson was open to some form of human genetic engineering. The dilemma of how to use the genetic information available

37. Anderson, "Genetic View of Human Nature," 53.
38. Bruce R. Reichenbach and V. Elving Anderson, *On Behalf of God: A Christian Ethic for Biology* (Grand Rapids, Mich.: Wm. B. Eerdmans Publishing Co., 1995), 294–95.
39. Gustafson, "Normative View of the Human," 46.

through predictive testing, particularly in making judgments about therapeutic abortions, underscores the need to address this topic.

This exploration has obvious risks. As the Jewish bioethicist Laurie Zoloth-Dorfman observes, the "power to describe and define the normal human is itself a normative act: it derives its essential meaning from power relationships and truth claims that then construct the possible world."[40] The philosopher Hans Jonas, who was a participant at the symposium at which Gustafson delivered his paper, responded that his proposal could result in "terrifying" possibilities leading to the "standardizing or homogenizing of mankind."[41] Writing some twenty years later, ethicist Roger Shinn cautions, "Individuals and societies, moved by an invincible impulse, treasure their own normality and seek to impose it on the world at large. Afflicted with self-regard, they universalize their particularities."[42]

In a society with a legacy of discrimination, this topic has particular risks. As cell biologist Fred Ledley commented, the effort to define a normal human genome "is dangerous because the notion that there could be a normative human genome also implies that deviations from the normal sequence would be abnormal or undesirable." He anticipated that "this would reinforce the tendency to stereotype individuals in terms of characteristics which deviated from the ideal."[43] It is not accidental that persons from communities with a history of suffering from discrimination have been particularly sensitive to the potential of genetic science to aggravate these problems.

The fact that some genetic mutations occur disproportionately within particular ethnic and racial communities increases the risks for new forms of discrimination. Tay-Sachs disease, a single gene disorder with devastating neurological defects that are universally fatal at an early age, has been found almost exclusively in the Ashkenazic Jewish population. Sickle-cell disease, causing a virulent form of anemia, occurs predominantly among African Americans. The incidence of cystic fibrosis is much higher among those of white Northern European descent. Given the United States' history of drawing sharp distinctions among people on the basis of race and ethnicity, scientific information about the prevalence of certain genetic disorders among specific groups creates a powerful potential for stigmatizing them, particularly if there has been a previous history of social discrimination.

40. Laurie Zoloth-Dorfman, "Mapping the Normal Human Self," in Peters, ed., *Genetics,* 196.
41. Quoted in Roger Lincoln Shinn, *The New Genetics: Challenges for Science, Faith, and Politics* (Wakefield, R.I., and London: Moyer Bell, 1996), 97.
42. Shinn, *New Genetics,* 98.
43. Quoted in ibid., 98.

The response of the Jewish community to genetic testing shows how the benefits and dilemmas are inextricably woven together. With strong support from Jewish religious as well as medical leaders, millions of members of the Jewish community in Israel and in the United States have been tested for carrier status for Tay-Sachs disease and counseled on how to avoid giving birth to children with this disorder. Major *halahkic* authorities (Orthodox interpreters of Jewish law) have also ruled favorably on the permissibility of permitting abortion when the fetus tests positively for Tay-Sachs. As a result, the number of children born with this condition in the Jewish community has declined dramatically.[44] Is this a success story? Zoloth-Dorfman offers several cautions about the Jewish community's enthusiasm for genetic testing. She reports that in United States and Israeli ultra-Orthodox circles, where arranged marriage is still common, one increasingly accepted criterion is having negative carrier status for several genetic disorders. Discrimination in marriage eligibility extends to carriers for genetic diseases like Gaucher's disease and cystic fibrosis, which do not necessarily have severe symptoms and often can be controlled with medication. She anticipates that these practices will accelerate as more genetic tests are discovered and that pressures for genetic selection and therapeutic abortions will also increase, even when the genetic abnormalities diagnosed are not severe.[45] Viewing these developments through the lens of the Holocaust, Zoloth-Dorfman foresees that genetics will serve as a new basis for exclusion and social marginalization. She fears that those marked with genetic dispositions by predictive genetic testing will not be assisted but instead will find in society "an increased tendency to leave outside the discourse, to step over in the street, to 'exclude from the benefit package' in the newest language of health care reform."[46] Therefore, she cautions that the HGP should proceed within a community that is fully aware of its history and of some essential human obligation for one another.[47]

Troy Duster and others also foresee that the genetics revolution may lead to new forms of social stratification and vulnerability to a genetically based form of social Darwinism. He cautions that now, as in other periods of social, economic, and political turmoil, there is increased appeal of genetic explanations to privileged persons. Duster is particularly concerned about lack of awareness of the history of gross human rights abuses committed in the name of eugenics earlier in this century or those too willing to dismiss this social history. He warns that the United States is now heading down a similar road

44. Zoloth-Dorfman, "Mapping the Normal Human Self," 192.
45. Ibid., 191–93.
46. Ibid., 196.
47. Ibid.

fueled by an unfounded faith in the connection between genes and social outcomes.[48]

Ironically, the findings of genetic science also offer a caution against the illusion of perfectibility, one manifestation of which is the desire of parents for a "normal child," free of genetic and congenital liabilities. This takes us back to the discussion of genetic testing and therapeutic abortion. Yet, geneticists estimate that so-called normal people generally have five to seven lethal genes and carry an even larger number of genes that make them susceptible to developing multifactorial diseases in which genetics plays some role. There is probably no one without at least a few genetic liabilities.[49]

Finally, yet another reason that genetic science complicates the task of defining what is normatively human is that it accentuates our differences rather than our similarities. As noted, with the exception of identical twins, each person has a distinct genome. This means that human beings are clearly born unequal in terms of their genetic endowments. What will this mean for the conceptions of equality and human dignity that underlie our political culture? Here a religious perspective that affirms the innate and ultimate worth of all persons may offer an important corrective to potential tendencies to reduce human dignity to genetic criteria and standards of normality. Ted Peters offers the following axiom: "God loves each human being regardless of our genetic make-up and, therefore, we should love one another according to his model."[50]

THE CHALLENGES OF SOCIOBIOLOGY

Proponents of sociobiology (later relabeled "evolutionary psychology" and "developmental or behavioral biology"), one of the first comprehensive intellectual responses to the new genetics, put forward a conception of human nature based on extreme genetic determinism and scientific reductionism that challenges many of the fundamentals of a religious worldview. Books written by two biologists, Edward O. Wilson's *Sociobiology: The New Synthesis*[51] in 1975 and *On Human Nature*[52] in 1978, and Richard Dawkins's *The Selfish Gene*[53] in

48. Troy Duster, "Persistence and Continuity in Human Genetics and Social Stratification," in Peters, ed., *Genetics*, 218–38.

49. Ted Peters, "Genes, Theology, and Social Ethics: Are We Playing God?" in Peters, ed., *Genetics*, 4–5.

50. Ibid., 33.

51. Edward O. Wilson, *Sociobiology: The New Synthesis* (Cambridge, Mass.: Harvard University Press, 1975).

52. Edward O. Wilson, *On Human Nature* (Cambridge, Mass.: Harvard University Press, 1978).

53. Richard Dawkins, *The Selfish Gene* (Oxford and New York: Oxford University Press, 1976).

1976, purport to show that all human traits and social behavior can be reduced to a genetic basis. Their description of human nature consists of an extensive list of universals, including such diverse phenomena as dancing, athletics, territoriality, patterns of aggression, kin altruism, xenophobia, warfare, and sexual practices, thought to characterize all societies and to be genetic in origin. These works further claim that natural selection constitutes the major evolutionary force that has molded virtually all the characteristics of species, including Homo sapiens.[54] Because they believe that genes, not organisms, are the basic unit of evolution,[55] the usual conception of the relationship between genes and the body in which they are located is reversed. In Wilson's gene-centered view of evolution, "The organism is only DNA's way of making more DNA."[56] This understanding of human nature does not leave much room for transcendence or religion. Wilson attributes the predisposition to religious belief, "the most complex and powerful force in the human mind and in all probability an ineradicable part of human nature," to various evolutionary advantages religious beliefs and membership confer.[57]

As the title of Dawkins' initial work heralded, his thesis is that the "selfish gene" is the central evolutionary driver. According to Dawkins, human beings, like all animals, are basically machines created by our genes. Taking the license of writing about genes as if they had conscious aims, in *The Selfish Gene* Dawkins develops a theory of "genesmanship" in which the goal of the gene is to try to multiply itself in the gene pool. It does so by developing survival machines (bodies) through which it can survive and reproduce (95). What, then, is the relationship between the gene and its survival machines, like the human body? Dawkins posits, "The genes too control the behaviour of their survival machines, not directly with their fingers on puppet strings, but indirectly like the computer programmer" (56). In a characterization approximating Tennyson's famous phrase "nature red in tooth and claw," Dawkins claims that for a gene to be able to survive millions of years in a highly competitive world it would have to be ruthlessly selfish. According to Dawkins, this gene selfishness usually gives rise to selfishness in individual behavior. "Much as we might wish to believe otherwise, universal love and the welfare of the species as a whole are concepts which simply do not make evolutionary sense" (2).

Dawkins's reductionism and biological determinism extend to his interpretation of culture. In his scenario, in the struggle for survival genes produce brains, and brains in turn give rise to a new kind of replicator, termed "memes."

---

54. Wilson, *Sociobiology,* 67.
55. Ibid., 3.
56. Ibid.
57. Wilson, *On Human Nature,* 169.

Memes constitute units of cultural transmission or mental entities in the form of tunes, ideas, concepts, or ways of making things that are analogous to genes and follow a vaguely similar process of evolution. "Just as genes propagate themselves in the gene pool by leaping from body to body via sperms or eggs, so memes propagate themselves in the meme pool by leaping from brain to brain via a process which, in the broad sense, can be called imitation" (206). And, like genes, memes are selfish and try to dominate the brain's thought processes at the expense of rival memes. Dawkins treats the idea of God as a very old meme that probably originated many times by independent "mutation." He attributes its high survival value in the cultural environment (i.e., its continued perpetuation across generations) to its great psychological appeal as a "superficially plausible answer to deep and troubling questions about existence."[58]

Sociobiology preaches a form of genetic determinism. A central tenet of Wilson's synthesis of biology with human nature and behavior is that natural selection shapes human perceiving, thinking, and acting. "The genes hold culture on a leash. . . . The leash is very long but inevitably values will be constrained in accordance with their effects on the human gene pool."[59] Put another way, we are what we are because of our biology, specifically our genes. The human brain is but a product of evolution through which our genetic material expresses itself. Wilson claims self-knowledge is constrained and shaped by the emotional centers in the hypothalamus and limbic systems that evolved through natural selection.[60] Although he acknowledges that culture confers an array of options, he emphasizes that genetic tendencies constrain our choices. Innate dispositions, particularly our deepest emotions, shape the manner in which humans process raw information absorbed from the external world, interpret and react to these data, and determine how to respond. Seemingly contradicting his own assertions that human nature and behavior are genetically determined, Wilson appeals to his readers to make conscious choices to change their values and behavior so as to overcome "jerry-built foundations of partly obsolete Ice Age adaptations."[61] *Consilience,* his most recent book, seems to envision a more flexible linkage between genes and culture and again acknowledges the need to address reshaping our sense of collective meaning and purpose.[62]

58. Dawkins, *Selfish Gene,* 207. One of the goals of his later books is to undermine further traditional concepts of theism. In *The Blind Watchmaker* (New York: W. W. Norton and Co., 1986), for example, he argues that evidence of evolution reveals a universe without design.
59. Wilson, *On Human Nature,* 167.
60. Wilson, *Sociobiology,* 562.
61. Wilson, *On Human Nature,* 208.
62. Edward O. Wilson, *Consilience: The Unity of Knowledge* (New York: Alfred A. Knopf, 1998).

Perhaps the most disturbing dimension of sociobiology is its understanding of the development and nature of ethics. Like other forms of behavior, Wilson contends, ethics is a product of the emotive centers in our brains with the goal to promote genetic fitness. He proposes that ethical norms, by which he refers to our general sense of right and wrong, are shaped by our genes. "Human behavior—like the deepest capacities for emotional response which derive and guide it—is the circuitous technique by which human genetic material has been and will be kept intact. Morality has no other demonstrable ultimate function."[63] In *Consilience* he claims that causal explanations of brain activity and evolution "already cover the most known facts about moral behavior with the greatest accuracy and the smallest number of freestanding assumptions."[64]

One of Wilson's interpreters, the philosopher Michael Ruse, adds the element of deception to this scenario. By nature, humans are selfish and individualistic. In order to improve our ability to survive, natural selection has vested us with a capacity to be cooperative. To be effective, though, the genes somehow have to connive to convince us that we are behaving cooperatively because we believe it is right to do so, not because it is in our evolutionary interest.[65] Hence the emergence of ethics. In this rather convoluted explanation, Ruse characterizes moral beliefs as "no more than a collective illusion fobbed off on us by our genes for reproductive ends."[66]

Sociobiologists acknowledge that there are special circumstances in which animals and persons exhibit social, even seemingly sacrificial, behavior, but they seek to explain this away by reducing altruism to a biological survival strategy. By vesting the gene with a cunning, as well as a sense of intentionality, Dawkins, like Ruse, describes cooperation and social behavior as a good biological strategy for a gene to achieve its own selfish goals. He explains that to maximize opportunities for reproduction, it makes sense in some circumstances for an organism to take risks to protect members of its own kin who share its genes. This accounts for why altruistic behavior tends to be demonstrated to members of one's own kin. Additionally, animals, and by extension humans, engage in forms of mutually advantageous reciprocal altruism—the principle "You scratch my back, I'll ride on yours."[67] Dawkins strenuously denies that such forms of kin or reciprocal altruism are in any way comparable to traditional ethics.

63. Wilson, *On Human Nature,* 167.
64. Wilson, *Consilience,* 241.
65. Michael Ruse, "Darwinism and Determinism," *Zygon: Journal of Religion and Science* 22 (December 1987): 426.
66. Michael Ruse, "The Significance of Evolution," in Peter Singer, ed., *A Companion to Ethics* (Malden, Mass.: Malden Books, 1991), 506.
67. Dawkins, *Selfish Gene,* 179.

Not surprisingly, the few theologians and philosophers who have responded directly to the challenges of sociobiology tend to be critical. Stephen Pope, one of the theologians most open to a dialogue with sociobiology, identifies flaws that are noted by many other thinkers as well. In his book *The Evolution of Altruism and the Order of Love,*[68] Pope criticizes Wilson's work for displaying a false reductionism, a tendency to substitute purely speculative suggestions for rigorous scientific argument, and an unjustified mechanistic materialism. Likewise, Pope faults Dawkins for consistently using the "selfish gene" literally, not metaphorically, as an interpretative key to understanding all animal behavior and much of human behavior despite his awareness that genes, as microscopic molecules rather than "selves," cannot really be selfish. Pope attributes this tendency to Dawkins's apparent belief that individual motivation is only an expression of an inbuilt dynamic issued from the genes (100–101). Like other theologians, Pope has problems with the implied or sometimes explicit genetic or biological determinism in sociobiology. At least in its early stages, according to Pope, sociobiology "failed to examine ways in which biological tendencies are reshaped within human behavior," and so portrays human beings as "genetic automatons and unthinking slaves of their deep biological masters" (103). Pope is also uncomfortable with the manner in which sociobiologists slide too easily between descriptive and normative discourse.

Pope does find some use in behavioral biology, however, and seeks to appropriate some of its insights without its reductionism. While he does not believe that human behavior is directly coded by specific genes, he acknowledges that morality reflects the influence of evolution to the extent that the latter profoundly shaped some of the important levels of our emotional and cognitive capacities and predispositions as human beings. He points to traits, including love, that have a biological dimension and acknowledges that genetic causes provide the necessary, but not sufficient, basis for the exercise of human moral and emotional capacities. In contrast with the relentlessly egoistic view of the sociobiologists, he argues that humans have a genuine, albeit limited, capacity for altruism. He posits that altruism and other forms of social behavior are influenced by a variety of factors, only some of which are biological in origin. Utilizing biologist Ernst Mayr's distinction between "closed" and "open" behavior programs, Pope's position is that Homo sapiens, with our complex brains and capacity to store knowledge, have the most flexible or open behavioral program of any species. Nevertheless, he understands the scope of our freedom to be more restricted than many theologians assume: because human behavior reflects its genetic heritage, we are not free to create a "new humanity" (109). Like the

---

68. Stephen J. Pope, *The Evolution of Altruism and the Order of Love* (Washington, D.C.: Georgetown University Press, 1994), 100–101.

primatologist Frans de Waal,[69] Pope believes that our evolutionary heritage has conferred a spontaneous empathy rather than a one-sided calculation of reproductive profitability. He characterizes human beings as having innate capacities, particularly the disposition to form a mature emotional attachment to and concern for others for their own sakes, on which human prosocial motivations and morality build (120–22).

Sociobiology's account of the evolution of morality, with its suggestion that human beings are ethical solely because morality is a strategy to preserve their genes, has received considerable critical commentary. As various critics have noted, this position confuses biologically determined behavior with moral norms. Francisco Ayala, an evolutionary geneticist and philosopher, puts forward a view that acknowledges the evolutionary origins of morality but still affirms the objective and independent basis of ethical systems.[70] Like the sociobiologists, he acknowledges that the high intellectual abilities present in modern humans are an outgrowth of the process of evolution, directly promoted by natural selection. Unlike the sociobiologists, Ayala posits that the capacity for morality evolved, not because it was itself adaptive, but as an outgrowth of human intellectual development. Moral reasoning, that is, the proclivity to make ethical judgments by evaluating actions as either right or wrong, is rooted in our biological nature, according to Ayala. It is a necessary outcome of our intelligence. He identifies three facets of human intellectual development, each of which conferred high survival value, as central to the development of morality: the ability to anticipate the consequences of one's actions, to make value judgments, and to choose among alternative courses of action. Ayala, in contrast with the sociobiological account, views the moral codes that guide our decisions as products of culture, including social and religious traditions, and not biological evolution. According to Ayala, we make moral judgments as a consequence of our intellectual abilities, not as an innate way to achieve biological benefit.[71]

Ayala also makes the point that the justification of ethical norms on the basis of biological evolution or any other natural process is a reversion to the natu-

69. Frans de Waal, *Good Natured: The Origins of Right and Wrong in Humans and Other Animals* (Cambridge, Mass., and London: Harvard University Press, 1996).

70. See, for example, Francisco J. Ayala, "Human Nature: One Evolutionist's View," in Brown, Murphy, and Malony, eds., *Whatever Happened to the Soul?*, 31–48; "Biology Precedes, Culture Transcends: An Evolutionist's View of Human Nature," *Zygon: Journal of Religion and Science* 33 (December 1998): 507–24; and "The Difference of Being Human: Ethical Behavior as an Evolutionary Byproduct," in Holmes Rolston, III, ed., *Biology, Ethics, and the Origins of Life* (Boston and London: Jones and Bartlett Publishers, 1995), 113–36.

71. Ayala, "Difference of Being Human," 132.

ralistic fallacy, the confusion of "is" with "ought." He cautions that "because evolution has preceded in a particular way, it does not follow that that course is morally right or desirable. . . . Biological nature is in itself morally neutral."[72] Citing smallpox and AIDS as products of evolution, he queries whether efforts to eradicate them should be categorized as immoral. As for natural selection having some kind of special or privileged status, he claims that it is no more moral than the force of gravity.[73] Ayala also underscores the need to differentiate between genetic predispositions and genetic determinism. While a natural predisposition may influence our behavior, our biological nature does not constrain or force us to behave accordingly. Additionally, Ayala points out that the confusion of evolutionary processes with morality seems to justify a morality consistent with a social Darwinism most of us would find abhorrent.[74]

Perhaps the most penetrating and sophisticated critique of sociobiology comes in the recently published work *Genes, Genesis and God* written by Holmes Rolston, III. The book is based on his 1997–98 Gifford Lectures at the University of Edinburgh. Rolston, who has training in both philosophy and biology, carries on a dialogue with sociobiology through which he persuasively argues that genetic processes are not blind, selfish, and contingent. In contrast with sociobiologists' focus on the genes as discrete units within individual organisms, Rolston contends that the central Darwinian concepts of adaptation and fitness are ecological, not genetic, in nature. Examining the emergence of complex biodiversity through evolutionary history, Rolston points out that any "self" is embedded in an environment and part of a biotic community. Increasing complexity and diversity require increasing specialization of parts and roles, which in turn require increasing coaction, cooperation, and interdependence of evolving selves. Genes serve as the means to this end over many millennia.[75]

Rolston contends that the metaphor of the "selfish gene" cannot pass scrutiny either philosophically or scientifically. To counter the sociobiologists, he puts forward an alternative framework he terms genetic "sharing." Rolston acknowledges that genes are no more capable of "sharing" than being "selfish" in the deliberated, moral meaning of these terms. But, if a word sometimes employed in the moral world is to be stretched to serve in the amoral natural realm, then "sharing," according to Rolston, offers a more accurate interpretative frame of reference, without the pejorative undertones of "selfish," to

72. Ibid., 126.
73. Ibid.
74. Ibid., 128.
75. Holmes Rolston, III, *Genes, Genesis, and God: Values and their Origins in Natural and Human History* (Cambridge: Cambridge University Press, 1999), 66–68, 93–96.

describe the processes of genes transmitting, distributing, communicating, and recycling the genetic information they contain and conserve (46-49).

The fifth chapter of *Genes, Genesis, and God* contains a frontal attack on the claim that ethics emerge through biological evolution. Rolston argues that morality is not intrinsic to natural systems and that religion and ethics cannot be reduced to the phenomenon of biology (286). Like many of the religious thinkers cited in this chapter, Rolston views human ethics as products of culture, not nature. He believes that human morality represents a genuine breakthrough past biology and overrides natural selection. On the issue of selfishness versus altruism, he points out that the self that emerges through culture gains expanded interests and an enlarged sense of identity well beyond any genetic unit. In the process, the cultural self entwines its identity with others and becomes something of an altruist (281). In one of the more memorable passages in the book, Rolston states the following:

> The bold hypothesis of selfish genes dies the death of a thousand qualifications once again, because these genes live the life of ten thousand cultural interconnections, beyond the ten thousand genetic interconnections found before. Human altruism, with its genuinely emergent properties, "takes over" the biology; . . . The organism "takes off" into life. Much later the organism "takes off" into ethics. (282)

He also suggests that some insights in our human moral systems may be "transhuman," that is, applicable to all moral agents living in cultures that have been elevated above natural selection. Some of the ethical norms he so characterizes are: keep promises, tell the truth; do not steal; do to others as you would have them do to you; love your enemies (290). As such, Rolston believes that human ethics "reveals transcendent powers come to expression point on Earth" (291).

GENETICS AND CONCEPTIONS OF HUMAN SINFULNESS

The Western Christian theological tradition claims that sin is an inherent dimension in human nature. The doctrine of the Fall emphasizes that while human beings may be intrinsically free, we are "not able not to sin."[76] Sin has been described in a variety of ways across the centuries, among them as a rebellion against God, as a tendency toward violence, as selfishness and antisocial behavior, and as guilt and estrangement. With some simplification, it is pos-

---

76. Statement from Augustine, quoted in Hefner, "Determinism, Freedom, and Moral Failure."

sible to group the various interpretations of sin put forward by Western religious thinkers in two categories. Hefner identifies these two versions of original sin as the first sin, a historical act of ancient forebears named Adam and Eve that is inherited through the ages, and the primordial sin of our origin, that is, the sin intrinsic to being human.[77] According to traditional Christian doctrine, human sin, however characterized, can only be overcome through the gift of divine grace.

How, then, should we understand the relationship between our genetic composition and sin? Genetic science, of course, obviates the biblical literalism that attributes human sin to the decision of Adam and Eve to eat of the tree of knowledge. The rejection of Lamarckian genetics rules out the possibility that acquired characteristics can be inherited by subsequent generations. Thus human nature could not have originated as good and then been corrupted because of the behavior of our early human ancestors. Moreover, evolutionary history also makes no room in its time scheme for an Eden story, that is, a point prior to which human nature was benign and after which it was fallen. Instead, science views nature as neither fixed nor eternal, but subject to change and evolution.[78]

But what about views of primordial sin that affirm human proclivities toward selfishness, violence, and antisocial behavior but do so independently of a myth of the Fall? Does our biological inheritance condemn us to be sinful in some way? Is aggression or violence fixed within our genetic code? Are human beings doomed to be violent? Is violence a trait we have inherited from our great ape ancestors or our early human forebears? And, can genetics offer an empirical basis for understanding the insights of Augustine and other traditional theologians about the heritability of human disorder?

Genetic science does provide some evidence of genetic contributions to behavior, including violence, but these insights must be applied with a great deal of caution. Genetic research underscores that genetic inclinations for good and evil, for selfishness and altruism, evolve together and are acquired through the same evolutionary process.[79] While our capacities, including those for moral and spiritual life, are conditioned in some ways by our biological inheritance, this is far from proving we are biologically determined. (The complex topic of the relationship between genes, determinism, and freedom will be discussed further in a subsequent section.) And, it is important to emphasize that genetic explanations of human behavior, particularly those that find their way into popular media, usually extrapolate too quickly and too simplistically from genes to assumptions regarding the biological determinants of behavior.

77. Hefner, "Determinism, Freedom, and Moral Failure."
78. Peters, *Playing God?* 86.
79. Cole-Turner, *New Genesis,* 88.

That said, claims that selfishness and violence are somehow biologically built into human nature are currently receiving considerable attention. The selfish gene theory put forward by sociobiologists and its various successor disciplines is one proponent of this perspective. Nevertheless, in its classic form, sociobiology claims that genes, not their carriers, are selfish. Although Wilson characterizes humankind as an aggressive species, he attributes the incidence and severity of violence, not to selfish or aggressive genes or a pervasive aggressive instinct, but to factors in the environment, particularly social stress.[80]

In *Demonic Males: Apes and the Origins of Human Violence*,[81] a work that has received considerable attention, primatologists Richard Wrangham and Dale Peterson resurrect the theory that hunting, killing, and extreme aggressive behaviors are inherited biological traits. While twenty-five years ago most scholars believed that human aggression was relatively unique, Wrangham and Peterson contend that the inclination to kill other members of one's species is a defining mark of both humans and chimpanzees. Since humans and chimpanzees share these violent urges, they assume that human violence has long evolutionary roots and is likely to be fixed. In another article, Wrangham claims that chimpanzees are conservative species and therefore a good model for the ancestor of the prehuman hominids.[82] The book attributes the origins of this "demonic" tendency to the existence of patrilineal, male-bonded communities. Wrangham and Peterson make the claim that only two animal species, humans and chimpanzees, live in such patrilineal male-bonded kin groups and hypothesize that these groups enable males to form aggressive mutual support coalitions with each other to attack outsiders. To explain why humans and chimpanzees are so different from bonobos, our equally close genetic cousin who are one of the most peaceful and socially oriented species, Wrangham and Peterson attribute the apparent absence of predatory violence among bonobos to the loss of male coalitionary skills. Their theory is that bonobo females form their own alliances and, unlike chimpanzee and human females, prefer to mate with less aggressive males. Why is this? A key factor in their thinking is that differences in the nature of the food supply among the groups shaped distinctive social patterns.[83]

80. Edward O. Wilson, "Human Decency Is Animal," reprinted in Connie Barlow, ed., *From Gaia to Selfish Genes: Selected Writings in the Life Sciences* (Cambridge, Mass., and London: MIT Press, 1994), 167–70.
81. Wrangham and Peterson, *Demonic Males*.
82. R. W. Wrangham, "Ape, Culture, and Missing Links," *Symbols* 2 (1995): 2–9, 20, cited in Robert W. Sussman, "Exploring Our Basic Human Nature: Are Humans Inherently Violent? *Anthro Notes* 19 (1997): 2.
83. Wrangham and Peterson, *Demonic Males*, 220–30.

There are many problems with this theory, however. Several anthropologists have criticized the book on the grounds that data do not support their characterization of the chimpanzee as a violent species. Wrangham and Peterson's assumption that contemporary chimpanzee behavior reveals something about early hominids is another source of contention.[84] Their claim that violence in the social structure reflects the nature of the food supply belies their description of violence as inborn and hereditary. Moreover, bonobos, like chimpanzees, like to eat meat and have the ability to catch monkeys, but nonetheless refrain from hunting them or undertaking aggression against other bonobo groups. The variety of habitats in which humans have evolved, with the nature of the food supply different in specific areas, also makes it problematic to correlate universal traits. Moreover, other primatologists have provided a very different interpretation of our evolutionary ancestry. As the title of Frans de Waal's book *Good Natured* implies, his characterization of chimpanzees emphasizes their sociability and incipient morality, not their inherent violence.[85]

What about the evidence from genetics? Behavioral geneticists, using two different modes of analysis, molecular genetics and population (statistical) genetics, have made claims to have identified specific genes or genetic defects that apparently confer a predisposition to violence. But, like the work of primatologists, these studies need to be subjected to careful scrutiny. One much cited body of research deals with the link between the XYY trisomy (an extra Y chromosome) and male violence. A genetic study of prisoners in the 1960s found that seven of the 197 men in the sample (3.5 percent) carried the XYY trisomy. Despite the absence of evidence about the frequency of the XYY trisomy in the general population, the authors of the study speculated that the 3.5 percent rate found in the prison population might be twenty times higher than the frequency in the normal population. They then generalized from that meager data to claim that men with forty-seven chromosomes were "mentally subnormal male patients with dangerous, violent, and criminal propensities."[86] The studies of men with the XYY genotype that followed during the 1960s all chose as subjects men who were identified as problematic rather than those who were functioning normally within society and, unsurprisingly, tended to confirm these results.[87] Given this bias in methodology, recent evaluations do not find this body of work credible.

84. Sussman's article "Exploring Our Basic Human Nature" criticizes Wrangham and Perston's work on both points, as have other reviews of their book.
85. Frans de Waal, *Good Natured,* 209–12.
86. Garland E. Allen, "Modern Biological Determinism: The Violence Initiative of the Human Genome Project and the New Genetics," in Robert W. Sussman, ed., *The Biological Basis of Human Behavior* (Needham Heights, Mass.: Simon and Schuster Custom Publishing, 1997), 378.

Research has shown a possible link between aggressive behavior and disturbances in levels of the chemical serotonin. Serotonin transmits nerve signals in the brain and plays a role in regulating sleep, sexual behavior, appetite, and impulsivity. There is a suspicion that genes, as yet unidentified, influence serotonin metabolism, making some people more susceptible to impulsivity, particularly under stress.[88] This falls far short of a genetic explanation of human violence and sin.

In 1993, a team of gene hunters conducted a study of a Dutch extended family in which fourteen men, but none of the women members, were characterized by engaging in various forms of antisocial behavior, including acts of aggression, arson, attempted rape, and murder. The fact that all the affected males were related through unaffected females suggested X-linked recessive inheritance, and genetic analysis found that the males had an abnormal gene that coded for monoamine oxidase A, an enzyme that breaks down neurotransmitters in the brain. On that basis, researchers surmised that an accumulation of neurotransmitters might be one possible cause of violent behavior. Nevertheless, they were cautious about their findings, acknowledging that their study does not conclusively determine a cause-effect relationship between the defective gene and violent behavior.[89]

Three studies of the links between genes and violence have made use of detailed adoption records available in Scandinavian countries. None provide conclusive answers, and the results of the three are inconsistent. One study in Denmark of 14,427 adopted men and their biological fathers found a statistically significant link between genes and property crime, but not for violent crime. Another Danish study of twins, one of which had committed an act of violence, resulted in a slightly greater correlation among identical than fraternal twins for engaging in violence. The difference was not statistically significant, however. A Swedish adoption study did uncover a significant link, but it was between violent crime in the father and alcoholism in the son.[90]

In addition, a series of statistical studies have purported to discover evidence of the genetic basis of crime. One often cited is an analysis of data of 2,621 criminals and their families conducted by a demographer for the Bureau of Justice Statistics. The study found that more than half of all juvenile delinquents and more than one-third of adult criminals in local and state institutions have

---

87. Peters, *Playing God?* 67.
88. Juan Williams, "Violence, Genes, and Prejudice," *Discover* (November 1994): 93–95.
89. Anderson, "Genetic View of Human Nature," 64.
90. Rosie Mestel, "What Triggers the Violence Within?" *New Scientist* (26 February 1994): 32.

family members who had also been incarcerated. Some criminologists made the claim that these data demonstrate that criminality runs in families.[91]

What do these findings really mean? It is relevant to note that all of these studies have been criticized on methodological and conceptual grounds. Problems identified in the research purporting to study a genetic basis for criminal and other social behavior include the following: failing to use clearly defined terms, such as what constitutes a criminal act; reducing complex processes of behavior to a single dimension or entity; relying on statistical analysis of variance within a population to determine heritability without any analysis of the genetic components involved; and engaging in extreme forms of genetic reductionism.[92] As Elving Anderson cautions, these studies show that "careful attention must be given to the terms used in the public media or in professional diagnosis to describe behavioral problems. Labels such as 'mean' gene, 'aggressive' gene, or 'criminal' gene are unfortunate since they prejudge the situation and imply a level of understanding that usually is not present."[93] He therefore argues against reducing aggressive behavior to biology, or viewing it as a static phenotype or the outcome of genetic processes.

To conclude that there is not yet definitive genetic evidence for a correlation between specific genes and antisocial or aggressive behavior does not, of course, say anything about the existence or nonexistence of sin. Two contemporary theological interpretations of sin are consistent with the findings of genetic science but do not fall into a simplistic biological trap. The first of these is the account of Philip Hefner. He suggests redefining the religious symbol of original sin as "the dissonance between the pre-human information that we carry in our genome and the distinctively human, the dissonance between societal culture and individual 'selfish' human nature, and the innate fallibility and vulnerability that marks our character as humans."[94] Building on Paul MacLean's concept of the "triune" brain, Hefner postulates that the human neocortex has been grafted on reptilian and ancient paleo-mammalian brain forms whose ancient programs still condition aspects of human behavior. He hypothesizes that we inherit from our predecessors genetic programs often inappropriate for contemporary circumstances. This then requires us to negotiate an inner chasm of alienation between the prehuman and the genuinely human, but we often fail. Hefner also identifies sinful dispositions with the conflict between our conditioning by "selfish" genes and our need to live a complex social existence. Additionally, both our genes and our culture are finite and fallible and not fully

91. Allen, "Modern Biological Determinism," 377–78.
92. Ibid., 378–79.
93. Anderson, "Genetic View of Human Nature," 64.
94. Hefner, "Determinism, Freedom, and Moral Failure," 119–20.

adapted to all future contingencies.[95] According to Hefner, sin is inherent in human nature because it is a constituent of the dissonance between genes and culture, between human origins in prehistory and the requirements of contemporary life. The very processes that contribute to the evolution of the human leave human beings internally divided. His theory is that awareness of sin and its concomitant, a sense of guilt and estrangement, originates from our inherent inability to satisfy and reconcile the messages delivered to our central nervous system by the reptilian, paleo-mammalian, and neocortex dimensions of the brain. Alienation and its various symbol systems reflect tensions between the biological and cultural strands of our heritage.[96]

Marjorie Hewitt Suchocki offers another constructive alternative to traditional theologies of sin. Like Hefner, she affirms the reality of sin and she seeks to develop a notion of original sin stripped of its mythic structures. Her objective is to provide some explanation for the persuasiveness of sin and yet avoid implicating God as creator of an imperfect creation. Unlike Hefner, however, she consigns the origins of sin and its evil consequences predominantly to nurture rather than nature. Suchocki understands sin as the rebellion against creation. In her book *The Fall to Violence*[97] she writes, "Sin is unnecessary violence against any aspect of existence, whether through act or intent, whether consciously chosen or otherwise" (16). Her argument is that neither the traditional definition of sin as a rebellion against God nor its corollary concept of original sin as rooted in human freedom is adequate as an account of the myriad ways that we inflict destruction upon ourselves, one another, and our "environing earth" (16-22). According to Suchocki, sin through violence is rooted in human nature and in the human situation. Drawing on the work of two scientists, one focusing on archaeological research and the other on innate behavior patterns in birds and animals, she postulates the universality and physiological basis of aggressive instincts in humans (90–99). Suchocki also identifies human solidarity and social inheritance as other sources of sin. Because we inherit and are shaped by the assumptions and values of previous generations, their prejudices, hypocrisies, and structures of domination are conveyed to us, and will in turn be passed along to our children. This relatedness means that the sins of the past shape human subjectivity through time. Individual self-consciousness once formed becomes constitutive of the self and difficult to transcend. Thus, societies serve as the bearers of sin to which their "children will adhere even before they have the means of assent . . . before they have the

95. Ibid., 114–16.
96. Hefner, *Human Factor,* 123–43.
97. Marjorie Hewitt Suchocki, *The Fall to Violence: Original Sin in Relational Theology* (New York: Continuum Books, 1994), 16.

means to exercise either consent or denial toward the corrupting sin" (118). Thus she comes to the position that original sin, embodied in social structures and cultures, creates sinners (126).

GENETICS, FREEDOM, AND DETERMINISM

Of the topics considered in the literature, one of the most important is the assessment of the extent to which genes shape human nature and determine human behavior. Specifically, how does evidence from genetic science recast the age-old theological and philosophical discussions of freedom and determinism, and what are the implications for moral responsibility? Previous sections of this book have argued against making a simple correlation between genes and behavior. Behavioral geneticists speak in terms of probabilities and dispositions, not genetic causes. The pathways from genes to human behaviors are far more complex than a crude genetic determinism implies. Elving Anderson cautions, "In some ways the gene story is surprisingly simple, but it must not be interpreted simplistically."[98] He compares our genes with a blueprint that contains essential information about the design of a specific building but requires an architect to interpret the plan and develop a sequence for implementing it. Without the plan—the genes—nothing would happen. During the translation from blueprint into building (the body structure or phenotype), however, there are many possibilities for changes subject to internal and external environmental factors.[99] Genes and the environment interact throughout life. The way in which the genes are expressed depends on the environment, and conversely, the effect of the environment is mediated through its influence on the genes. Anderson concludes:

> Genes are now known to be less stable and more subject to regulatory factors than we used to think, and the pathways from genes to expressed traits are more complex and less predictable. The history of an organism becomes important, with each developmental step dependent on prior events that continually alter the internal environment. Thus the effects of individual genes have to be described in terms of probabilities rather than rigorously determined outcomes.[100]

Understanding genetic influences as predispositions or limiting factors still leaves a broad potential sphere of human freedom and moral accountability. An individual's genome sets boundaries on various traits and potential, for example, on body type, athletic ability, and intellect. It does not, however, determine

98. Anderson, "Genetic View of Human Nature," 54.
99. Ibid., 55.
100. Ibid., 57.

how someone will organize his or her life within those parameters. Genetic science leaves a broad sphere of choice and personal responsibility intact. Biologist R. David Cole comments, "Most genes merely 'predispose' us to biological characteristics, such as athletic ability, intelligence, or violent behavior. How these characteristics come to be expressed depends on complex interactions among genetic and nongenetic factors."[101] He suggests that the pattern of gene expression in the brain and body be regarded as the substrate on which the human spirit continually acts and in the process modifies the substrate for subsequent interaction.[102]

On Behalf of God, coauthored by Elving Anderson and Bruce Reichenbach, a philosopher teaching at a Christian college, characterizes genetic-environmental influences as operating along a continuum. At one end, causal conditions are weak and individual choice and freedom greatest. At the other end, particularly in relationship to some genetically based diseases and disabilities, causal factors are so compelling that individual freedom and accountability are severely constrained. Reichenbach and Anderson locate human actions in most circumstances somewhere near the middle. Some genetically based diseases, for example, schizophrenia, cystic fibrosis, and Huntington's disease, are sited at the end where freedom is significantly reduced. The appropriate place on the continuum of various other conditions with genetic components that affect human behavior, alcoholism, for example, is still subject to controversy, as are others where the genetic contribution is still undetermined.[103]

Compatibilism, or soft-determinism, is the philosophical position that seems most consistent with the findings of genetic science. Compatibilists hold that freedom and determinism address different issues. Determinism addresses questions about the causes of biological or physical states, such as genes and the environment, while freedom deals with human choices stemming from our motivation and desires. As characterized by Louis Pojman, compatibilism acknowledges that behavior is shaped by antecedent causal conditions, though not necessarily in a mechanistically determined way, but acknowledges that we still have a sphere of freedom and concomitant moral responsibilities. The distinction between voluntary and involuntary behavior is key. For proponents of compatibilism, the critical element is not whether an act or event has causal antecedents but whether an agent was free of

---

101. R. David Cole, "Do Genes Control Us?" in John P. Burgess, ed., *In Whose Image? Faith, Science, and the New Genetics* (Louisville: Geneva Press for the Office of Theology and Worship, Presbyterian Church [U.S.A.], 1998), 65.
102. Ibid., 66.
103. Reichenbach and Anderson, *On Behalf of God,* 262.

internal or external constraints.[104] Philip Kitcher is very helpful in clarifying this point. As he states,

> Freedom does not consist in the absence of determination but in the way the action is determined. To posit randomness or indeterminism at the biological level would not bring us one step closer to understanding human freedom. This is because freedom must be seen as a form of determination—that is, determination by a human subject. To act freely is to make choices in light of evaluation. To act freely is to determine an action based on what one values and to do so without enslavement to compulsions from within or constraints from without.[105]

To be free is to be able to act in accordance with our values, preferences, and desires. If by definition free acts are those done voluntarily because we have reasons to do so, then it stands to reason that agents can be held accountable. Moral responsibility depends not on whether a decision made or an action taken is causally determined but whether it is consistent with what a person wanted and whether she or he could have acted differently. Having a predisposition or sensitivity that is genetically based may incline someone toward a specific form of behavior, but it does not predetermine a specific course of action. A person's genetic makeup may also make it harder for some to control particular kinds of conduct. Nevertheless, only in few disorders do genes affect the capacity to be able to act in accordance with moral norms and principles. Reichenbach and Anderson offer the example of someone who has a genetic disposition toward alcoholism. They point out that unless he or she were somehow forced to accept a first drink, we would rightly hold that individual morally responsible for his or her behavior while under the influence of alcohol.[106] As recovering alcoholics learn, a genetic disposition places a greater not lesser burden of responsibility on someone to take appropriate precautions. To be genetically inclined toward a certain behavior still leaves us free to choose or resist.

Of the various theological discussions of genetics and human freedom, Ted Peters' book *Playing God?* contains the most careful analysis as well as the strongest criticism of genetic essentialism or the gene myth. Peters offers insightful criticism of the notion that persons are determined by their genes. His book argues forcefully that science does not support the view that humans are the sum total of their DNA and nothing more. It also provides an eloquent

---

104. Louis P. Pojman, "Freedom and Determinism: A Contemporary Discussion," *Zygon: Journal of Religion and Science* 22 (December 1987): 410–13.
105. Philip Kitcher, *Vaulting Ambition: Sociobiology and the Quest for Human Nature* (Cambridge, Mass.: MIT Press, 1990), 24.
106. Reichenbach and Anderson, *On Behalf of God,* 277.

defense of the existence of human creativity, moral responsibility, and freedom. According to Peters, molecular biology has provided little or no evidence supporting a philosophy of human determinism that undermines traditional philosophical and theological conceptions of human freedom. He raises the question of whether human freedom requires that we liberate ourselves from nature in the form of our own DNA. His answer is that it does not. "Nature, including our genetic makeup, establishes the particular conditions for the particular ways in which we as persons will exercise our freedom."[107] Peters concludes that because freedom is exercised at the level of the person in the form of deliberation, decision, and responsible action, determinism at the genetic level, even if proven, does not obviate having free moral will.[108] He reminds us that God's freedom is the source of human freedom. God's call draws human consciousness beyond its physical makeup, including the DNA bequeathed by our evolutionary history, toward a future of infinite possibility.[109]

GENETICS, HUMAN ESSENCE, AND THE SOUL

What are the implications of genetic science for understanding the human essence, portrayed in classical theology as the soul or spirit? This work has argued that the evidence from genetic science does not warrant accepting a reductionist view of the human person. It has maintained that human beings are more than the sum total of their genes or some combination of genes and environmental influences. A nonreductionist point of view acknowledges that higher-level, more complex human capacities depend upon lower-level biological processes, but it also contends that these human abilities or functions cannot be solely explained by or reduced to their biological underpinnnings. This is because new principles of explanation, modes of behavior, and processes of causality emerge at higher, more complex levels of organization.[110]

Nevertheless, genetics, like neuroscience research, makes it difficult to maintain a dualistic conception of a self that is divided into a body and soul. Therefore, the findings from genetic science do not rest easily with religious doctrines which posit that the soul is completely distinct from the body and consists of a fundamentally different kind of being. Genetics does make problematic traditional Christian confessions of faith that describe human beings

107. Peters, *Playing God?* 160.
108. Ibid., 176.
109. Ibid., 160–61.
110. Warren Brown, "Conclusion: Reconciling Scientific and Biblical Portraits of Human Nature," in Brown, Murphy, and Malony, eds., *Whatever Happened to the Soul?* 215–16.

as two different substances in one person, an immortal and immaterial soul which can never die and a mortal material body. Data from genetics also effectively undermine positions, such as Pope John Paul II's modified creationism, that affirm the human soul's immediate and direct creation by God at the moment of conception.[111] It is possible, however, to formulate a notion of the human essence that is neither reductionistic nor dualistic.

Just as Christianity is fundamentally an incarnational faith in which God took on human form and literally became embodied, genetic science requires an integrated and embodied view of the human person. As Reichenbach and Anderson comment, "human personhood cannot be reduced to a purely immaterial or spiritual notion, as sometimes occurs when people identify themselves with souls. We are essentially and fundamentally embodied beings, with a genetic heritage from our parents, their parents, and so on. This genetic heritage affects all parts of us."[112] Genetic science requires a theological rediscovery of the sacredness of the body and a more unitary conception of the self. It is important to note that this is a rediscovery. Seyyed Hossein Nasr shows that traditional religions, both the primal and the Abrahamic faiths, once considered the body to be sacred.[113] The philosophical dualism that came to characterize Western Christianity, particularly during the past few centuries, reflects the influence of Descartes, as well as the resurgence of gnostic and patriarchal strands within Christian tradition. Modern science has also influenced and accelerated the increasing objectification and secularization of the understanding of the body. Like the religious thinkers grappling with the findings of genetic science, many contemporary theologians, particularly those with feminist inclinations, have sought to reintegrate spirit and matter, intellect and body. This final section will consider ways in which it is possible to conceptualize the human essence that are consistent with contemporary science.

A recently published volume, *Whatever Happened to the Soul?*, represents a major effort by a multidisciplinary group of scholars in biology, genetics, neuroscience, cognitive science, philosophy, and theological and biblical studies to strive for greater consonance between contemporary science and Christian faith. In its opening chapter, Nancey Murphy, a philosopher and theologian, describes the approach of this group of scholars as a "nonreductive physicalist" account of the person. "Nonreductive" indicates the rejection of contemporary philosophical and scientific views that claim the person is "nothing but" a body. "Physicalism" signals their agreement with scientists and philosophers

111. Clifford, "Biological Evolution and the Human Soul," 164–68.
112. Reichenbach and Anderson, *On Behalf of God,* 293.
113. Seyyed Hossein Nasr, *Religion and the Order of Nature* (New York and Oxford: Oxford University Press, 1998), 236.

who hold that it is not necessary to postulate a separate metaphysical entity, the soul or mind, to account for human capacities and distinctiveness. A reductive materialism treats the person as a physical organism, whose emotional, moral, and religious experiences will ultimately be explained by the physical sciences. In contrast, nonreductive physicalism conceptualizes the person as "a physical organism whose complex functioning, both in society and in relation to God, gives rise to 'higher' human capacities such as morality and spirituality."[114] Various chapters in the volume argue that the souls of humans are a physiologically embodied property of human nature and not an entity with a distinctive existence, awareness, and agency.

Psychologist Warren Brown's essay in the volume proposes an understanding of the soul as a dimension of human experience that arises out of personal relatedness. This relatedness has three dimensions: subjective processes of self-relatedness and self-representation, interindividual relatedness, and relatedness to God. According to Brown, these experiences of relatedness to others, to the self, and most particularly to God endow a person with the attributes traditionally ascribed to the concept of the soul.[115] He further suggests that personal relatedness is an emergent property. As defined by Brown, "An emergent property is a unique mode of functioning that becomes possible on the basis of both a significant increase in the capacity of some number of lower-level abilities and the interaction among these capacities."[116] While analogues to these fundamental human mental abilities or functions are present to some degree in nonhuman species, particularly primates, they are substantially greater in humans. The expansion of certain areas of the brain endowed humans with advanced mental powers and capacities that have had significant implications for the scope and quality of human relatedness. Enhanced capacities he identifies as critical for personal relatedness include the development of language; an ability to consider the thoughts and feelings of another person; a conscious historical memory of events, persons, times, and places; conscious mental control of behavior; an ability to anticipate future implications of behaviors and events; and emotion modulation by complex cognition to guide behavior and decision making.[117]

In another essay in the volume, Joel Green, a New Testament scholar, argues that a nonreductive physicalist account of the person is compatible with the

114. Nancey Murphy, "Human Nature: Historical, Scientific, and Religious Issues," in Brown, Murphy, and Malony, eds., *Whatever Happened to the Soul?* 25.
115. Warren S. Brown, "Cognitive Contributions to the Soul," in Brown, Murphy, and Malony, eds., *Whatever Happened to the Soul?* 99–102.
116. Ibid., 102.
117. Ibid., 103.

conception of human nature in Scripture and early Christian teaching.[118] He acknowledges that popular Christianity has tended to assume that the Bible portrays anthropological duality, but claims this is not supported by a textual analysis. He refers to the near consensus among biblical scholars that the Hebrew scriptures do not have a dualistic conception of personhood. In the Old Testament, humans do not possess a body and soul, but are human only in their fully integrated, embodied existence.[119] While acknowledging that there is more disagreement among New Testament specialists and more diversity in the texts themselves, he concludes that the New Testament is not as dualistic as the traditions of Christian theology and past lines of biblical interpretation have implied.[120] He shows that particular texts do not mean to convey specific details about human anthropology or have a conception of a disembodied soul. Even Pauline language, while not consistent in all cases, tends to understand embodied existence as the norm.

A nonreductionist physicalist approach fits with a trend in recent theology proposing a relational interpretation of the symbol of the image of God. Douglas John Hall, one proponent of such a relational conception, insightfully points out that there are various problems with the traditional identification of the *imago Dei* as a quality of human nature. While theologians have often been inclined toward substantialistic claims that the human species possesses certain characteristics or qualities that render it similar to the divine, they have disagreed as to the nature of this distinctive endowment. Theologians throughout history have been influenced by the values of the particular culture in which they worked. Thus, they have alternatively elevated differing human qualities, including rationality, intellect, freedom, and will, depending on which is the most highly evaluated.[121] He proposes an alternative view, namely, an understanding of the image of God as an inclination or proclivity occurring within the relationship of the Creator and human creatures. In his reformulation, "The human creature images (used as a verb) its Creator because and insofar as it is 'turned toward' God. To be *imago Dei* does not mean to have something but to be and do something: to image God."[122] Like the contributors to *Whatever Happened to the Soul?*, Hall conceptualizes this inclination

118. Joel Green, "'Bodies—That Is, Human Lives': A Re-Examination of Human Nature in the Bible," in Brown, Murphy, and Malony, eds., *Whatever Happened to the Soul?*, 149–73.
119. Ibid., 158.
120. Ibid., 172–73.
121. Douglas John Hall, *Imaging God: Dominion as Stewardship* (Grand Rapids, Mich.: Wm. B. Eerdmans Publishing Co., 1986), 88–97.
122. Ibid., 98.

or proclivity as a capacity for relationships—with other persons, with the Creation, and with God.

In a similar manner, Karen Lebacqz offers a view of the soul as a symbol of the covenant between God and each person. Building on the concept of the soul in the work of Helmut Thielicke, Lebacqz characterizes the soul as an "alien dignity" conferred by God. For Thielicke and also for Lebacqz, that human dignity is "alien" does not mean that it comes from outside of the person but that it is bestowed by God and is therefore always present with each of us. Precisely because human dignity is alien, it does not have to be earned and it cannot be lost. The alien dignity that confers the basic inalienable worth of every person rests on God's love, which permeates our being to its very core.[123] "'Soul' is not an individual possession but a statement about relationship," according to Lebacqz. "Soul has to do with our standing before God."[124] Given this understanding, it is possible for her to affirm that the "unique relationship of the individual person to God is not determined by our DNA. Instead it derives from God's active grace and God's desire to love us as we are."[125]

Offering another, albeit complementary, perspective, Ronald Cole-Turner defines the human soul as a set of capabilities defined by genes, but not entirely determined by them. He writes:

> According to Christian theology, human beings are like other animals in that we are made of the dust of the ground, but we are unlike all other animals in several important ways. Our mental capacities are far greater, our emotional sensitivities far more subtle, and our social relationships are more complex and rich than those of any other species. We alone have the capacity for language, for moral awareness, for free moral choice, for art, and, perhaps most important, for a relationship with God, a relationship which we believe will continue forever. These special capacities, taken together, are the human soul.[126]

Cole-Turner also proposes thinking of the self or soul as the coherence within the complexity of the human organism, a coherence which is geneti-

---

123. Karen Lebacqz, "Alien Dignity: The Legacy of Helmut Thielicke for Bioethics," in Allen Verhey, ed., *Religion and Medical Ethics: Looking Back, Looking Forward* (Grand Rapids, Mich.: Wm. B. Eerdmans Publishing Co.), 44–49.
124. Karen Lebacqz, "Cloning: Asking the Right Questions," *Ethics and Policy: Newsletter of the Center for Ethics and Policy at the Graduate Theological Union* (Winter 1997): 4, quoted in Peters, "Cloning Shock," 18.
125. Ibid.
126. Ronald Cole-Turner, "At the Beginning," in Cole-Turner, ed., *Human Cloning*, 124.

cally conditioned but also transcends that conditioning.[127] This coherence is not fixed and unchanging. In relationship with God, through God's grace, our lives and our very being can become more coherent, more focused on that which is good, and more capable morally and spiritually. He cautions that it is important not to think of this transformational process in dualistic terms, for example, that a right relationship with God affects the soul but not the body. Rather, he emphasizes that this transformation penetrates the soul and body and by so doing alters the center of our self, our person.[128]

In yet another reconceptualization of the soul cognizant of genetic science, Anne Clifford puts forward a theological proposal for what she terms "generationalism." Clifford, who is Roman Catholic, nonetheless is critical of the official Roman Catholic teaching that the human soul is separate from the body, inserted by God into the cells of each human embryo at the moment of conception. Generationalism is intended to be more consonant with the mechanisms of evolution, including the element of contingency or randomness in the origins of each human person and the human species, and the findings that many traits and aptitudes in the individual develop within limits that are genetically inherited. Because she envisions God as continuously acting creatively in the world through its natural processes, Clifford does not have need of an interventionist Creator to affirm that humans have a capacity for a relationship with God. Clifford understands the soul "as a metaphorical naming of the compilation of those elements that make each of us a unique individual with a capacity for transcendence."[129] As such, the soul refers to qualities affected by genetic inheritance but is not reducible to them. For Clifford, the soul is synonymous with the center of human individuation. It includes properties of the "speculative intellect" that confer the human capacity for contemplation and for relationship with the "all-encompassing mystery and inexhaustible depth," named as "God." She posits that the soul and body are separate but interpenetrating entities: occurrences in the body affect the soul and, conversely, "soul events" (which are not defined or explained) affect the body. In Clifford's generationist theology, the dignity of the human is affirmed in the metaphorical designation *imago Dei*. It serves as a reminder that "the image of God describes not a primordial state of the first human who evolved, but the destiny toward which each human and the human community, as a whole, are called."[130]

---

127. Cole-Turner, *New Genesis*, 88.
128. Ronald Cole-Turner, "Human Nature as Seen by Science and Faith," in Burgess, ed., *In Whose Image?* 129.
129. Clifford, "Biological Evolution and the Human Soul," 169.
130. Ibid., 171.

CONCLUSION

It has taken more than twenty years for other theologians and religious ethicists to take up Gustafson's 1969 challenge to reformulate theological anthropology in light of the scientific findings from the study of evolution and genetics. As the survey of the literature indicates, much of the work dealing with the
implications of genetics for theological anthropology is relatively recent, dat-
ing from the mid-1990s. A serious engagement or dialogue between genetics
and theology on the topic of human nature is just beginning. Of the works
highlighted here, none are full-length books explicitly attempting to formulate a comprehensive theological anthropology based on current scientific
knowledge. Peters's *Playing God?* and the collection of essays in *Whatever
Happened to the Soul?* come the closest, but neither focuses on this task. Most
of the writings reviewed in this chapter are in the form of chapters of books
or articles and sometimes only paragraphs or pages. Many deal with narrow
issues or topics. This is quite understandable given the complexity and significance of their task. There is much yet to be done.

Much of the writing examined in this chapter can be broadly thought of as
a form of "response theology." I am so categorizing it because its authors appear
to have been stimulated not so much by the ever-growing body of findings from
the genetic sciences and their theological implications as the simplistic reductionism and determinism characteristic of the media reporting and the hype by
some scientists. Exaggerated claims of sociobiologists to be able to trace human
behavior and morality to its genetic foundations have been particularly instrumental in prodding several ethicists and theologians to clarify their own perspectives. In doing so, Wilson, Dawkins, and Ruse, among others, have inadvertently done theology and ethics a great service.

The effort to construct an updated theological anthropology truly represents
a serious effort to engage in religious ethics at the frontiers of science. Of the
topics considered in this work, it comes the closest to a constructive dialogue
between theology and science. The thinkers reviewed in this chapter are generally in dialogue with a body of scientific findings rather than a specific dialogue partner, but they seek to engage and respect the science as well as the
integrity of their own discipline. While not trained in science, theologians and
ethicists generally are knowledgeable about the science and take it seriously.
Some have been members of multidisciplinary working groups in which scientists participated. In one case, the Reichenbach and Anderson book *On
Behalf of God,* a senior geneticist collaborated with a religious philosopher.
Nevertheless, these writing are works of theological and ethical reflection and
not science offered in normative and interpretative guise.

Much like the constructive intersection between theology and the natural sciences that Gustafson proposes,[131] the reconceptualization of human nature has been informed and even altered by concepts, information, and theories proffered by genetic science and its interpreters. The body of work represents an important step toward modifying or replacing traditional nonevolutionary, fixed, unchanging, and essentially dualistic concepts of human nature with views that are more consistent with the findings from contemporary scientific research. The revisionist reconsideration of the respective roles of culture and biology in the shaping of human nature and the theological interpretations of human sin, freedom, and the human essence are particularly notable. In all of these efforts the genetic science is filtered through the authors' religious perspective. Synthesis goes beyond empirical research to affirm God as the ultimate author and giver of life. And perhaps far more than science will ever be able to do, this literature respects the complexity, transcendence, and mystery of the human person.

So where does this exploration of genetic science and human nature take us? Genetic science illuminates but does not explain human nature. Like consciousness, human personhood can best be understood as an emergent or higher-order phenomenon. As an emergent phenomenon, personhood is not additive but instead is multiplicative and complex. It may be possible for science to analyze many of the factors influencing human behavior. Clearly biology, as well as culture, plays a significant role. Nevertheless, personhood by its very nature is not reducible to the sum of its parts. Nor can it be fully explained by modern biochemistry and genetic science. As Arthur Peacocke, who is both a scientist and a theologian, has written, "God has made human beings thus with their genetically constrained behavior—but, through the freedom God has allowed to evolve in such creatures, he has also opened up new possibilities of self-fulfillment, creativity, and openness to the future that requires a language other than that of genetics to elaborate and express."[132] The mystery and gift of personhood transcend any current or future scientific explanation.

131. James M. Gustafson, *Intersections: Science, Theology, and Ethics* (Cleveland: Pilgrim Press, 1996), 4.
132. Arthur Peacocke, *God and the New Biology* (San Francisco: HarperSanFrancisco, 1986), 110–11.

Chapter Six

Contributions and Limitations of Religious Ethics

This study began with the affirmation that religious ethics can potentially make a significant contribution both to the religious community and to broader societal efforts to grapple with the choices and dilemmas arising from the genetics revolution. It did so for a variety of reasons. Religious perspectives on genetics can offer broad frameworks of understanding and the moral vision so necessary to deal with these complex issues. Theologians and ethicists can draw on centuries, indeed millennia, of reflections about the nature of the person, human relationships, and social responsibilities. In contrast with the radical individualism so prevalent in our society, most religious traditions have both a conception of human beings as basically social and interdependent and a commitment to the common good. Religious thinkers also tend to interpret human life and destiny in more inclusive contexts of meaning and purpose than do secular philosophers and ethicists.

Nevertheless, religious thinkers have many obstacles to surmount before they can shape a moral response to the genetics revolution. According to James Gustafson, a theocentric perspective requires that practical moral questions be asked as follows: "What is God enabling and requiring us to be and to do?"[1] While I agree in principle with Gustafson, I am doubtful that it is possible to discern divine mandates for most choices and decisions related to genetics. Some commentators apparently assume that religious communities and thinkers have positions based on their heritage that they can readily apply to particular issues as they arise, but clearly that is not the case. Written within the context of prescientific societies, the foundational texts of most religious communities do not speak directly to the many dilemmas raised by genetic

---

1. James M. Gustafson, *Ethics from a Theocentric Perspective,* vol. 2, *Ethics and Theology* (Chicago and London: University of Chicago Press, 1984), 1.

advances. Moreover, philosophical, ethical, and theological concepts relevant to the intellectual milieu of past centuries do not easily illuminate the interpretation and analysis of contemporary science. Additionally, religious principles and norms are likely to be formulated in such an abstract manner that they need to be operationalized to become sufficiently concrete to be pertinent to empirical scientific developments. And, since many of the issues and choices before us today are unprecedented, inherited norms and experience, even broadly conceived, may not be applicable. At the least then, traditional ethical and theological building blocks need to be informed by, and in some cases revised through, a dialogue with science.

Preceding chapters surveyed religious literature written on behalf of specific communions and by individual religious ethicists and theologians addressing issues related to genetics, cloning, and genetic patenting. Chapter 5 also reviewed efforts to develop an updated theological anthropology consistent with the findings of genetic science. This chapter evaluates these efforts to assess the distinctive contributions and limitations of undertaking religious ethics at the frontiers of genetic science. It focuses on the six issues identified in the introduction: First, what are the methodological issues and options related to undertaking religious ethics at the frontiers of genetic science? Second, what kinds of conceptual building blocks do various religious thinkers use to address these topics? Third, in what ways, if any, do religious thinkers tend to differ from their secular counterparts? Fourth, what implications does the interface between religion and genetic ethics have for theology, particularly theological anthropology? Fifth, is religious ethics on science and technology necessarily bound by historical religious traditions, or is it possible to engage meaningfully in broader theological and ethical analysis across confessional boundaries? And sixth, how can the religious community most meaningfully contribute to deliberations on genetics in a pluralistic secular society, and what are the costs and trade-offs for religious thinkers of attempting to develop a public theology on genetics that addresses the wider society?

EVALUATION OF THE LITERATURE

A 1980 letter from the general secretaries of three major religious communities—Protestant, Catholic, and Jewish—to President Jimmy Carter made a pledge: "The religious community must and will address these fundamental questions [related to genetic developments and societal applications] in a more urgent and organized way."[2] Has it done so? Literature reviewed in this study attests to the interest of religious communions and thinkers in genetic discov-

2. Letter from Dr. Claire Randall, General Secretary, National Council of Churches, Rabbi Bernard Mandelbaum, General Secretary, Synagogue Council of America,

eries and applications. Nevertheless, the review of this literature concluded that the religious contributions, while significant, fell considerably short of the systematic and serious treatment warranted. The same can be said of the work on cloning, genetic patenting, and the reinterpretation of human nature in light of genetic discoveries.

During the past twenty years, various ecumenical bodies and many of the major Christian communions in the United States have formulated policy statements on issues related to genetics and commissioned pastoral and study resources for their members. WCC organized its first consultation on genetics as early as 1973, focusing on issues of genetic counseling,[3] and then dealt with genetics at its 1979 World Conference on Faith, Science and the Future at the Massachusetts Institute of Technology. Following that conference, WCC convened a working group that prepared the 1982 report *Manipulating Life: Ethical Issues in Genetic Engineering*.[4] In 1989, the WCC subunit on Church and Society issued another report, *Biotechnology: Its Challenges to the Churches and the World*.[5] And in 1980, the National Council of Churches of Christ in the U.S.A. organized its first task force, whose membership included both scientists and several theological ethicists, which spent three years preparing a report entitled *Human Life and the New Genetics*.[6] Subsequently, the National Council of Churches appointed another panel which in 1984 produced a book entitled *Genetic Engineering: Social and Ethical Consequences*.[7] Then, in 1986, the Governing Board formally adopted a statement entitled "Genetic Science for Human Benefit," which was published as a sixteen-page pamphlet.[8]

Bishop Thomas Kelly, General Secretary, United States Catholic Conference to President Carter, 20 June 1980. The letter is reproduced in the President's Commission for the Study of Ethical Problems in Medicine and Biomedical and Behavioral Research, *Splicing Life: The Social and Ethical Issues of Genetic Engineering with Human Beings* (Washington, D.C.: U.S. Gov't Printing Office, 1982), App. B, 95.

3. This chronology of ecumenical discussions on genetics follows Roger Lincoln Shinn, "Genetics, Ethics, and Theology: Ecumenical Discussions" (paper prepared for the Genome Consultation of the Center for Theology and the Natural Sciences, August 1992).

4. WCC Church and Society, *Manipulating Life: Ethical Issues in Genetic Engineering* (Geneva: WCC, 1982).

5. WCC Church and Society, *Biotechnology: Its Challenges to the Church and the World* (Geneva: WCC, 1989).

6. *Human Life and the New Genetics: A Report of a Task Force Commissioned by the National Council of Churches of Christ in the U.S.A.* (New York: NCC, 1980).

7. Panel of Bioethical Concerns, *Genetic Engineering: Social and Ethical Consequences*, Frank M. Harron, ed. (New York: Pilgrim Press, 1984).

8. National Council of Churches of Christ in the U.S.A., "Genetic Science for Human Benefit" (New York: Office of Research and Evaluation, adopted by the Governing Board 22 May 1986).

Of the documents within the Roman Catholic tradition with implications for genetics and genetic engineering, "Instruction on Respect for Human Life in Its Origin and on the Dignity of Life (Donum Vitae),"[9] issued by the Congregation for the Doctrine of the Faith in 1987, is perhaps the most significant. Unlike most of the ecumenical Protestant documents listed above, it has the status of a magisterial statement seeking to clarify and restate official teaching. Other resources setting forth a Catholic perspective include an address Pope John Paul II made on medical ethics and genetic manipulation in 1983 to participants in the World Medical Association convention.[10] In 1990, the Catholic Health Association of the United States issued *Human Genetics: Ethical Issues in Genetic Testing, Counseling, and Therapy,*[11] developed by an interdisciplinary research group to serve as a resource for ethical consultation and decision making. A working party of the British Catholic Bishops Joint Committee on Bioethical Issues undertook a four-year study of human genetics and produced a resource that considers both somatic (nonheritable) and germ-line (heritable) interventions.[12]

Eight major North American Protestant denominations and at least one European communion, the Church of Scotland, have addressed genetics issues in some form. As might be anticipated, these denominational documents are very different in focus, purpose, and emphasis, as well as the process by which they were drafted. Of the group, seven—the United Methodist Church, the UCC, the Episcopal Church, the Presbyterian Church (U.S.A.), the Reformed Church in America, the Evangelical Lutheran Church in America, and the Southern Baptist Convention—have drafted reports, policy statements, or study resources on genetic science, genetic engineering, or procreational ethics, and an eighth, the United Church of Canada, has prepared a brief for submission to the (Canadian) Royal Commission on New Reproductive Technologies.

There is also a growing ethical and theological literature on genetics by moral theologians in the form of individually authored book-length studies, articles and edited collections of articles, and chapters of broader works.

9. Congregation for the Doctrine of the Faith, "Instruction on Respect for Human Life in Its Origin and on the Dignity of Life (Donum Vitae)," 1987, reproduced in Kevin D. O'Rourke, O.P., J.C.D., S.T.M., and Philip Boyle, *Medical Ethics: Sources of Catholic Teaching,* 2d ed. (Washington, D.C.: Georgetown University Press, 1993).
10. Pope John Paul II, "The Ethics of Genetic Manipulation," *Origins* 13 (17 November 1983): 386–89.
11. *Human Genetics: Ethical Issues in Genetic Testing, Counseling, and Therapy* (St. Louis: Catholic Health Association of the United States, 1990).
12. Working Party of the Catholic Bishops Joint Committee on Bioethical Issues, *Genetic Intervention on Human Subjects* (London: Catholic Bishops Joint Committee on Bioethical Issues, 1996).

Nevertheless, fewer than a dozen book-length studies written by religious thinkers were published in the period between 1980 and 1998, despite acknowledgment of the significance of the discoveries in the field of genetics. There are also two edited collections on genetics based on contributions by religious ethicists. Several of these works, particularly the individually authored book-length volumes, make a notable contribution toward identifying the moral and religious implications of genetic developments. Nevertheless, this literature is far from a comprehensive treatment of the ethical issues raised by genetic advances.

Other topics related to genetic science have also attracted only limited and intermittent religious attention. Within four months of the announcement of the successful cloning of a lamb from an adult cell, at least five official religious bodies had issued statements opposing human cloning. Three of these were North American—the United Methodists, Southern Baptists, and the UCC. The Vatican and the Church of Scotland also made statements critical of the prospects of human cloning. Prompted at least in part by requests from the media, theologians and ethicists from a wide range of backgrounds also quickly contributed preliminary reflections on the ethical and religious meaning of human cloning. Thus far, however, only one book dealing with religious perspectives on cloning, a collection of short essays prepared in the summer of 1997, has been published.[13]

Concerns that genetic patenting demeans the dignity of life and/or intrudes on divine prerogatives have led a wide range of religious bodies, well beyond the Christian community, to criticize patents on life-forms and genetic sequences. The best known of these is the 1995 "Joint Appeal Against Human and Animal Patenting," endorsed by leaders of some eighty religious faiths and denominations, including representatives of mainline Protestant denominations; Catholic, evangelical, charismatic, and Orthodox churches; and Jewish, Muslim, Buddhist, and Hindu communities. The controversy over this statement in turn engendered further commentary by various religious thinkers on the topic. Yet, despite the public attention and turmoil in the religious community, only two book-length studies have been published representing religious perspectives on the topic. The first is the proceedings of a weekend workshop organized by the Institute for the Theological Encounter with Science and Technology,[14] the other a collection of papers commissioned by a dialogue group operating under the aegis of the AAAS.[15]

13. Ronald Cole-Turner, *Human Cloning: Religious Responses* (Louisville: Westminster/John Knox Press, 1997).
14. *Patenting of Biological Entities: Proceedings of the ITEST Workshop, October 1996* (St. Louis: ITEST Faith/Science Press, 1997).
15. Audrey R. Chapman, ed., *Perspectives on Genetic Patenting: Religion, Science, and Industry in Dialogue* (Washington, D.C.: AAAS, 1999).

Despite the early recognition that genetic research had significant implications for conceptions of human nature, work on updating traditional understandings of theological anthropology has been slow in coming, far slower than the ethical analysis generated by specific developments. Without a doubt, many of the ethicists writing on genetics during the past twenty years had some sense that genetic discoveries required reconsideration of traditional interpretations of human nature, but they deferred the undertaking. This meant that evaluations of the implications of genetic discoveries tended to be based on interpretations of human nature that were at least partially outmoded by these and other scientific findings. In the 1990s, serious efforts were finally begun. Several were responding to the implied genetic essentialism and determinism of scientists, the media, and popular culture. Others can be considered evaluations of the claims of sociobiology. Still others, taking account of discoveries in the neurosciences as well as genetics, have reinterpreted the conception of the soul and the image of God. Overall, however, only a small number of scholars have dealt with the topic of human nature, and most of this literature focuses on narrow aspects rather than a more synoptic review and recasting of religious views.

Periods of attention to genetic developments within the religious community have tended to be followed by years of seeming inattention. Involvement has rarely been sustained. After an initial burst of writing in the 1960s, there was a decade during which very few theologians, ethicists, or religious communities dealt with genetics or genetic engineering. Then, in the second half of the 1980s and early 1990s most of the ecumenical and denominational statements were produced. After another hiatus, there was another wave of activity in the late 1990s, in both scholarly works and a cluster of second-generation denominational resources. These latter works finally provide a far more thoughtful and in-depth treatment.

Religious attention to cloning and genetic patenting has not been sustained either. News of Dolly's creation and the speculation about the applicability of nuclear transfer technology to humans quickly galvanized many official bodies and religious ethicists into taking a position on human cloning. But after the initial few months of commentary during the first half of 1997 and the publication of a collection of essays in November of that year,[16] little else was written or published on the topic through the first quarter of 1999. Few bodies or persons offering a religious perspective commented on discussions subsequent to developments related to cloning or draft legislation to regulate cloning. Similarly, aside from the recommendations of a group of religious

16. Cole-Turner, ed., *Human Cloning.*

ethicists commissioned by Geron Corporation,[17] there has been little in the way of in-depth commentary from mainline religious thinkers or bodies about the religious implications of stem cell research. At the time of this writing, the groups within the religious community who have expressed a point of view have done so primarily to protect the moral status of the embryos from which embryonic stem cells are derived.

In much the same way, there was a flurry of activity on genetic patenting in the early 1980s when the Supreme Court issued its precedent-breaking decision to allow the patenting of genetically altered organisms. Then, in 1987, the antibiotechnology activist Jeremy Rifkin solicited signatures from religious leaders on a petition opposing the patenting of genetically altered animals. In 1995, the Joint Appeal was issued, but there was virtual silence on the topic in the eight years in between. Despite expressions of concern, those opposing patenting of life-forms on religious grounds have been slow to articulate adequately their theological and ethical grounding for doing so. That there is at least a small body of literature expressing religious perspectives is more a result of the reactions the Joint Appeal generated within and outside the religious community than a commitment to develop a theological understanding of patenting. It should also be noted that two of the three dialogues with religious thinkers on this topic were organized by secular organizations with theologically trained ethicists on staff, namely, the AAAS and The Hastings Center.

Given the rapid changes in the technology and the new issues that consequently emerge, the tuning-in and then tuning-out pattern characteristic of religious ethics on genetics has frequently meant that religious ethics is out of date or does not address the most pressing questions. The relative neglect of the potential application of genetic therapies for enhancement purposes is one example. Ten or fifteen years ago, when many of the denominational task forces were being convened, it was far less relevant to evaluate potential enhancement applications. Today, however, it is a moral dilemma that must be faced. Indeed, secular ethicists and scientists have convened conferences and research projects devoted to this topic and written entire books. Yet, other than the significant literature on so-called designer children,[18] little in-depth analysis has been forthcoming from the religious community on this topic. Heritable germ-line interventions are now on the horizon, but not

17. Geron Ethics Advisory Board (Karen Lebacqz, chair, with Michael M. Mendiola, Ted Peters, Ernlé W. D. Young, and Laurie Zoloth-Dorfman), "Research with Human Embryonic Stem Cells: Ethical Considerations," *The Hastings Center Report* 29 (March–April 1999): 31–36.
18. Ted Peters, *For the Love of Children: Genetic Technology and the Future of the Family* (Louisville: Westminster/John Knox Press, 1996).

necessarily on the agenda of religious ethicists. Indeed, a leading genetic scientist has already submitted a preprotocol to the NIH Recombinant Advisory Committee to undertake somatic genetic therapy on a fetus which may alter germ cells as well. The promising new approaches to genetic therapies that attempt to correct genetic misspellings rather than to insert a corrected copy of the mutated gene may have the same result. Yet, AAAS's working group on this topic, which does include religious ethicists, seems to be one of the few initiatives dealing with this set of moral issues. Here it is relevant to note the relative lack of incentives and funding for religious thinkers to specialize in genetic science or even the broader field of religious ethics on science and technology. In contrast with secular counterparts who have opportunities for specialization, religious ethicists, most of whom teach at seminaries with small faculties, tend to have pressures to be generalists or at least to be knowledgeable about and offer classes on a broad range of topics. Moreover, it has been far more difficult for religious ethicists to access research grants, particularly from the Ethical, Legal, and Social Issues Program on the HGP, which has funded much of the work to date. Foundations have also generally been reluctant to underwrite research projects that proceed from a religious perspective. And, the one foundation focusing on the interface between science and religion is not much interested in ethics.

One of the factors accounting for the lack of consistent attention to various dimensions of the genetics revolution and the lack of a more integrated treatment is that the community of religious thinkers working on these issues is quite small. Some commentators have been alarmed that there are only about a thousand genetics professionals, M.D. geneticists and genetic counselors, available in the United States.[19] Yet few people have expressed concern about the handful of religious thinkers, mostly Protestants from mainline denominations, addressing issues related to genetic science. Many of the same people play multiple roles, serving on denominational and ecumenical task forces, drafting resources for churches, and writing their own articles and books. While knowledgeable, these few represent a relatively narrow range of religious and ethical perspectives. Surprisingly and disappointingly, not many Catholic moral theologians have written extensively on genetics. And even fewer thinkers from non-Christian backgrounds have joined the discussions.

The relative absence of Jewish, Muslim, Hindu, or Buddhist voices and perspectives reflects a variety of factors. Not all faith traditions have developed

19. Thomas H. Murray, "Introduction: The Human Genome Project and the Future of Health Care," in Thomas H. Murray, Mark A. Rothstein, and Robert F. Murray, Jr., *The Human Genome Project and the Future of Health Care* (Bloomington and Indianapolis: Indiana University Press, 1996), ix.

methodologies and approaches for addressing contemporary bioethical and genetics issues. In some communities there is even fundamental disagreement as to whether their scriptures should or can be used as the basis for claims about views on topics in medical ethics, let alone biotechnology. The absence of a centralized ecclesiastical structure or the existence of an official body to speak for or commission a study for the development of positions has obviously been an impediment for many communities. Some, the Jewish normative tradition, for example, have placed great emphasis on discussion, dialogue, and interaction as the means to interpret texts to fit new circumstances,[20] but there have not been opportunities to convene groups on genetics. It is also understandable that thinkers situated in regions distant from genetic research and testing centers would be less concerned about these issues.

Given this situation, I would like to repeat a comment made in the conclusion to chapter 2. It is difficult to overstate the importance of involving a greater diversity of religious thinkers and religious perspectives in the considerations of issues related to the applications of genetics and biotechnology. We must engage ethicists from Jewish, Muslim, Buddhist, and Hindu backgrounds in discussions of these ethical dilemmas. Only then will they be able to offer guidance within their own communities and contribute to the development of a more authentic multireligious perspective. Perhaps the furor over cloning will encourage efforts in that direction. Nevertheless, it should be acknowledged that thinkers from some of these traditions will confront a daunting task due to the lack of groundwork for addressing contemporary scientific issues.

It is equally important to attract a greater diversity of voices within the Christian community. As significant as the contributions of thinkers from the major Protestant denominations have been, they cannot represent the full range of religious sensitivities and perspectives within Christianity. It would enrich the dialogue on genetics to have more ethicists explicitly utilizing contemporary theological approaches, specifically, writing from a feminist, process philosophy, liberation, and black theological perspective. Greater efforts should also be invested in encouraging participation from representatives of Christian communities from the global South.

There is a special need for women thinkers to become more involved in the deliberations on genetics. The few female religious ethicists writing on genetics have contributed thoughtful and insightful articles, often with somewhat different orientations and perspectives than male ethicists and theologians, whether or not they are explicitly utilizing a feminist approach. Ethical

20. Noam J. Zohar, *Alternatives in Jewish Bioethics* (Albany: State University of New York Press, 1997), 8–9.

reflections by female ethicists tend to be more sensitive to dimensions of justice, social relationships, and the implications for the poor and marginalized
groups. Unfortunately, the roster of these works is relatively scanty and mostly in the form of articles or chapters in books. Karen Lebacqz has written on
the HGP and privacy issues[21] and served as the chair of the Geron Ethics
Advisory Board on stem cells; Lisa Sowle Cahill, a specialist on reproductive
technologies, has also testified and written on human cloning[22] and stem
cells;[23] and Elizabeth Bettenhausen has written on genetic testing.[24] Laurie
Zoloth-Dorfman, perhaps the most significant Jewish ethicist writing on the
ethical implications of genetics, has recently begun to devote more attention
to genetic issues and stem cells.[25] Given the importance of this topic and
their potential contribution, I hope some female ethicists will decide to invest
more of their time and attention to genetic issues.

METHODOLOGICAL ISSUES

Surprisingly, there is little explicit concern in most of the religious literature on
genetics with methodological issues. The continuing ferment in bioethics over
approaches and models of moral reasoning has little counterpart in the literature on genetics. There are few analogies to the debates in secular ethics between
consequence-based and deontological or obligation-based moral theorists.
Argumentation over universalism versus particularism common in postmodernism have little resonance in religious ethics on genetics. Nor is there much
discussion of the respective strengths and weaknesses of principalism and casuistic thinking. Despite the many complications related to applying traditional

21. See, for example, Karen Lebacqz, "Fair Shares: Is the Genome Project Just?" and
"Genetic Privacy: No Deal for the Poor," both in Ted Peters, ed., *Genetics: Issues of Social
Justice* (Cleveland: Pilgrim Press, 1998), 82–110, 239–54.
22. Lisa Sowle Cahill's major contribution to the discussions of cloning was her written and oral testimony to the NBAC, 13 March 1997 (Washington, D.C.: Eberlin
Reporting Service), 51.
23. Lisa Sowle Cahill, "The New Biotech World Order," *The Hastings Center Report* 29
(March–April 1999): 45–48.
24. Elizabeth Bettenhausen, "Genes in Society: Whose Body?" in Roger A. Willer, ed.,
Genetic Testing and Screening: Critical Engagement at the Intersection of Faith and Science
(Minneapolis: Kirk House Publishers for the Evangelical Lutheran Church in America,
1998), 94–115.
25. In addition to the articles she has written—for example, Laurie Zoloth-Dorfman,
"Mapping the Normal Human Self: The Jew and the Mark of Otherness," in Peters,
ed., *Genetics*, 180–204—she is serving as a member of an AAAS working group on the
ethical and theological implications of human germ-line intervention and on the
Geron Ethics Advisory Board.

theological concepts and norms identified in this study, few thinkers have given explicit attention to this subject matter. This suggests that the authors surveyed may assume that doing religious ethics on genetics does not raise fundamental questions about methodology or, alternatively, they may have decided not to deal with these issues. In fact, the former may be closer to the mark than the latter. James Gustafson's writings represent the exception and for that reason have been helpful in offering a framework for consideration of these issues.

Dialogue with Science

In his work *Intersections: Science, Theology, and Ethics,* James Gustafson differentiated eight models or ways that other disciplines, including science, have been and could be related to theological ethics.[26] Most of the literature on genetic science reviewed in this volume constitutes examples of what Gustafson described as theological "redescription." In his typology, this refers to works in which the findings and potential applications of genetic science are reexplained or given additional meaning.[27] Put another way, much of the ethics to date has sought to explain scientific developments and to assess their implications to a religious audience. The initial thrust focused on the import of genetic science and the significance of the human community engaging in genetic engineering and thus altering nature. These works tended to reassure religious audiences that such interventions were generally consistent with religious perspectives. A second round of works dealt more with the implications of the HGP and human genetic therapy, again generally endorsing the appropriateness of these activities.

A few works constitute examples of another model whereby information, explanations, interpretations, and values from other disciplines affect the content of theology and theological ethics. In these works, the intersection requires a revision of traditional theological and ethical theses. Gustafson cites Philip Hefner's *The Human Factor: Evolution, Culture, and Religion*[28] as an example,[29] a study, which was reviewed in chapter 5. Hefner interprets evolutionary processes as God's project. While Hefner often cites data from science, he still uses traditional theological themes to interpret its wider significance.

26. James M. Gustafson, *Intersections: Science, Theology, and Ethics* (Cleveland: Pilgrim Press, 1996), 136–46.
27. Ibid., 138.
28. Philip Hefner, *The Human Factor: Evolution, Culture, and Religion* (Minneapolis: Fortress Press, 1993).
29. Gustafson, *Intersections,* 137–38.

Holmes Rolston III's *Genes, Genesis and God*[30] provides another example in which the author employs his knowledge of science, in this case an extensive analysis of genetic processes, to reinterpret the relationship between biology, ethics, and religion.

Of the topics considered in this volume, the effort to construct an updated theological anthropology best fits Gustafson's model or theme of seeking some general coherence between science, theology, and ethics.[31] Thinkers reviewed in chapter 5, for example, Stephen Pope's exchange with sociobiology over the evolution of ethics[32] and the various reinterpretations of the nature of the soul, generally seek to engage and respect the science as well as the integrity of their own discipline. Two books, *On Behalf of God*[33] and *Whatever Happened to the Soul?*,[34] resulted from collaborations between scientists and religious thinkers. Much like the constructive intersection between theology and the natural sciences proposed by Gustafson, the reconceptualization of human nature in these works has been more interactive or two-directional. Their revisionist reconsideration of the respective roles of culture and biology in the shaping of human nature and the theological interpretations of human sin, freedom, and the human essence are particularly notable. In all of these efforts, the theology is informed and even altered by findings from genetic science, and the interpretation of the implications of genetic developments is filtered through the authors' religious perspective. And far more than science will ever be able to do, this literature respects the dignity and mystery of the human person.

Nevertheless, this body of work is still quite small and some of the most significant work has been inspired more by findings in the neurosciences than genetics. It also tends to be highly specialized, with more on the development of ethics than an attempt to provide a synoptic understanding of what it means to be human in light of the findings of genetic science. Another limitation is that the work dealing with theological anthropology has yet to be connected

---

30. Holmes Rolston III, *Genes, Genesis and God: Values and Their Origins in Natural and Human History* (Cambridge, U.K., and New York: Cambridge University Press, 1999).
31. Ibid., 143.
32. Stephen J. Pope, *The Evolution of Altruism and the Ordering of Love* (Washington, D.C.: Georgetown University Press, 1994) and "The Evolutionary Roots of Morality in Theological Perspective," *Zygon: Journal of Religion and Science* 33 (December 1998): 545–56.
33. Bruce R. Reichenbach and V. Elving Anderson, *On Behalf of God: A Christian Ethic for Biology* (Grand Rapids, Mich.: Wm. B. Eerdmans Publishing Co., 1995).
34. Warren S. Brown, Nancey Murphy, and H. Newton Malony, eds., *Whatever Happened to the Soul? Scientific and Theological Portraits of Human Nature* (Minneapolis: Fortress Press, 1998).

in a meaningful way with ethical analyses of the implications of genetic discoveries or efforts to prescribe appropriate applications. In part this reflects the sequence of the work, with ethics generally preceding theological reconstruction. It also results from the character of the ethical analysis, much of which has been a kind of response ethic, generated by developments, many unanticipated, in the science. This sequence is problematic, however, because ethical analyses and prescriptions, to the extent they are rendered, often reflect underlying conceptions of human nature. And, it is as yet unclear as to whether and how religious thinkers will connect these updated conceptions of human nature with prescriptions for what kinds of genetic applications and interventions are good or appropriate, and development of norms recommending what ought or ought not be done.

The need for an interactive and ongoing dialogue between genetic science, theology, and ethics is a recurring theme in this study. As noted, though, only a few of the thinkers whose works were reviewed have engaged in the thoroughgoing dialectical conversation with science so essential, especially if the religious community is to hone and reformulate its intellectual tools. In many of the works scientific developments are compartmentalized to frame or introduce the discussion of the ethical implications. Once science provides the setting, religious ethicists often proceed with a relative traditional approach to ethical analysis. Moreover, genetic science is frequently dealt with at a level of generality—the interpretation of the meaning of all genetic engineering, the ethical implications of genetic testing and screening as a category—rather than at a level of greater specification. There are, of course, important exceptions, for example, Ted Peters' insightful analysis of and dialogue with the body of scientific literature on behavioral genetics and genetic determinism in *Playing God?*[35] and Holmes Rolston III's masterful treatment of genetics, values, and ethics in *Genes, Genesis and God.*

Modes of Ethical Discourse at the Frontiers of Genetic Science
In his book *Intersections,* Gustafson distinguishes between four complementary modes of ethics: ethical discourse, prophetic discourse, narrative discourse, and policy discourse.[36] The first of these, ethical discourse, sets forth how one ought to act in particular circumstances. More specifically, it evaluates the moral justification for particular courses of action. Prophetic and narrative discourse present broader questions about worldviews, vision, and basic values. The former is more general than ethical discourse and usually takes two

35. Ted Peters, *Playing God? Genetic Determinism and Human Freedom* (New York and London: Routledge, 1997).
36. Gustafson, *Intersections,* 35–55.

forms, indictments and utopian thinking, both of which tend to be framed in passionate, metaphorical language. Narrative ethics deals with the selection of stories and narratives appropriate for shaping moral ethos and character. Policy discourse involves more practical issues regarding alternative possibilities for public policy. Gustafson also emphasizes that none of the modes of discourse is sufficient: at different moments or for specific purposes, one or another may be more appropriate.

Much of the ethical literature surveyed in this study does not easily fit into any of Gustafson's categories. It most closely approximates the model characterized as ethical discourse, but it tends to be broadly interpretive and descriptive rather than prescriptive. It is likely that the authors were motivated by the intent to establish normative boundaries for the applications of genetic science. Most of the literature, however, focuses more on identifying the meaning of genetic discoveries than on providing guidance as to how to proceed. To put it another way, much of this body of works attempts to sensitize readers to the many issues specific genetic research and applications raise rather than to recommend guidelines on how to resolve these dilemmas. Frequently, the authors punt, underscoring the need for caution or for further societal discussion before proceeding, as, for example, in the writings on human germ-line interventions that will be heritable. While societal education and discourse is a worthwhile goal in dealing with new technologies, it is extraordinarily difficult to find an appropriate forum and have a meaningful review. Moreover, why should the public or policy makers be expected to have greater wisdom than the professional ethicists unable or unwilling to offer guidance?

Another problem is that the level of abstraction at which norms are presented makes them difficult to apply as action guides. The ethical framework in the United Church of Canada's brief on genetics is typical of the level of generality and abstraction in these works. Among the principles it proposes are: life is a gift of ultimate value and must be so respected; human beings are essentially relational rather than individual; justice and compassion are at the heart of being human; medical technologies must be carefully scrutinized for their costs to human beings and their utilization of scarce resources.[37] Other sets of guidelines are similarly abstract. Roger Shinn's six guidelines for evaluating genetic developments include the following: "Genetic investigation and practice directed toward healing are beneficent—provided they guard against excessive risk, rash denials of human frailty, and partisan definitions of normality. . . . We can intervene [in nature], with due caution, to protect signifi-

---

37. The Division of Mission in Canada, "A Brief to the Royal Commission on New Reproductive Technologies on Behalf of the United Church of Canada" (approved by the Executive of the Division of Mission, 17 January 1991), 3.

cant values. . . . An ethically responsible program of genetic research and practice . . . will recognize the mystery of selfhood and will seek to protect free-
dom-in-community. . . . Diversity is an asset to be treasured."[38] While norms
so formulated can sensitize the religious community and decision makers
about values to take into account, they require far more intellectual development before they can be utilized to evaluate specific courses of action. Shinn
quite appropriately characterizes his six guidelines as referring "less to precise
decisions than to the personal and cultural climate in which decisions are
made."[39] If this description were to be slightly rephrased so that the norms
referred less to precise guidelines than to personal, ethical, and religious considerations for people of faith making decisions, it would be relevant to much
of the literature contributed by religious thinkers.

What is unfortunate is that these general and abstract guidelines and principles are neither developed further nor applied to analyze specific issues. If
religious ethics had proceeded to do so, it could have made a real contribution
to dealing with the dilemmas raised by genetic applications. Virtually no religious ethicists have attempted to formulate middle axioms, let alone to employ
them to evaluate specific issues. Middle axioms have been described as "more
concrete than a universal ethical principle and less specific than a program that
includes legislation and political strategy. They are the next steps our own generation must take in fulfilling the purposes of God."[40] The failure to develop
middle axioms has hampered efforts to operationalize religious concerns.
Therefore, none of the principles and norms identified in this literature can
offer clear directions, priorities, or limitations for the application of genetic
power. Instead, ethicists frequently affirm the need to take ethical considerations into account and to draw specific boundaries, but fail to offer models on
how to do so. When they do reach conclusions, they often do so on the basis
of moral intuition rather than moral reasoning.

Prophetic discourse is a second of Gustafson's categories. Characteristically,
prophetic ethics tends to be macro in orientation and occupied with the roots
of what is perceived to be fundamentally and systematically wrong. Such discourse is usually passionate and sometimes apocalyptic. It combines metaphors
and analogies in the marshaling of evidence to stir up emotions.[41] Some of the
religious literature clearly aspires to engage in prophetic inquiry, but these

38. Roger Lincoln Shinn, *The New Genetics: Challenges for Science, Faith, and Politics*
(Wakefield, R.I., and London: Moyer Bell, 1996), 107–20.
39. Ibid., 120–21.
40. John C. Bennett, *Christian Ethics and Social Policy* (New York: Charles Scribner's
Sons, 1946), 76–77, quoted in J. Philip Wogaman, *Christian Moral Judgment* (Louisville:
Westminster/John Knox Press, 1989), 49.
41. Gustafson, *Intersections*, 41.

works rarely do so successfully. In part, this reflects the difficulties of engaging in prophetic discourse in relationship to science and technology. In comparison with other subject matter, there is a greater need to base prophetic calls on clear analysis and arguments, in this case based on knowledge of scientific developments. This is not a simple task and only a few thinkers, scientist and ethicist Leon Kass for one, have managed to do so.

In its 1991 resolution "On Implications of Genetic Research and the Church's Response," the Presbyterian Church (U.S.A.) commits itself to engage in prophetic inquiry concerning the theological and ethical issues raised by the HGP. It defines prophetic inquiry as "the means by which we use the wisdom of modern technology and science integrated with the teachings of biblical tradition in order to move more fully toward God's kingdom of wholeness and justice."[42] But, the analyses of the potential challenges of genetic research, testing, and applications in this and many other of the resources does not differ noticeably from many secular evaluations. Resources developed by or for specific communities often are quite superficial and therefore lack the grounding on which to make a prophetic call.

Much of the public policy work on genetic developments has emanated from social policy or church and society units within the major denominations, some of which are critical of certain aspects of genetic development. A clear instance is the 1995 Joint Appeal. One analyst, a former staff member of the United Methodist Board of Church and Society, defends this statement on the grounds that its proponents were using a framework of prophetic argument. In his article, John Evans appears to assume that a prophetic orientation does not need to undergird or support its indictment by a clearly formulated argument, let alone reasoning based on knowledge of the subject matter.[43] While it is true that prophetic discourse differs in its mode of reasoning from more conventional ethical reasoning, this doesn't excuse sloppy thinking. Moreover, the very fact that society tends to be resistant to prophetic approaches would suggest the advisability of having accurate facts, careful ethical reasoning, and precise conclusions, particularly when dealing with a technical issue such as genetic patenting. Otherwise, religious advocates are more likely to appear unknowing than prophetic.

One of the reasons the religious response to genetics is less prophetic or even incisive than it might be is the failure to deal consistently and thoroughly

---

42. Presbyterian Church (U.S.A.), 202d General Assembly (1990), "On the Implications of Genetic Research and the Church's Response," *Social Policy Compilation* (Louisville: Advisory Committee on Social Witness Policy, 1992), 775–77.
43. John H. Evans, "The Uneven Playing Field of the Dialogue on Patenting," in Chapman, ed., *Perspectives on Genetic Patenting,* 57–74.

with the justice dimensions of issues. The works reviewed in this volume often recognize that genetic discoveries and applications have significant justice implications, but this observation does not translate into the development of a consistent justice trajectory in these works. Titles can be deceptive. For example, few of the essays in the collection *Genetics: Issues of Social Justice*[44] actually focus on justice and one of the most significant of these is written by a sociologist from a secular perspective. Moreover, like other norms and principles, the commitment to justice is often stated abstractly without clearly spelling out what it means or requires in a particular circumstance.

Also, the treatment of justice issues rarely deals with the important role commercial interests play in shaping the priorities for genetic research or the implications of commercialization for future applications of genetics. Various authors comment in passing that corporate aims and the requirements of distributive justice might be incompatible; for example, the Working Group of the Society, Religion and Technology Project of the Church of Scotland deals briefly with science, funding, and the commercial context in its *Engineering Genesis: The Ethics of Genetic Engineering in Non-Human Species.*[45] But few of these works spell out this important point. Even the religious critics of patenting focus primarily on the symbolic issues related to the patenting of life and its potential impact on human dignity. Their concerns with patenting regimes rarely address the larger issues of the market's influence over genetic developments. One of the most perceptive treatments of this topic occurs in a recent article in which Lisa Sowle Cahill evaluates the proposals of a group of ethicists advising a biotechnology company on human stem cell research. Cahill perceptively points out that statements advocating "global distributive justice and equitable access," as does the work of the Geron Ethics Advisory Board, will not have much meaning unless the ethicists deal with what she terms "the new biotech world order." This is because social justice commitments to equitable access to genetic services, especially for those whose needs are greatest, face new and daunting challenges in a global market economy."[46] She rightly notes that the biotechnology corporations driving genetic development are likely to derive greater profits in a global context of vastly unequal access to health care and other human goods. Clearly, this topic requires priority attention from religious ethicists addressing genetics.

44. Peters, *Genetics.*
45. See, for example, the comments in Donald Bruce and Ann Bruce, eds., *Engineering Genesis: The Ethics of Genetic Engineering in Non-Human Species* (London: Earthscan Publications for the Working Group of the Society, Religion and Technology Project, Church of Scotland, 1998), 259–63.
46. Cahill, "New Bioetch World Order," 45–46.

Potential Secularization of Religious Ethics on Genetics

An essay written by LeRoy Walters, director of the Kennedy Institute of Ethics and professor of philosophy at Georgetown University, contrasts the early work of various religious thinkers on genetics with more recent analyses of human genetic intervention. He terms the former "cosmic theology" and characterizes the latter as a casuistic approach.[47] As characterized by Walters, the cosmic mode takes the long view examining the question of genetic intervention in the context of evolution, the divine role in creating and sustaining the world, and human responsibility vis-à-vis the creation. Casuistic genetic analysis, according to Walters, considers near-term technical possibilities and attempts to make determinations among potential applications of new genetic knowledge.[48] Walters implies that an authentic theological approach requires the broad lens of cosmic theology and that a narrower focus on specific moral issues or cases inevitably leads to a secular ethical approach.

Does this suggest that religious thinkers who address specific topics, such as justice or enhancement issues, can only do so adequately by taking a secular approach? It is instructive to look back on what occurred in the development of modern bioethics, the study and formulation of the ethics of health care and the biological sciences, and to ask whether history is repeating itself. Thirty-five years ago, religious thinkers played a central role in establishing bioethics as a specialization or focus of work. Several of the midwives to the birth of bioethics included major Protestant theologians and ethicists associated with the neoorthodox movement—Helmut Thielicke, Karl Barth, and Dietrich Bonhoeffer. Others who were involved have been characterized as maverick thinkers familiar with religious thought and theological ethics, like Daniel Callahan, a Catholic philosopher who went on to found The Hastings Center, and Joseph Fletcher, an Episcopal ethicist who became increasingly secular in orientation. Catholic moral theology was represented by such thinkers as Bernard Häring, Richard McCormick, S.J., and Charles Curran.[49]

As the field developed and became more specialized, however, the public voice of religious thinkers became marginalized. A variety of factors apparently contributed to this development. One was increasing secularization of the roles some of these thinkers assumed. As theologians participated in the life of the secular university, their role and status in their own community changed,

---

47. LeRoy Walters, "Human Genetic Intervention and the Theologians: Cosmic Theology and Casuistic Analysis," in Lisa Sowle Cahill and James F. Childress, eds., *Christian Ethics: Problems and Prospects* (Cleveland: Pilgrim Press, 1996), 235–49.
48. Ibid., 235.
49. David H. Smith, "Religion and the Roots of the Bioethics Revival," in Allen Verhey, ed., *Religion and Medical Ethics: Looking Back, Looking Forward* (Grand Rapids, Mich.: Wm. B. Eerdmans Publishing Co., 1996), 9–18.

as did their ability to speak on behalf of their community. When bioethics entered the clinical realm, there were pressures to use a common language and concepts accessible to patients. Language dependent on a particular religious tradition was not considered appropriate. Relatedly, there were pressures for bioethics to strive for some form of universal understanding across groups in society. The paradigm of modern bioethics entered medicine in the United States at a time when it was adopting the language of the market and an orientation toward the medical consumer. Religious traditions, with their vision of persons in community, did not fit a paradigm in which members are assumed to act like nothing more than self-interested consumers who are uninterested in their responsibilities to others.[50]

There were other factors relating to the methodological reorientation of bioethics. At the end of the 1970s and in the early 1980s, under the increasing influence of contemporary moral philosophy in the United States, bioethics developed a preoccupation with the elaboration of normative criteria or principles and the ethical theory that provides a theoretical underpinning for them. This approach came to be known as principlism. This methodological transition constituted a step toward the development of a rationally consistent and autonomous discipline, but it was to push religious bioethics to the margins because its potential contribution was more in the form of a broad religious or moral vision than the philosophical precision demanded by principlism.[51] One of the two authors of the "bible" of principlism, *Principles of Biomedical Ethics,*[52] James Childress, a Quaker with theological training, provides an example of someone who seems to have decided at this point to adopt a philosophical rather than a theological orientation. One interpretation of Childress's thoughts finds that many of his core principles have a religious underpinning,[53] but theological convictions do not furnish the premises from which his moral conclusions are derived.

The loss of a distinctively religious voice has had major implications for the field of bioethics. Warren Reich comments on the tendency of practitioners to exclude the search for meaning on the part of a moral agent, a meaning that

50. Stephen E. Lammers, "The Marginalization of Religious Voices in Bioethics," in Verhey, ed., *Religion and Medical Ethics,* 19–34.

51. Warren Thomas Reich, "A New Era of Bioethics," in Verhey, ed., *Religion and Medical Ethics,* 96–101.

52. Tom L. Beauchamp and James F. Childress, *Principles of Biomedical Ethics,* 4th ed. (New York and Oxford: Oxford University Press, 1994).

53. Courtney Campbell, "On James F. Childress," in Allen Verhey and Stephen E. Lammers, *Theological Voices in Medical Ethics* (Grand Rapids, Mich.: Wm. B. Eerdmans Publishing Co., 1993), 130–35.

is crucial to moral decisions.[54] Other critiques of secular bioethics, many by long-term practitioners, point to other deficiencies, for example, the degree to which secular bioethics' orientation assumes the paramountcy of individualism and the consequences this has for shaping and distorting its issues, the social construction of realities, and its priorities. By conceptualizing the individual not as a means but as an end, entitled to self-rule or autonomy, bioethics depicts the society as a set of atomistic and self-ruling individuals. It thereby encourages disregard of community bonds and strips away relationships that are morally central within a community.[55] Several commentators believe that the loss of a distinctively religious voice in medical ethics has contributed to these trends and encouraged a form of moral philosophy for use in the marketplace. And, it has deprived society of the wisdom, knowledge, and moral sensitivities of long-established religious traditions.[56]

But, to assume religious thinkers dealing with genetics are about to opt for a secular orientation would be erroneous. In recent years, only one religious ethicist, Roger Shinn, has chosen to write a book-length study of genetics for a general, predominantly secular audience.[57] Others may have sought to reach beyond the religious community, sometimes because of invitations to participate in a multidisciplinary dialogue group or to contribute articles to an edited collection.[58] Nevertheless, it is noteworthy that in doing so they usually maintain a religious orientation, or at least religious themes, and sometimes even utilize a theological vocabulary. Although some of the ethicists Walters points to as practitioners of casuistic thinking, while trained as theologians, do utilize secular philosophical reasoning, they are predominantly from the generation of bioethicists who made this switch at an earlier point in time.[59] In

54. Reich, "New Era for Bioethics," 110.
55. Susan M. Wolf, "Introduction: Gender and Feminism in Bioethics," in Susan M. Wolf, ed., *Feminism and Bioethics: Beyond Reproduction* (New York and Oxford: Oxford University Press, 1996), 14–19.
56. Daniel Callahan, "Religion and the Secularization of Bioethics," in Daniel Callahan and Courtney S. Campbell, eds., *Theology, Religious Traditions, and Bioethics: A Special Supplement to The Hastings Center Report* 20 (July/August 1990): S4.
57. Shinn, *New Genetics.*
58. Some examples of religious ethicists' contributions to predominantly secular volumes are essays by Ronald Cole-Turner, Ted Peters, and Roger Lincoln Shinn in Mark S. Frankel and Albert H. Teich, eds., *The Genetic Frontier: Ethics, Law, and Policy* (Washington, D.C.: American Association for the Advancement of Science, 1994); also see essays by Ronald Cole-Turner, Ted Peters, and C. Ben Mitchell in Chapman, ed., *Perspectives on Genetic Patenting;* and Ronald Cole-Turner's contribution to Erik Parens, ed., *Enhancing Human Traits: Ethical and Social Implications* (Washington, D.C.: Georgetown University Press, 1998).
59. Walters, "Human Genetic Intervention," 242.

fact, this characterization would fit Walters as well. Walters's distinction between cosmic theology and casuistic analysis is itself suspect, at least as defined and applied in his article. Many of his citations are not so much examples of casuistic or case-oriented thinking, as this term is usually used, as they are focused analyses of particular topics or aspects of genetics. And, at least some of these works are as profoundly theological as his first category. It is also noteworthy that, in contrast with the situation in bioethics, most of the religious thinkers working on genetics teach within seminaries and not universities.

Perhaps most importantly, Walters's anticipation of the loss of a genuinely theological voice or explicitly religious perspective is contradicted by the nature and quality of the work currently being done by religious thinkers on genetics. Chapter 5, for example, discussed the very significant explorations of genetics implications for theological anthropology, much of which is of a relatively recent vintage. Walters himself points to a renaissance of cosmic theology and the possibility of a new synthesis that integrates casuistic thinking with cosmic theology. He anticipates that a broader approach to human nature could look at human characteristics in light of millennia of evolution, and in light of the findings of behavior genetics, which is precisely what many religious thinkers have done.[60]

In contrast with Walters, I believe that the major question is not whether religious thinkers address genetic science with a broad or narrow lens but whether they can meaningfully apply relevant theological and ethical perspectives with the analytical rigor achieved by philosophically trained secular thinkers. To do so, religious thinkers will have difficult and complex task— offering a broad vision in the identification of issues melded with specificity, analytical precision, and thoroughness in treatment. As Gustafson notes, statements about science and theology make some general sense at a high level of abstraction. But they often become quite dense and require more specialized competencies and analyses when the subject matter becomes more specific.[61] Thus far, religious thinkers have tended to engage genetics predominantly at a relatively high level of generalization or abstraction. In part this is because religious work on genetics often surveys a wide range of issues and topics, devoting only a short space to each. Secular ethical analyses of genetics tend to have a greater focus and thereby provide more in-depth treatment. To provide a few examples, many religious ethicists and policy statements developed on behalf of religious communities mention issues of justice, but frequently they either list their concerns or identify general principles, such as the need to assure access to the medical benefits of genetic applications. Indeed, whole

60. Ibid., 244–46.
61. Gustafson, *Intersections,* 128.

volumes have been devoted to this topic by secular ethicists.[62] Although religious assessments of genetic therapy generally affirm the inappropriateness of
utilizing these techniques for enhancement purposes, the topic rarely attracts
the attention it warrants or the attention necessary to deal with the complex
issues it raises. In comparison, a recent publication entitled *Enhancing Human
Traits: Ethical and Social Implications,* edited by Erik Parens, a philosopher with
The Hastings Center, fills this vacuum, albeit from a secular perspective.[63]

CONCEPTUAL BUILDING BLOCKS

The manner in which thinkers select, weigh, develop, and apply fundamental conceptual building blocks plays an important role in shaping their evaluation of the ethical implications of particular scientific and technological
innovations. Some norms and concepts—for example, the notion of humanity as stewards or co-creators, the concern with playing God, an emphasis on
human dignity, the prospect of commodification—appear time and again in
the analysis of the implications of genetic developments. While I originally
assumed that doing religious ethics at the frontiers of genetic science was a
matter of identifying relevant theological norms and concepts, I came to realize that the religious thinkers had a far more challenging task before them.
Theology and religious ethics are typically based on sweeping first-order
principles, such as love of neighbor, and/or abstract concepts, for example,
human dignity. The original meaning affixed to these concepts emerged in
response to very different contexts than we face today. In most cases, the cultures were prescientific and the theologians' dialogue partners were more
likely to be philosophy than science or technology. As such, they rarely have
precise content. Nor can they easily be applied to empirical data. These building blocks, therefore, require redefinition, specification, and operationalization
to be relevant for ethical analysis of genetic science. A recurrent theme in this
study is that this process of operationalizing abstract theological concepts
necessitates a multifaceted and multidisciplinary dialogue between science
and the theology where each is open to the other's contribution.

   As noted, this task is made all the more complex because many of the concepts function more like metaphors or symbols. Metaphors refer to "any aspects
of experience that have ever functioned or will ever function as the basis for

62. See, for example, Timothy F. Murphy and Marc A. Lappé, eds., *Justice and the Human
Genome Project* (Berkeley, Los Angeles, and London: University of California Press,
1994), and Maxwell J. Mehlman and Jeffrey R. Botkin, *Access to the Genome: The
Challenge to Equality* (Washington, D.C.: Georgetown University Press, 1998).
63. Parens, ed., *Enhancing Human Traits.*

interpreting the whole of reality."[64] Therefore various religious claims, for example, the assertion that humans are created in the image of God, tend to evoke a range of meanings over time and within different theological contexts rather than to have a fixed and carefully defined content. Historically this characteristic has been an asset because it has enabled religious traditions to adjust and adapt to varying situations, but it also makes these symbols or concepts difficult to serve as standards or criteria by which to develop guides for action.[65] To do so requires updating the norms, concepts, and metaphors drawn from sacred texts, tradition, and theology through an interface with science; clarifying and refining their meaning; and developing criteria by which they can be applied to contemporary issues.

The literature reviewed in this study shows the limitations of inherited theological concepts and metaphors for undertaking ethical analysis of genetic science as well as the lag in updating and revising them. Chapter 2, for instance, dealt with problems in applying the notion of stewardship. The concept of stewards, which is rooted in Scripture, characterizes the vocation of humanity as a servant who has been given the responsibility for the management and service of something belonging to another, in this case the Creator. According to this formulation, as servant-managers, humanity cannot fundamentally alter or dispose of the property of another.[66] While stewardship may provide the grounding for an ecological vision, emphasizing the need to care for and preserve God's creation, it is much less fruitful when applied to issues related to genetic engineering. This is because the classical notion of stewardship predates the discovery of evolution and assumes a static, finished, and hierarchically ordered universe in which every creature and life-form had its own place. In such a universe, stewardship implies respecting the natural order and not seeking to change it. However, twentieth-century science undermines these assumptions, showing that nature is dynamic and ever evolving. This suggests it is appropriate for humanity to make at least some changes in the order of things. But, on what basis should we draw a line between what is appropriate for a steward and what is a transgression? The denominational statements that employ a stewardship paradigm do not usually make an effort to update, reinterpret, or deal with the dilemmas of applying this model to a dynamic and ever-changing creation.

---

64. Wogaman, *Christian Moral Judgment,* 17.

65. Jan Christian Heller, "Religiously Based Objections to Cloning," in James M. Humber and Robert F. Almeder, eds., *Human Cloning* (Totowa, N.J.: Humana Press, 1998), 161.

66. Douglas John Hall, *The Steward: A Biblical Symbol Come of Age* (New York: Friendship Press, 1982).

The book *On Behalf of God: A Christian Ethic for Biology,* written by religious philosopher Bruce Reichenbach and geneticist V. Elving Anderson, is one of the few works that attempts to update the concept of stewardship so as to be able to apply it to genetics.[67] Drawing a Christian ethic of stewardship from the opening chapters of Genesis, they interpret this ethic as having three components: the human responsibility to fill the land, to rule the land, and to work with and care for the property of the owner. In contrast with traditional stewardship models, they also draw on one of Jesus' parables (Matt. 25:14-30). Utilizing these resources, they draw the conclusion that stewards are charged with seemingly contradictory obligations to both preserve and change, conserve and risk, the property entrusted to them. To argue for the permissibility of change, Reichenbach and Anderson reject tenets of classical theology that portray God as knowing all possibilities, controlling all actualities, and instead portray God as a risk taker, especially in the divine relationship with free human beings (65–66). Given this understanding of the human mandate, they then wrestle with the central questions of what we are obligated to change, what other kinds of changes are permissible, for what purposes are we to change creation, and what are the limits of the change (40–72).

Reichenbach and Anderson posit that science and technology should be held to the same accounting as all other stewards: "They must address concerns about what is worth knowing in light of human needs, about what is worth doing in light of potential human good, and about what scientists should be doing in light of the development of their own moral character" (62). But, what does that mean in terms of setting priorities or drawing limits? Reichenbach and Anderson do not offer a clear answer. One problem is that they seek guidelines for genetic engineering in a source unsuited to provide them with answers. Scripture cannot offer prescriptions for complex contemporary conundrums related to science and technology. Another limitation is that once their stewardship model is developed, Reichenbach and Anderson do not draw middle axioms for its applications. While the chapters dealing with specific issues, two of which address aspects of genetic science, are factually illuminating and their analysis and recommendations insightful, this is largely despite, not because of, their efforts to apply their ethic of stewardship to the issues at hand.

Resources based on the alternative concept of humans as God's partner, created co-creator, or co-creator at least begin with a theological model that is more relevant to scientific discoveries in biology and genetics. In contrast with the stewardship model, the various formulations of humans as God's partner, created co-creator, or co-creator begin with the acknowledgment that "scientific research has revealed to us that creation is not fixed, but ongoing" and that

---

67. Reichenbach and Anderson, *On Behalf of God.*

"God calls us to be involved in the process."[68] This perspective typically relates human creativity with the continuing quest for knowledge and extends it to decoding and learning to control the intricate powers compressed in genes of DNA molecules.[69] Two theologians, Philip Hefner[70] and Ted Peters,[71] have been central to the effort to develop the concept of humans as created co-creators. Hefner, the concept's originator, uses it primarily to illuminate the human role within the process of evolution. He asserts that the distinctive essence of the created co-creator is the freedom to participate in God's ongoing activity and thereby to share in the image of God. His explication is highly abstract. Peters has sought to apply the concept of created co-creator to genetics, but again it remains more a metaphor of human creativity and freedom. On the whole, however, the theological concept of co-creation or partnership does not generate a clearer delineation of appropriate applications or limitations for genetic engineering than does the stewardship model used in other resources. Like the stewardship-oriented documents, however, the theological affirmations of co-creation are not translated into specific precepts or middle axioms that can then provide the basis for ethical analyses and policy recommendations. Instead, both remain more a metaphor than a critical framework for analysis.

One of the consequences of the failure to operationalize these concepts is that the positions of documents and resources utilizing the metaphor of stewardship may not be different from those that prefer co-creation or partnership. For example, it was rumored through the religious grapevine that the task force which authored the United Methodist policy statement on genetics swung between using models of stewardship and co-creation, depending on the configuration of attendance at meetings, but with little consequence for the content or its recommendations. Cole-Turner concludes his book *The New Genesis* with an emphatic rejection of the notion of humanity being imaged as God's co-creator. Yet, he offers theological affirmations that conceptualize genetic engineering as an extension of God's creating and redeeming activity, which differ only slightly from Hefner's and Peter's views that God works through both natural processes and human initiatives to achieve genetic changes.[72]

---

68. Presbyterian Church (U.S.A.), 195th General Assembly (1983), "The Covenant of Life and the Caring Community," *Social Policy Compilation* (Louisville: Advisory Committee on Social Witness Policy, 1992): 10.

69. National Council of Churches, "Genetic Science for Human Benefit," 14–15.

70. Hefner, *Human Factor.*

71. Peters, *Playing God?*

72. Ronald Cole-Turner, *The New Genesis: Theology and the Genetic Revolution* (Louisville: Westminister/John Knox Press, 1993), 109.

"Playing God" has come to be used as shorthand for concerns that it is inappropriate for humans to change the way other living organisms or human beings are constituted and amounts to usurping the creative prerogative of God. As noted in chapter 2, several religious ethicists have made a notable contribution to analyzing this phrase, but more in the line of deconstructing its meaning than giving it positive content. Claims that genetic engineering amounts to playing God have served as a rallying cry for a variety of critics, many of them secular thinkers. Nevertheless, as ethicist Roger Shinn notes, "Theology, even in all its diversity, has traditionally taught that God acts through the processes of nature, which long antedated humankind, who sometimes serve and sometimes resist the divine will."[73] Thus, according to Shinn, the phrase "playing God" does not readily provide an answer as to whether specific biomedical acts are a sign of God's activity or human defiance.[74]

Despite the title of his book, *Playing God?*, Ted Peters tends to be disparaging of the usefulness of that enigmatic phrase. Like many other religious thinkers, he argues that the primary role of the phrase "playing God" is to serve as a warning and that it has very little cognitive value when looked at from the perspective of a theologian.[75] He suggests that it can have three overlapping meanings. The first has to do with a sense of awe about learning fundamental secrets of nature, a kind of belief that we are on the threshold of acquiring Godlike knowledge and powers. The second relates to wielding power over life and death, something that the medical profession routinely exercises. The third, which Peters considers the most relevant to genetics, is the use of science to alter life and influence evolution.[76] Peters disputes what many critics claim, that genetic engineering and other reproductive technologies go beyond the limits of a reasonable dominion over nature or at least provide temptations in that direction. His elevation of human freedom and creativity as God's created co-creator provides a wide latitude for human intervention, so much so that it is difficult to draw any boundaries or limits.

The concept of human dignity and the related affirmation that human beings are created in the image of God figure prominently in religious ethics dealing with genetic applications, cloning, and genetic patenting. Despite the long history of theological development and its important role in this literature, there is still a lack of intellectual clarity and precision as to what is being implied and what is required to uphold the dignity and worth of the person. Do appeals to human dignity carry fundamentally different connotations from

73. Shinn, *New Genetics,* 144.
74. Ibid., 144, 154–55.
75. Peters, *Playing God?* 2.
76. Ibid., 10–11.

a religious as compared with a secular perspective? How does human dignity relate to the physical body and bodily integrity? Relatedly, what are the foundations of human personhood, and does a nondualistic but nonreductionist conception of personhood vest human DNA with a sacred status? None of these important questions have yet been answered. Few thinkers have even addressed them.

Cloning Human Beings, the report and recommendations of the NBAC, identifies seven ways in which the theological conception of creation in God's image has been interpreted in Western religious tradition: (1) moral agency is inherent in the human self and creates moral responsibilities, including respect for the equal freedom and agency of other persons as well as personal responsibility for one's actions before one's conscience, others, and ultimately God; (2) humans, since they are created in the image of God, are fundamentally equal, and their equality transcends any differentiation based on gender, race, class, or ethnicity; (3) human beings are relational and social creatures; (4) human diversity, including gender diversity, also reflects the image of God and provides positive warrants for the expression of human sexuality; (5) the person is revealed and expressed through the body, not merely as a disembodied mind or will or an intellectual or spiritual essence; (6) as embodied selves, human beings are in nature and transcend nature; and (7) although human beings are created in God's image, they are finite and fallible, with limited capacities to predict and direct the course of actions they initiate.[77] Many, if not most, of these themes appear and reappear in the literature reviewed in this study. The dilemma is that many authors fail to specify which of the several interpretations they have in mind. In some cases, they slide into a different approach without seemingly being aware they are doing so.

Utilizing an analysis of the phrase "image of God," as a case study, Jan Heller makes the point that core symbols cannot easily serve as standards or criteria by which a particular action may be judged, either prospectively or retrospectively, as right, wrong, or permissible under specified conditions, particularly in relationship to scientific developments. According to Heller, their surplus of meanings often leads to contradictory recommendations.[78] One of the principal tensions he identifies is whether the exercise of human creativity in the effort to understand and manipulate nature should be interpreted as an appropriate expression of the image of God or a human usurpation of a role that is properly reserved for God. As noted in chapter 2, this dilemma underlies the difficulties religious thinkers have in drawing boundaries between what is

77. NBAC, *Cloning Human Beings: Report and Recommendations* (Rockville, Md.: NBAC, 1997), 43–44.
78. Heller, "Religiously Based Objections to Cloning," 161.

appropriate and inappropriate in human genetic engineering and human genetic intervention. Heller contends that religious objections to cloning fail to answer this question in a meaningful way and therefore are not able to show what should be regarded as forbidden or wrong with cloning as compared with other interventions into natural human reproductive processes. Nevertheless, Heller rightly acknowledges that much of religious thinkers' discussion about the implications of cloning for human dignity is insightful and helpful.[79]

Some of the discussions about the implications of genetics for human dignity also raise a related concern about commodification. The concept of commodification figured prominently in the religious critiques of cloning and genetic patenting. Despite Heller's rather harsh assessment of the religious critique of human cloning, he does acknowledge that concerns that cloning will objectify and commodify human life may have promise as the basis for ethical analysis because of their greater specificity. Here he is referring to the arguments that clones will be used as a means to others' ends, or, once created, clones will be treated by others with less respect than is morally warranted, given their status as human beings.[80] As noted in chapter 4, both opponents of patenting and other religious ethicists expressed the view that patenting of human DNA and tissues would promote a commodified view of the person inconsistent with human dignity. Yet, despite the importance of this claim, none of those involved in the debate on patenting specified clearly how commodification diminishes human dignity.

Chapter 4 described religious analyses of patenting as a theology in process, and its conclusion identified a variety of subjects deserving of greater attention and development. Some of the issues concerned the theological status of various intellectual property claims, such as the difference between making intellectual property claims to categories of life and owning tangible property in land or animals. Others required the development of a theology of property that would delve more deeply into the implications of affirming God as creator to our understanding of the basis, scope, and limits of human intellectual property rights. Commodification was a third subject, needing both a clearer explanation as to what is meant by commodification and a specification as to how commodification diminishes human dignity. The ontological, ethical, and theological status of DNA was another item on the list.

The need to gain greater clarity and depth about the concept of human dignity and its relationship to the affirmation of the human being as created in the image of God is a critical task. Given the many meanings traditionally attached

79. Ibid., 162–68.
80. Ibid., 169–70.

to the concept of human dignity, at the least, religious thinkers should be more precise as to what is implied in affirming the dignity and worth of a person. They also should answer more clearly a series of questions: Does the concept of human dignity necessarily carry different connotations from a religious as compared with a secular perspective, for example, in the human rights literature? If so, what are the specific dimensions of a religious approach to human dignity? How does human dignity relate to physical body and bodily integrity? What limitations does human dignity impose and why for genetic testing, somatic or germ-line gene therapy, cloning, and/or the commercialization of human DNA? What does a commitment to protecting human dignity require in specific circumstances? What are the implications of a nondualistic, physicalist account of the person for conceptions of human dignity?

As noted in several chapters, the failure to concretize and give specific content to intellectual building blocks has a corollary in the frequent absence of intermediary criteria or middle axioms. Not that middle axioms are a form of religious philosophical principlism; rather, they might serve as the next step in operationalizing the content of specific concepts. Perhaps the best way to describe them is as concept subcomponents that can serve as a concrete means to assess the ethical implications of specific acts, developments, or policies. The lack of such criteria makes it exceedingly difficult to apply concepts or religious principles to empirical data. As a result, religious ethicists frequently operate at a level of intuition rather than careful analysis.

CHALLENGES TO THEOLOGY

Another issue this volume has sought to address is the challenges contemporary developments in the biological sciences, particularly genetics, pose to traditional theologies. The plurality of traditional theologies makes it difficult to generalize across various communities, but at least the following can be noted. First, the genetic revolution makes it even more important to come to terms theologically with evolution in nature and in human development. One of the most significant divides in the literature surveyed is each author's position on evolution. Of the religious thinkers writing on genetics, a very small number are consistently creationists who refuse to accept evidence for evolution. A larger group of religious thinkers, however, are still reluctant to place human beings fully within the evolutionary process. Some, like Pope John Paul II, are modified creationists who accept that the human body is the product of an evolutionary process but, in keeping with tradition, assume that God directly intervenes in the creation of each person, adding the soul or shaping the human essence. Many others, perhaps the majority, have not as yet explicitly dealt with and come to terms with these issues. There has been surprisingly little systematic theological exploration of the implications of evolution for understanding human nature.

Second, developments in genetics raise a series of issues traditional theological formulations cannot answer and thereby challenge contemporary theologians to go beyond their inherited traditions. Virtually every one of the conceptual building blocks applied to genetic science requires further intellectual development to be able to discern and resolve the perplexing ethical choices posed by genetics. To name but a few, drawing clearer boundaries for appropriate forms of genetic engineering appears to be related to further development of concepts of stewardship and/or co-creation. The possibility of human cloning should stimulate thinking about the sources of human identity, human dignity, and human uniqueness. The genetic patenting controversy underscore the need for improved theological understandings of property, particularly intellectual property, human dignity, and the nature of DNA. Developments in genetic science reraise age-old questions about what is the "normatively human" in an exacerbated form. To evaluate and respond to proponents of sociobiology views of genetic reductionism and hypotheses about genetic determinism, religious thinkers have to address questions about the relationship between nature and nurture in the evolution of morality in a new and more sophisticated manner.

Third, genetic science raises new questions about the relationship between our genetic heritage and sin. It undermines the Christian doctrine of original sin as the first sin, a historical act of ancient forebears. Modern genetics rules out the possibility that acquired characteristics, like behavioral changes, can be inherited by subsequent generations. Genetic research indicates that our capacities, including those for moral and spiritual life, are conditioned by our biological inheritance, but this is far from proving that specific behavioral proclivities of any kind, whether to violence and selfishness or to altruism and compassion, are biologically determined. This leaves considerable room for interpretations of the origins and nature of sin in the human condition.

Chapter 5 reviewed two very different contemporary theological interpretations of sin that are consistent with the findings of genetic science and do not fall into a simplistic biological trap. The first was Philip Hefner's redefinition of original sin as "the dissonance between the pre-human information that we carry in our genome and the distinctively human, the dissonance between societal culture and individual 'selfish' human nature, and the innate fallibility and vulnerability that marks our character as humans."[81] The other, more compelling, view is that of Marjorie Hewitt Suchocki, who considers sin partially

81. Philip Hefner, "Determinism, Freedom, and Moral Failure," in Peters, ed., *Genetics*, 119–20.

biological in nature but primarily the product of social inheritance as embodied in social structures.[82] There are, of course, many other options beyond these two alternatives. The important thing is that any treatment of sin consider the biological or genetic components in a manner cognizant of the findings of genetic science.

The most notable challenge, as well as advance, in theological clarification and conceptual development comes in drawing the implications of genetic science for understanding the human essence, portrayed in classical theology as the soul or spirit. Genetic research, like work in the neurosciences, makes it difficult to maintain a dualistic conception of a self divided into a body and soul. The findings from genetic science therefore make problematic the religious doctrines that describe the soul as completely distinct from the body and consisting of a fundamentally different kind of being. To take genetic science seriously requires an integrated and embodied view of the human person. This has prompted some theologians and ethicists to reformulate a notion of the human essence that is neither reductionistic nor dualistic.

One promising line of interpretation, discussed in chapter 5, is the development of a nonreductive physicalist account of the person by a multidisciplinary group of scholars in the recently published collection *Whatever Happened to the Soul?*[83] Many articles in the volume reconceptualize the soul as a physiologically embodied property of human nature and not an entity with a distinctive existence, awareness, and agency. Several of the authors propose an understanding of the soul as a dimension of human experiences that arises out of personal relatedness. According to one of these essays, written by psychologist Warren Brown, experiences of relatedness to others, to the self, and most particularly to God endow a person with the attributes that traditionally have been attributed to the soul.[84]

As noted in chapter 5, a nonreductionist physicalist approach fits with a trend in recent theology proposing a relational interpretation of the symbol of the image of God. It also is consistent with the work of several theologians defining the human soul as a set of capabilities defined by genes but not entirely determined by them. Ronald Cole-Turner, for example, suggests thinking of the soul or self as the coherence within the complexity of the human organism, a coherence that is genetically conditioned but also transcends that conditioning.[85] In

---

82. Marjorie Hewitt Suchocki, *The Fall to Violence: Original Sin in Relational Theology* (New York: Continuum Books, 1994).

83. Warren S. Brown, Nancey Murphy, and H. Newton Malony, eds., *Whatever Happened to the Soul? Scientific and Theological Portraits of Human Nature* (Minneapolis: Fortress Press, 1998).

84. Warren S. Brown, "Cognitive Contributions to the Soul," in Brown, Murphy, and Malony, eds., *Whatever Happened to the Soul?* 99–102.

like manner, Karen Lebacqz offers a view of the soul as a symbol of the covenant between God and each person.[86] For Anne Clifford, the soul is synonymous with the center of human individuation.[87]

DISTINCTIVENESS OF RELIGIOUS ETHICS

This query relates back to the question of defining the nature of religious ethics at the frontiers of science: Are there specific approaches, sensitivities, or criteria that distinguish religious and secular ethicists? While religious communities and speakers do not speak with one voice, they do tend to differ from many secular ethicists. This contributes both to the strength and, in some cases, the limitations of their work.

One of the contributions religious perspectives provide is to offer broad frameworks of understanding and commitment so necessary to deal with these complex issues. A religious centering by its very nature offers a vision in which persons are responsible beyond their own self-interest to the ultimate source of grounding of their lives and being. Resources written by the religious community typically emphasize a need for science and technology to serve the welfare, common good, and fulfillment of the broader human society. The symbols and metaphors that complicate the ethical analysis of religious thinkers may also incline them to deal with the broader implications of specific discoveries and applications.

That religious ethicists tend to go beyond an individualistic perspective may reflect their own sense of connectedness to a community, a tradition, and ultimately the divine. Religious thinkers also often have a social conception of personhood. In contrast with the secular approach based on individual rights and on notions of reproductive and medical privacy, many religious thinkers hold up the importance of a framework that places individuals within the context of community and upholds the importance of considerations of the common good. In her commentary written for a UCC working group considering ethical and theological considerations related to cloning, Karen Lebacqz wrote the following about the Christian vision:

> In that vision, all individual rights are always concordant with a fundamental commitment to the good, including the demands of justice. No one has

85. Cole-Turner, *New Genesis,* 88.
86. Karen Lebacqz, "Alien Dignity: The Legacy of Helmut Thielicke for Bioethics," in Allen Verhey, ed., *Religion and Medical Ethics: Looking Back, Looking Forward* (Grand Rapids, Mich.: William B. Eerdmans Publishing Co., 1996), 44–49.
87. Anne Clifford, C.S.J., "Biological Evolution and the Human Soul," in Ted Peters, ed., *Science and Religion: The New Convergence* (Boulder, Colo.: Westview Press, 1998), 172.

"rights" independent of a concern for the social whole and for the well-being of God's creation. All "rights" involve responsibilities. While it is difficult to delineate exactly the range of these responsibilities, or the limits that they might place on the exercise of individual rights, we know that unless we take a relational view of the world, we fail to capture the purposes of a God who so loved us that God sent God's only begotten son that all people might have life and have it abundantly.[88]

Lisa Cahill, in her testimony to the NBAC, made an appeal to go beyond the confines of the principles of autonomy, individuality, and individual freedom to consider other social goods, particularly the interdependence of all in the society we create for ourselves and our children. Like many other religious thinkers, Cahill's frame of reference was the character of a good society and what we can do concretely to move in the appropriate direction.[89] Likewise, Aziz Sachedina stated in his testimony that the central ethical question for Islam was how cloning might affect interhuman or interpersonal relationships. He asked whether human advancement in biotechnology-created relationships would jeopardize the very foundation of human community.[90]

While this study has criticized the failure of religious thinkers to focus more systematically and in greater depth on justice issues, for example, in the discussion of genetic patenting, it's important to note that religious thinkers generally are more sensitive than their secular counterparts to justice considerations. Justice traditions within the religious community and concerns for the needs of those lacking a voice in decision making play a role in the response to genetic technologies and cloning. Also, the understanding of justice and its requirements is significantly broader among religious ethicists. Many secular philosophers and ethicists, particularly those influenced by the "Georgetown mantra" based on the Tom Beauchamp and James Childress *Principles of Biomedical Ethics,*[91] identify justice as only one of several principles central to biomedical ethics. And, they often treat justice as of less importance than other principles, particularly respect for the autonomy of patients. Justice is typically explicated in secular literature primarily in terms of fairness in one-on-one relationships, as between a provider and a patient. In contrast, religious ethicists

88. Karen Lebacqz, "Some Ethical and Theological Considerations about Cloning" (paper written for the UCC Genetics Working Group, 1998, quoted with the permission of the author).
89. Lisa Sowle Cahill, Testimony to the NBAC, 14 March 1997 (Washington, D.C.: Eberlin Reporting Service), 50.
90. Aziz Sachedina, Testimony to the NBAC, 14 March 1997 (Washington, D.C.: Eberlin Reporting Service), 16–21.
91. Beauchamp and Childress, *Principles of Biomedical Ethics.*

view justice as constitutive of systems as well as individual relationships. They are more likely to question the basis on which broader societal patterns of benefits and burdens are distributed. Religious ethicists often go beyond principles of formal justice and empirical research dealing with various risks, costs, and benefits to a more egalitarian approach to justice. When religious ethicists deal with justice issues they also often mention the need for preferential access for the disadvantaged. Again, to quote Lebacqz, "Justice requires that we see ourselves as bound in a covenant of life with life, in which individual freedom and choice is always coupled with a sense of social responsibility and a particular concern for the poor and oppressed. This is what it means to have a biblical perspective on justice."[92] Lebacqz also emphasizes that a Christian perspective evaluates technological achievements in the context of global justice. Because cloning will not be available to the poor and oppressed around the globe, but only to the wealthy and privileged, she concludes that it violates the demands of a wide-ranging biblical justice.[93] Nevertheless, much of the discussion of justice is brief and cursory in the religious literature on genetics. Understandings of the requirements of justice often remain more implicit than explicit, and concerns are rarely developed adequately.

In contrast with the tendency of secular ethicists to emphasize the positive potential contributions of genetic technologies, many religious thinkers evince what might be described as a presumption of caution. That is, they place greater priority on anticipating and preventing potential problems than on favoring technologies and applications because they may bring future benefits. Writing for the Evangelical Lutheran Church, Roger Willer characterized this approach as "critical engagement," meaning that Christians generally support genetic science but are required to evaluate any particular genetic discovery or application according to criteria informed by faith and Christian sources.[94] This difference in emphasis is considerable when comparing the religious approach with the comments of some secular thinkers on cloning. Some secular thinkers, for example, argued that it would be premature to close off research opportunities on the grounds that only a few people are likely to reap benefits and claimed that it would be prejudicial to ban an entire line of research because of possible unethical applications. In contrast, religious thinkers tended to be more mindful of those who were likely to be harmed than those who were likely to benefit. They sought to protect important societal values, even if this puts constraints on science and technology.

92. Lebacqz, "Considerations about Cloning."
93. Ibid.
94. Roger A. Willer, "Introduction," in Willer, ed., *Genetic Testing and Screening*, 8.

This presumption of caution has its limits, primarily because the approach to genetics is generally hopeful and supportive. The tensions intrinsic to balancing hopes and fears, accepting the benefits while still offering a warning about some of the likely consequences, are embodied in the writings of Philip Hefner. In one of his essays on genetics, Hefner offers a perceptive critique of the prevailing worldview in our society, including how it impinges on genetics, and suggests that the Christian faith and theological perspectives offer a constructive alternative.[95] Hefner characterizes the tapestry of ideas, commitments, values, hopes, and fears that currently forms the background of what we say and do as a "fix-it" mentality. He argues that this approach to life reflects the innate human capacity to co-create and shape nature, but that it also results in a failure to acknowledge our status as creatures in nature with fundamental limitations and flaws. Another problem with the fix-it disposition, according to Hefner, is its tendency to segregate and ostracize those who deviate from the norm and treat persons with disabilities as needing to be fixed rather than valuable in their own right. He finds corrections in Christian theological perspectives on finitude, ambiguity, and failure, and most importantly in the belief that humans are weak and sinful.

Does the religious literature on genetics, specifically those works written by Christians, offer a real alternative to the prevailing fix-it or "hammer and nails" approach to life? Not really. Yes, there are some very significant cautions about proceeding with remaking human nature or the world around us. Hefner, for example, warns that the HGP, as well as the growing emphasis on genetic testing, reflects the prevailing worldview. But, theological conceptions of humanity as co-creators or partners in completing or correcting the flaws in the creation, ironically popularized through some of Hefner's own writing, tend to support, even sacralize, efforts at genetic engineering. And, theologians and ethicists who refrain from using these images are little different in their underlying views on genetics. Moreover, most of the religious analysis of genetics shares the societal desire for health and physical well-being that Hefner attributes to the prevailing worldview, as well as the strong hope that genetics will significantly contribute to healing and improved health. Thus, despite their discomfort with the impact of genetic technologies, few, if any, religious ethicists stand apart from this consensus and oppose these developments. Human cloning constitutes the one exception where members of the religious community were more likely to utter the "prophetic no."

95. Philip Hefner, "The Genetic 'Fix': Challenges to Christian Faith and Community," in Willer, ed., *Genetic Testing and Screening*, 73–93.

RELEVANCE OF TRADITIONAL CONFESSIONAL
FORMULATIONS AND BOUNDARIES

Postmodernism has encouraged some religious, as well as secular, thinkers to emphasize the distinctiveness and particularities of their heritage and to question the relevance of broader communities of belief and commitment for ethical analysis. These ethicists, for example, the founders of a journal entitled *Christian Bioethics,* assume that meaningful ethical reflection by religious thinkers must necessarily begin with the traditions of particular communities. An article in the first issue written by one of the editors of this journal to set forth its perspective contends that bioethics requires a vision of the good moral life and that the various Christian communities have very different approaches to this topic. The article argues that to address specific issues, such as birth, suffering, life, death, and stewardship, it is necessary to situate them in confessional frameworks of moral thought and theology. The journal also tends to be disparaging of secular attempts to develop universal moral theory, such as the Beauchamp and Childress project to identify a widely shared set of principles to serve as the basis for resolving moral dilemmas.[96] According to the critique in *Christian Bioethics,* these efforts ignore the need for a content and context to interpret and apply principles or universals. The editors are also critical of previous efforts to departicularize Christian bioethics, claiming that a "facile ecumenism" reduces the content of Christian morality to the lowest common denominator.[97]

Without arguing the specifics of these claims, a few observations are warranted. First of all, many of the topics on which *Christian Bioethics* has focused are more rooted in traditional Christian thought than the issues raised by the genetic revolution. Issues addressed by the journal have been devoted to suffering, double-effect, authority, end-of-life decision making, euthanasia, physician-assisted suicide, and the moral integrity and spirituality of Christian health care professionals. Doctrines and traditional methodologies can be applied more readily to discussions about the beginning and end of life than to the appropriate limitations of human intervention into the genetic basis of life. Second, the authors contributing to the journal tend to have more conservative and traditional approaches to religion than most of the ethicists writing on genetics. The position and perspective of the editorial board undoubtedly have attracted like-minded contributors. Differences in religious affiliation between the bioethicists writing for the journal and the thinkers dealing with genetics

---

96. Beauchamp and Childress, *Principles of Biomedical Ethics.*
97. Kevin William Wildes, S.J., "The Ecumenical and Non-Ecumenical Dialectic of Christian Bioethics," *Christian Bioethics* 1 (1995): 121–27.

may also be a factor. As noted, the majority of ethicists addressing genetics come from mainline Protestant backgrounds, whereas many of the articles published in the journal are by Catholic, Orthodox, and more conservative Protestant authors. Few, if any of the Protestant denominations have set up an authoritative system of moral teachings by which to answer troubling ethical questions, but Catholic doctrine, particularly about the origin of life and status of the embryo and fetus, does offer a framework from which to proceed. Third, medical ethics frequently requires a less profound interface with science than does genetics.

Those advocating the importance of inherited traditions for shaping bioethics and, by extension, work on genetics and biotechnology often fail to take three important factors into account. The first is that most religious traditions are more diverse and pluralistic than their position implies. To describe religious ethics as community-embedded or tradition-embodied does not necessarily determine how the heritage will be used or the shape of the resulting ethical stance. Nor does it acknowledge that major issues, including the relevance of foundational texts to contemporary issues, may be contested within, as well as across, various traditions. This is the case even within communities in which the official teaching is considered binding, and even more so in others. Interpretations of the teaching, the authority of sources, and appropriate methodologies for applying the tradition to contemporary issues are often contested.

Writing about Catholic responses to official church teachings on sexuality, a central topic within Catholic doctrine, Lisa Sowle Cahill identifies four groups: traditionalists, revisionists, skeptics, and the alienated, each of which represents a different position on the role of the magisterium in shaping Catholic practical morality. According to Cahill, traditionalists accept the full authority of magisterial teaching and believe there is no basis for dissent. Revisionists accord magisterial teaching considerable weight but acknowledge that it may be flawed. In such circumstances they believe the appropriate response is to seek reformulation. Skeptics are doubtful about the authority of magisterial teaching and openly dissent from church teaching that appears to be misguided. The alienated treat magisterial teaching as the source against which their views are defined.[98]

This means that a spokesperson for the National Conference of Catholic Bishops is likely to affirm official church teachings on the moral status of the fetus and embryo, but Roman Catholic theologians and ethicists often offer a

---

98. Lisa Sowle Cahill, "Can We Get Real about Sex," *Commonweal* 67 (1990): 497–503, cited in Paul Lauritzen, "Catholic Magisterial Teaching as a Source for Bioethics," in P. F. Camenisch, ed., *Religious Methods and Resources in Bioethics* (Dordrecht, The Netherlands: Kluwer Academic Publishers, 1994), 309–10.

range of positions. Testimony given to various bodies on Roman Catholic views involving human embryonic stem cell research exemplifies this dichotomy. In January 1999, Richard Doerflinger, the Associate Director for Policy Development at the Secretariat for Pro-Life Activities of the National Conference of Catholic Bishops, presenting the views of the Catholic bishops' to a Senate hearing, emphasized the unacceptability of using cells derived from deliberately destroyed human embryos in federally funded research.[99] Similarly, testifying before NBAC in May 1999, Edmund Pellegrino, Professor of Medicine and Medical Ethics at Georgetown University, argued against the moral acceptability of research involving embryonic stem cells obtained from *in vitro* fertilized blastocysts and embryonic primordial germ-line cells from aborted fetuses. He indicated that his objections were grounded in the teachings of the Roman Catholic Church about the moral status of the fetus and embryo; the insufficiency of utilitarian arguments that would justify destruction or discarding of embryos; and practical difficulties of effectively regulating the practice.[100] In contrast, Margaret Farley, a Roman Catholic theologian teaching at Yale University, emphasized the diversity of perspectives on this issue within Roman Catholic moral tradition in her testimony to NBAC. She stated that there are clear disagreements among Catholics on a range of issues, including conflicting assessments of the moral status of the human embryo, assisted reproductive technologies, and the use of aborted fetuses as sources of stem cells. Her own position is that the human embryo in its earliest stages does not have the moral status of a person, and therefore its use for certain kinds of research can be justified.[101]

Similar constituencies and disagreements characterize many other religious communities where there is a need or desire to represent an official or semi-official position. Currently, for example, heated discussions are going on among Jewish bioethicists about the use of *halakahkic* material as the basis for claims about the Jewish view on disputed topics in medical ethics.[102]

99. Richard M. Doerflinger, "Testimony on Behalf of the Committee for Pro-Life Activities, National Conference of Catholic Bishops," Hearing on Legal Status of Embryonic Stem Cell Research, Senate Appropriations Subcommittee on Labor, Health and Education, 26 January 1999, <http://www.senate.gov/-appropriations/labor/Doerf1-26-99.htm>

100. Edmund D. Pellegrino, M.D., "Testimony Regarding Human Stem Cell Research," National Bioethics Advisory Commission, Washington, D.C., 7 May 1999, text distributed at the hearing.

101. Margaret A. Farley, Ph.D., "Roman Catholic Views on Research Involving Human Embryonic Stem Cells," National Bioethics Advisory Commission, Washington, D.C., 7 May 1999, text distributed at the hearing.

102. Zohar, *Alternatives in Jewish Bioethics,* 6.

The second important factor not taken into account is that when and if particular thinkers draw on their religious heritage, the manner in which they do so and apply it to genetics, genetic patenting, or cloning may differ quite significantly from another theologian or ethicist from the same community. Contemporary theological orientations—feminism, process thinking, liberation and justice perspectives—often matter more than, or at the least interact with, traditional confessional resources. Because traditions are quite diverse, thinkers have many options as to the manner in which they can appropriate and interpret their relevance for specific issues arising from genetic science. Thus, theologians within the same religious community do not necessarily agree with one another, and if they do so, it may have more to do with their shared sensitivities to particular concerns or their vocabularies than with confessional doctrines.

Third, the genetic revolution has brought many issues to the fore for which there is little direct relevance within any of the traditions. This is the very reason for the title of this work, *Unprecedented Choices.* Confessional formulations and dogmas that originated in response to doctrinal debates of another century rarely provide a satisfactory grounding for the dilemmas resulting from contemporary science and technology. As Albert Moraczewski, the representative of the National Conference of Catholic Bishops, noted in his testimony to the NBAC on the Catholic church's position on cloning, "Neither sacred Scripture nor the Catholic Church's moral tradition have explicitly and fully treated this issue."[103] That is not to say there is nothing in the tradition from which to craft a response, but those teachings and ethical principles that most readily apply often tend to be the more universalistic norms shared across communities. And, hasty policy statements written in response to scientific developments simply do not carry much moral authority.

While it is true that there is a considerable denominational literature on various topics related to the genetics revolution, the statements and publications rarely, if ever, have a strict confessional grounding. Most resources prepared under the sponsorship of a particular community are only loosely linked with historical doctrines and earlier policy positions. Instead, the purpose of the various denominational efforts appears more to develop materials that will appeal to and service their particular constituencies. This does not, of course, mean that there are no differences in these documents. However, the distinctive orientations, reasoning, and positions infusing the documents seem more to reflect the composition of their respective drafting committees or task

103. Albert Moraczewski, Testimony to the NBAC, 13 March 1997 (Washington, D.C.: Eberlin Reporting Service), 52.

forces than the denominational origins. As an example, *Wrestling with the Future: Our Genes and Our Choices* defines the basic moral framework shared by Anglicans/Episcopalians as follows: (1) a belief that a moral order pervades creation that is grounded in God's wisdom and is partially accessible through the gifts of reason and grace; (2) a conviction that living a moral life is essential to our relationship with God; (3) an understanding that the moral life has social dimensions rooted in the body of Christ; and (4) a commitment to the values of love and justice based on the belief that each person, as a creature made in the image of God, has unique worth.[104] Undoubtedly these principles not only could be affirmed by Anglicans, but would characterize core beliefs of virtually all Christians and with a slight change in wording many Jews and Muslims as well. If the various statements, resolutions, and resources commissioned by official bodies were stripped of identifiers, it might be difficult to figure out the affiliations of many of them.

Obviously most religious thinkers do not begin with a tabula rasa. Nevertheless, given the unprecedented character of many genetic developments, ethicists generally have considerable latitude as to how they interpret and dialogue with their tradition. Even when the process of conceptual development reflects historical doctrinal and methodological perspectives, the relationship is rarely linear. An examination of the contributions on cloning by various religious thinkers underscores that religious affiliation may impose certain boundaries and offer methodological approaches and ethical and theological themes, but it rarely determines the content, the emphasis, or the conclusions drawn by theologians and ethicists. It concludes that a careful examination of the work of particular ethicists and theologians clearly indicates that something more complex is happening than the mechanical application of traditional doctrines.

That traditional confessional boundaries do not necessarily predetermine ethical reasoning was shown by comparing the views on cloning of religious ethicists from the same traditions. To be more specific, both Elliot Dorff and Moshe Tendler ostensibly represented a shared Jewish tradition, but their differences in seeking to interpret the relevance of the Jewish heritage to cloning were striking. Moreover, although both drew conclusions that the Jewish tradition permitted cloning, at least under some circumstances, the Chief Rabbi of Israel issued a blanket prohibition against any research in cloning.[105] The three Lutheran theologians who participated in the cloning debate had even

104. Cynthia B. Cohen, Chair, Committee on Medical Ethics, *Wrestling with the Future: Our Genes and Our Choices* (Harrisburg, Pa.: Morehouse Publishing, 1998).
105. Dr. Moshe Tendler, Testimony to the NBAC, 14 March 1997 (Washington, D.C.: Eberlin Reporting Service), 10.

more profound disagreements. Much as Paul Ramsey argued thirty years ago, Gilbert Meilaender found cloning problematic because it would sever the connection between marriage and begetting children. Meilaender also emphasized that humans do not have the freedom to make and remake ourselves.[106] In contrast with Meilaender's position, Philip Hefner wrote about cloning against the horizon of the human person as created co-creators, "creatures of nature who themselves intentionally enter into the process of creating nature."[107] Ted Peters, a third Lutheran theologian, argued that cloning did not pose any fundamental theological problems and dismissed fears that cloning would compromise human identity and violate human dignity.[108]

Although Lisa Cahill and Albert Moraczewski share a Roman Catholic background, they also offered very different perspectives on cloning. Because Moraczewski spoke for the National Conference of Catholic Bishops, he was grounded in the church's official teachings. As in her writings, Cahill drew on a Catholic natural law tradition as modified by a feminist perspective. While Moraczewski's testimony reiterated official church teachings on marriage and sexuality and attempted to apply them to the new issue of cloning, Cahill never mentioned Catholic doctrine. Instead she chose to focus on two issues— the need to resist the technological imperative and related market forces and the importance of going beyond autonomy and informed consent when engaging in moral reflection on cloning. When she dealt with the issue of the family it was to note the cross-cultural variety and the importance of the biological relationship between parents and children as a symbol of reproductive, domestic, and social partnership.[109]

Divisions within the religious community on genetic patenting frequently did not reflect confessional backgrounds as much as other differences in approach. In a number of cases, critics were drawn from communities whose leader(s) endorsed the Joint Appeal. Perhaps the most salient point of disagreement occurred between professional ethicists and theologians who specialize on science and technology on the one side and staff members of the church's social justice/social action agencies on the other. Some of the latter were so intent on making a splash with their critique of patenting that they

106. Dr. Gilbert Meilaender, Testimony to the NBAC, 13 March 1992 (Washington, D.C.: Eberlin Reporting Service), 62–64.

107. Philip Hefner, "Cloning as Quintessential Human Act," e-mail transmission, 13 March 1997.

108. Ted Peters made these remarks on a panel discussion at the AAAS Forum on Cloning, 25 June 1997, in Washington, D.C., reported in Vincent Kiernan, "The Morality of Cloning Humans: Theologians and Philosophers Offer Provocative Arguments," *Chronicle of Higher Education* (18 July 1997): A13–14.

109. Cahill, Testimony.

proceeded opportunistically with few preliminaries, like learning the specifics about patenting law or taking care in the drafting of their position statement. The former tended to be so concerned about exhibiting their professional credentials and retaining their credibility within the scientific community that they were sometimes reluctant to acknowledge that the patenting of life raised real ethical issues.

What does this suggest about the possibilities of working across traditional religious boundaries? The one effort to develop a position on an interreligious basis, the Joint Appeal, was not a resounding success. Chapter 4 presented a critique of both its content and its failure to conform to basic standards for the formulation of public theology. The Joint Appeal process also resulted in the anomaly of a Southern Baptist ethicist with a conservative Christian theology ostensibly speaking on behalf of a diverse religious coalition including Muslim, Hindu, Buddhist, and Jewish groups. In defense of the Joint Appeal proponents, they did not intend the statement to be a carefully crafted work of theology or ethics. Instead, it was more in the nature of a publicity ploy to gain attention for the concerns of a broad spectrum of religious leaders that patenting was contrary to the dignity and sanctity of life. For all these reasons, the Joint Appeal experience does not appear to be very informative about the possibilities of developing religious ethics on a broader basis.

Although it may sometimes seem to be the case, I do not believe that the choice is between a noncontextual philosophical universality or a "facile ecumenism" on the one side and the particularity of religious traditions on the other. The diversity of religious traditions can enrich ethical deliberation on genetics without constraining analysis and reflection within narrow confessional boundaries. Take the perceptive comment Courtney Campbell made on religion and moral meaning in bioethics. Writing in 1990, he suggested that "the answers to the conventional bioethics questions of 'who should decide?' or 'what should we do?' often—if we felt free to allow them to do so—would push back to the fundamental issues that require a substantive account of the purpose of human life and destiny. These are common questions of meaning that religious communities have devoted considerable attention to in their theologies, rituals, and practical ethics."[110] These common questions of meaning and their relevance to genetics might provide an appropriate starting point for an interreligious dialogue. Perhaps now is the time for various communities to explore the commonalities and differences of their respective efforts to grapple with the genetics revolution.

110. Courtney S. Campbell, "Religion and Moral Meaning in Bioethics," in Callahan and Campbell, eds., *Theology, Religious Traditions, and Bioethics*, 6.

The need for a serious interface between science and theology may also open up possibilities for working across traditional religious boundaries. It may be feasible for groups of ethicists from a wide range of religious backgrounds to work together in a science-religion framework developing and explicating concepts and issues. This is not to say that they will necessarily agree, but even so, their interaction would no doubt enrich all of their thinking. As an example, the AAAS currently has a multidisciplinary working group on ethical and theological issues related to human germ-line intervention in which there are religious ethicists from a wide variety of backgrounds as well as secular ethicists. Although most have sought to draw on their heritage, the issues are so unprecedented that ethicists quickly realized they were in unchartered territory. The process of moral reasoning in this group has benefited from discussions in which the insights and sensitivities of each ethicist then stimulated and contributed to the thinking of others. Moreover, the group appears to be moving toward consensus on several significant points.

If religious groups want to have an impact on public policy on genetic issues, greater collaboration would certainly contribute to their doing so. Historically each communion has spoken in its own voice. Ecumenical or interfaith initiatives, when they have taken place, have just added yet another perspective. Even when several religious communities have similar positions, they offer different modes of reasoning. But this pattern undermines the credibility and effectiveness of religious perspectives. The multiplicity of viewpoints also inclines policy makers to dismiss religious constituencies as expressing narrow opinions that are not held by other groups. Although there are significant divisions, there are also many shared concerns on genetics within the religious community, as this study has certainly shown. Exploring greater cooperation in the policy domain would also strengthen linkages across religious boundaries.

PUBLIC THEOLOGY

Ronald Thiemann has defined public theology as "faith seeking to understand the relation between Christian convictions and the broader social and cultural context within which the Christian community lives."[111] Others, like Max Stackhouse, have emphasized that public theology seeks to give ethical guidance to the structures and policies of public life.[112] Both are relevant

111. Ronald F. Thiemann, *Constructing a Public Theology: The Church in a Pluralistic Culture* (Louisville: Westminster/John Knox Press, 1991), 21.
112. Max Stackhouse, *Public Theology and Political Economy* (Grand Rapids, Mich.: Wm. B. Eerdmans Publishing Co., 1987), xi.

characterizations of various ecumenical and denominational initiatives on genetics over the past twenty years. Whatever the limitations of the literature reviewed here, these works represent a very significant effort to come to terms with a complex topic shaping the social and ethical landscape during the second half of the twentieth century. Moreover, given the relative absence of secular voices and the implications of genetics revolution, the religious community quite appropriately sought to reach beyond its own members to inform a broader public, including policy makers.

Much of the thrust of this public theology, however, is more to underscore the need for public discussions and societal decision making than to prescribe particular policy directions. Positions of religious thinkers and agencies on two of the most controversial issues, human germ-line engineering and somatic cell nuclear cloning, for example, typically emphasize the need for a moratorium so as to permit ethical reflection necessary for developing guidelines. Although the various religious congregations and educational institutions in the United States potentially constitute one of the largest forums for ethical deliberation, the role proposed for the church or religious communions is surprisingly modest. While much of this literature eloquently justifies the religious community's addressing the genetic revolution, it usually does not envisage any religious body taking a leadership role in developing national policy on this topic. Instead, the various statements and works confine the role of churches to monitoring and participating in governmental, legislative, and public policy debates.

There have also been several instances when religious bodies sought to influence the formation of public policy. An example of the latter was the 1980 letter to President Jimmy Carter calling for the establishment of adequate mechanisms for public review and oversight of genetic engineering. This letter then led to the broadening of the mandate of the President's Commission for the Study of Ethical Problems in Medicine and Biomedical and Behavioral Research to genetic engineering and invitations to religious thinkers to participate in its deliberations. The 1995 Joint Appeal constituted another initiative, though perhaps more to record the religious communities' discomfort with the direction of patent policies than with the expectation of changing them. In 1997, several religious bodies, as well as religious scholars, intended to influence the shaping of public policy on human cloning through their statements, resolutions, and testimony before the NBAC.

The interface between faith, Christian and non-Christian, and public theology on genetics reflects the recognition of the significance of the genetics revolution for contemporary and future generations and the unprecedented nature of the choices it brings. As early as 1984, a publication of the National Council of Churches expressed the conviction that discoveries in human genetics might revolutionize our fundamental understanding of the world and the role of humanity. This publication anticipated that this turning point might have implications as far-reaching as Copernicus's finding that the earth revolves around the sun, Darwin's theory of evolution, and Einstein's theory of matter.[113] And several thinkers note that the capacity to genetically engineer forms of life and reshape human nature may eventually propel us toward the role of co-creators, hopefully with the recognition of our finitude and creatureliness. Given their analysis of the broad societal implications of genetic developments, religious communities gravitate toward the public arena both to raise various issues and to seek resolution of them. In taking these initiatives, religious communities and thinkers hold the conviction that "the church [religious community] has significant and distinctive things to say about a society wrestling with the questions and the meaning of genetic developments,"[114] and they are usually correct about this.

The activist character of American religion also propels faith bodies into social and political life as a manifestation of their sense of a religious calling in society. An earlier work by this author observed the following about Christian faith and politics: "A faith that is social, ethical, and incarnational . . . cannot countenance the liberal delineation of politics and religion as unrelated to each other. Such a separation of faith and politics, moreover, contradicts the biblical perspective that time and again affirms God as the ultimate source of meaning, authority, and inspiration over all spheres of life."[115]

A decade or so ago, several books and articles anticipated the development of a "naked public square" stripped of religious actors and perspectives,[116] but this, of course, did not occur with regard to religious input on various issues related to the genetics revolution. Religious participation in discussions about genetics has generally been welcomed and sometimes even solicited. This reflects, at least at some junctures, the growing public sense that developments like human cloning have authentic religious dimensions. Of course, there have been critical voices, some from the scientific community, arguing that "ancient theological scruples" have no appropriate role in the formation of public policy on genetic issues. The NBAC's justification of why it invited religious thinkers to offer their views on human cloning provides a powerful rejoinder to these claims. NBAC acknowledged that the United States Constitution prohibits the establishment of policies solely motivated by religious belief, but

113. Panel of Bioethical Concerns, *Genetic Engineering: Social and Ethical Consequences,* Frank M. Harron, ed. (New York: Pilgrim Press, 1984), 20.
114. Willer, "Introduction," in Willer, ed., *Genetic Testing and Screening,* 7.
115. Audrey R. Chapman, *Faith, Power, and Politics: Political Ministry in Mainline Churches* (New York: Pilgrim Press, 1991), 44.
116. Richard John Neuhaus, *The Naked Public Square: Religion and Democracy in America* (Grand Rapids, Mich.: Wm. B. Eerdmans Publishing Co., 1984).

explained that NBAC thought religious perspectives were especially important "because religious traditions shape the moral views of many U.S. citizens and religious teachings over the centuries have provided an important source of ideas and inspiration. . . . Although in a pluralistic society particular religious views cannot be determinative for public policy decisions that bind everyone, policy makers should understand and show respect for diverse moral ideas regarding the acceptability of cloning human beings."[117] Not only did NBAC set aside time to hear a diverse group of religious ethicists, it also devoted a chapter of its report on cloning to analyzing their viewpoints and recommendations. And the NBAC repeated this procedure in its hearings on the appropriateness of human stem cell research.

While the public witness of the religious community should be affirmed, the way in which it is sometimes executed is worthy of criticism. Chapter 4 offers several guidelines for public theology growing out of a critique of the Joint Appeal. First, for public theology to be consistent with the nature and mission of a religious actor, it should proceed from a clear religious rationale and reflect the priorities of the communions it is representing. In order to speak for, rather than to, the religious community, public theology should represent the views of a wide cross section of members of a faith communion, not just its leadership. To do so, it requires systematic education and wide-ranging consultation with members in advance of any public initiatives. Second, to be appropriate, public theology should be timely and at the very least explain why the religious community or communion has decided to address a specific issue in the public arena. Third, public theology must be well reasoned, informed, and understandable to persons within both the religious and secular communities. When public theology appeals to theological beliefs, even when those beliefs are not widely shared, the logical relationship between the beliefs and the conclusions should be comprehensible to believer and nonbeliever alike.[118] Fourth, to be credible, public theology should exhibit knowledge of relevant research and data related to the subject it is addressing. This is particularly the case on topics related to science and technology. Fifth, if public theology aims at changing public policy, it needs to be clear about what it is advocating as well as what it is criticizing.

To what extent did the public policy initiatives of religious spokespersons on genetic patenting and human cloning conform to these criteria? The analysis of the Joint Appeal concluded that it did not meet any of these conditions.

117. NBAC, *Cloning Human Beings,* 7.
118. Ronald Cole-Turner, "The Theological Status of DNA: A Contribution to the Debate over Gene Patenting" (revised version of a paper written for the AAAS Dialogue Group on Gene Patenting, originally presented 13 March 1997).

Opponents of patenting did claim a religious grounding, but it was poorly articulated. Moreover, the Joint Appeal did not build on a long-term and consistent concern with patenting issues in the religious community. Science and technology, let alone genetic issues or patenting, are barely on the agenda of most religious leaders and communions. Far from there being a religious consensus over patenting, those most knowledgeable about the topic tended to disagree with the position and theological rationale of the Joint Appeal and/or argued that the patenting of life-forms is peripheral to the primary issues before the religious community. The Joint Appeal was also problematic because it was neither timely nor related to specific developments in patent policy. Further, with few exceptions, the religious participants in the genetic patenting debate were not well informed about the specifics of patent law or the status of genetic patenting, which undercut their credibility. Nor did the critique of the Joint Appeal make clear the specific changes the coalition was advocating.

The religious witness on cloning came somewhat closer, particularly in being timely. The statements issues by various religious bodies, as well as the articles and testimony of religious ethicists, expressed a clear religious rationale understandable both to their own members and to the wider public. While it is difficult to know whether any of the thinkers or agencies represented the views of a strong cross section of members of their communion, some did seek broader membership support after the fact. In contrast with the Joint Appeal, whose timing represents something of a mystery, the input on cloning came at a point of public attention and discussion after the announcement of the cloning of a lamb, but then dropped away as Congress actually considered the text of specific bills. The statements addressing cloning were far more well reasoned, informed, and understandable to persons within the religious and secular communities than the Joint Appeal text. In addition, the cloning critics who argued for either a prohibition or a moratorium generally were clear about what they were advocating.

Engaging in public theology so as to offer ethical guidance to the structures and policies of public life requires making religious discourse publicly accessible. It is quite a challenge to explicate the religious basis of the claims made and the policies advocated while communicating with a broader public. Utilizing the experience of religious thinkers in the field of bioethics, several secular ethicists have expressed concerns about the feasibility of translating religious discourse into a common moral language appropriate to an interdisciplinary and public audience. Chapter 1 noted the claims of Leon Kass that there is little choice but for religious ethicists to leave their special insights at the door and to adopt secular categories and terminologies.[119]

---

119. Leon R. Kass, "Practicing Ethics: Where's the Action?" *The Hastings Center Report* 20 (January/February 1990).

Another problem, according to philosopher Jeffrey Stout, is that there is no universal and neutral ethical language, no Esperanto, into which theological formulations can be translated. Stout is not unduly disturbed because he does not infer that talk of God is irrelevant to public life or to society's ethical discourse.[120]

In contrast with some secular ethicists, Lisa Sowle Cahill argues in a 1990 article that there is not an independent realm of secular or philosophical discourse that is privileged because it is more reasonable, neutral, or objective, and less tradition-bound, than religious discourse. Instead, she points out that all ethicists attempt to speak out of, but beyond, a particular tradition. According to Cahill, it is best to construe public discourse "as embodying a commitment to civil exchanges among traditions, many of which have an overlapping membership, and which meet on the basis of common concerns."[121] She recommends that religiously motivated spokespersons develop policy initiatives on the basis of moral quandaries, moral sensibilities, moral images, and moral vocabulary shared among a variety of religious and moral traditions. If they do so, she anticipates that theologians and religious groups can contribute to public discourse by serving a critical function and cutting through cultural assumptions.[122]

Public theology related to genetics issues has generally focused on moral dilemmas, values, sensitivities, and images, utilizing both faith-specific language and a shared moral vocabulary. Faith language on genetics and biotechnology has usually been comprehensible precisely because it has transcended a particular community's positions and beliefs. By doing so, it has offered perspectives congenial to supporters of other moral traditions, including some forms of secular humanism. Rather than so-called God talk, religious ethicists have tended to ground their concerns and objections in terminology and concepts consistent with human rights principles and the ideals of a democratic society. They have emphasized norms such as protecting human dignity, assuring nondiscrimination, and promoting substantive justice and fairness while reasoning out of, but also beyond, specific religious traditions.

Has such an approach imposed a cost? Or, put another way, have theologians and ethicists consciously sacrificed "God talk" so as to be more comprehensible to a wider public? Not very often. In part this derives from an increasingly higher threshold of acceptance of theological language in the public arena on

120. Jeffrey Stout, *Ethics after Babel: The Languages of Morals and Their Discontents* (Boston: Beacon Press, 1988), 187.
121. Lisa Sowle Cahill, "Can Theology Have a Role in 'Public' Bioethical Discourse?" In Callahan and Campbell, eds., *Theology, Religious Traditions, and Bioethics*, 10.
122. Ibid., 10–14.

some of these issues, cloning, for example, than was anticipated in the earlier discussions about the public role of religion arising out of bioethics. The acknowledgment that many genetic discoveries raise religious questions has helped legitimate an explicitly religious presence in public discourse. The diffuse sense of anxiety about the implications of genetic engineering, especially applications directly affecting persons, may also contribute to openness to religious actors because they are viewed as representatives of a moral authority.

There is yet another reason why contributing to public discussions has not entailed stripping away theological layers of discourse. Most religious thinkers, even when writing for a religious audience, have placed their analysis of genetic discoveries primarily within an ethical rather than a theological framework. As noted, theological interpretations of genetics implications have lagged behind concerns about ethical dilemmas. This reflects a variety of factors, among them the difficulties and complexities of understanding genetic developments through traditional theological approaches and methodologies.

A FEW FINAL WORDS

This study began with the observation that the genetics revolution offers both a challenge and an opportunity to the religious community: a challenge to apply religious values and frameworks to new and unprecedented issues, and an opportunity to help interpret and illumine significant ethical choices before members and the broader society. Clearly, the literature on genetics surveyed in this study confirms that during the past twenty years a variety of religious bodies and thinkers have recognized and responded to the genetics revolution. Their work has made an important contribution to societal efforts to identify and begin to grapple with the choices and dilemmas arising from genetic discoveries and applications. This literature is quite wide-ranging in the topics and concerns it addresses. Most are Christian in background, but there are also signs of increasing interest among Jewish and a few Muslim ethicists. The major contribution of religious thinkers has been to sensitize and stimulate the moral imagination of the religious and secular publics and expand their ethical horizons. In so doing, they have affirmed the relevance of genetics to the realms of ethics and theology as well as science and medicine. By identifying the values and commitments that genetic discoveries challenge, this literature makes clear that nothing less is at stake than the moral compass and fundamental humanity of our and future societies.

But the works reviewed also underscore that religious ethics is still only potentially relevant to the task of shaping a moral response to the genetics revolution. Twenty-five years ago, James Gustafson observed that theology rarely yields precise and concrete directives for bioethical decision making.[123] On a similar note, Lisa Sowle Cahill noted in 1990 that theology, even within the religious community, is more likely to affirm fundamental values and commitments relevant to the bioethical decision making of religious persons than to yield specific norms.[124] The same could be said of the ethical literature on genetics and biotechnology subsequently written by religious thinkers. We are still at the very beginnings of attempting to understand what God is enabling and requiring us to do related to genetic processes and our newfound abilities to intervene and reshape nature. Few of the works reviewed in this volume offer specific guidance toward resolving the many ethical dilemmas and unprecedented choices resulting from genetic developments. Nor do they provide norms, methodologies, or guidelines to use in making these determinations. The various thinkers do not illuminate where to draw the precise boundary between genetic interventions representing responsible expressions of human stewardship, co-creation, or partnership with the divine and those that are extensions of human hubris or pride. Instead it can be said that the greatest value of these works is more in the issues they raise than in the answers they provide.

Is this role sufficient? I think not. I have greater aspirations for religious thinkers dealing with genetics. Given the magnitude of the issues—as set forth in the various analyses of the unprecedented challenges and choices related to genetic developments—it is not enough for them to stimulate the moral imagination. Unless religious ethicists begin to offer guidance on how to respond to these developments, they may become irrelevant to shaping our genetic future. Improved methodologies for interfacing religious ethics and genetic science and more systematic development of relevant conceptual building blocks can make a significant contribution. The most important task ahead will be to formulate a scientifically-based prescriptive ethics infused with religious insights and values.

---

123. James M. Gustafson, *The Contributions of Theology to Medical Ethics* (Milwaukee: Marquette University Theology Department, 1975), cited in Cahill, "Can Theology Have a Role?" 11.
124. Cahill, "Can Theology Have a Role?" 14.

Index